There seems to be a resurgence of interest in Thomas Aquinas and natural theology in this present time. I am all in favor of gleaning what we can from those who have gone before us, and Thomas is no exception. However, how should we evaluate this revival of Thomistic interest? We need to evaluate it because this revival of interest is primarily among Reformed theologians and pastors. We need to think about it because assertions of what constitutes classic theism abound (those assertions frequently appeal to Thomas and natural theology). Jeffrey Johnson has given us an important analysis of this subject. With his usual breadth of knowledge and insight, Jeffrey has given an even-handed assessment of Thomas and natural theology. I found this book to be incredibly helpful. Not everyone will agree with Jeffrey's assessment of Thomas and natural theology, but you won't be able to disagree lightly. I especially urge pastors to open this book and digest this important book.

—Dr. Brian Borgman,
Founding Pastor of Grace Community Church
Minden, Nevada

Thomas Aquinas casts a long shadow across the sacred halls of church history. Today, enthusiasm for Thomas's theism has even gained traction in the Reformed community. That's why Jeffrey Johnson's book is so timely and needed! Jeff homes in on the "fatal flaw" in Aquinas's theological method—namely, his natural theology. In an attempt to make philosophy the handmaiden of theology, Thomas sacrifices divine immanence on the altar of a pagan sort of transcendence that bears more affinity to Deism than to Christianity. In the end, Thomas's natural theology (which is based on a Greek metaphysic) functions as a kind of hermeneutical Procrustes' Bed upon which the Bible's testimony of a triune Creator-Redeemer is "resized" to match more closely the dimensions of Aristotle's Unmoved Mover. Such a methodology, as Johnson shows, distorts the biblical portrait of God the Father, Son, and Holy Spirit. Moreover, it undermines the sufficiency and authority of Scripture. I couldn't agree more! If you're entertaining contemporary calls to wed your Reformed theology to Thomism, I urge you to read Jeff's judicious critique.

—Dr. Robert Gonzales Jr.
Academic Dean and Professor of Biblical Studies
Reformed Baptist Seminary
Sacramento, California

Historical and theological retrieval and resourcement is on the rise in evangelical and Reformed circles, and as a lover of church history, I believe it is ultimately a good thing. However, the pendulum seems to be swinging to the extreme that all that is old is good, and therefore, all must be well-received. Jeffrey Johnson makes a compelling argument, that in the case of Thomas Aquinas, we should pause in our embrace of the "Angelic Doctor." He explains that Thomas was an innovator in his day who was deviating from the classical theology he received, and in doing so, made a fatal flaw at the root of his theological method that produced an inferior fruit. If Thomas's natural theology begins with man's reason and never truly reconciles with revealed theology, then we can never have a proper knowledge of God and thus never truly experience eternal life (John 17:3).

– Dr. Ryan L. Rippee
President and Professor of Church History and Theology
The Cornerstone Bible College and Seminary
Vallejo, California

There is an increasing trend toward theological retrieval from the patristic and medieval eras for the church today. The works of Thomas Aquinas, medieval theologian *par excellence*, are once again finding their way into the hands of many evangelicals. Perhaps too often, however, Aquinas is read in a vacuum, or his works in isolation, without a broader contextual understanding of his life, times, and influences. Dr. Johnson's book serves as a crucial corrective to those who embrace all things Aquinas without really comprehending his philosophical and naturalistic theology. Understanding the influence that Aristotle and Pseudo-Dionysius had on Thomas provides keen insight into Aquinas's understanding of God and his creation. This book rightly criticizes both the social trinitarians who elevate the diversity in God over his unity, but also many contemporary trinitarian scholars who so heavily emphasize the oneness of God that they fail to give adequate time and attention to his threeness. Johnson provides a necessary and needed warning to those who would wish to baptize Aquinas as an evangelical that, while there is much gold to glean in the writings of this theologian, his works should be carefully and biblically analyzed rather than unreservedly embraced. Pastors and scholars alike will greatly benefit from this deeper and broader survey of the philosophical theology of Thomas Aquinas.

– Jonathan J. Routley
Professor of Bible and Theology
Emmaus Bible College

Thomas Aquinas was a brilliant man, and his philosophical material in particular is fathoms-deep. Jeff Johnson's scholarly but gracefully readable text shows that his intellect notwithstanding, Aquinas's mingled metaphysics, mixed methodology, and promotion of "divine immobility" merit strong caution. There is much to consider and evaluate within the sprawling system called "classical theism"; Johnson's book helps us get solid footing for this task. He reveals why it is altogether improper to baptize Aristotle as Aquinas did, and no less problematic for him (and us) to embrace the undifferentiated mysticism of Dionysius. This is the book the church has needed on this subject. It is an urgent read by one of our best theologians.

– Dr. Owen Strachan
Provost and Research Professor of Theology
Grace Bible Theological Seminary
Conway, Arkansas

The view is increasingly promoted in Reformed circles today that to be historically Reformed one must be at some level a Thomist. I agree with Jeff's challenge to this notion especially when it comes to the Thomist idea of natural theology. Thomas Aquinas is not the only or best church-historical alternative for the Reformed Christian. It is clear that Calvin much preferred Augustine's approaches to many issues including the knowledge of God to that of Thomas. (He cites Augustine in a mostly positive way in the *Institutes* over 300 times, but Thomas only about 3 times and in a mostly negative way.) Jeff's book is a welcome contribution to the debate that is and should be going on in Reformed circles about the value of Thomism in general and the usefulness of his natural theology in particular.

– Dr. Sam Waldron
President and Professor of Systematic and Historical Theology
Covenant Baptist Theological Seminary
Owensboro, KY

Jeff Johnson has provided the church of Jesus Christ with a solid and insightful study of Thomas Aquinas with *The Failure of Natural Theology*. The author has done the necessary spadework and gets down into the details of Thomas's thought regarding natural theology, and he writes in a clear and compelling way. Specifically, Johnson targets Thomas's affirmation of Aristotle's idea of divine immobility as at the heart of his problem. Along the way, Johnson tackles the cosmological argument and the relation of philosophy and theology. The strength of Johnson's work here is its intrinsic Trinitarian foundation. This is a must-read whether you agree with the author or not. Future work on the significance of Thomas will necessitate reckoning with the argument set forth herein.

– Jeffrey C. Waddington, PhD
Pastor of Faith Orthodox Presbyterian Church
Glenside, Pennsylvania

THE FAILURE OF
Natural Theology

THE **FAILURE** OF
Natural Theology

A CRITICAL APPRAISAL OF THE PHILOSOPHICAL
THEOLOGY OF THOMAS AQUINAS

Jeffrey D. Johnson

NEW STUDIES IN THEOLOGY · FGP ·

FGP
ACADEMIC

The Failure of Natural Theology: A Critical Appraisal of the Philosophical Theology of Thomas Aquinas

Scripture quotations are from the ESV® Bible (The Holy Bible, English Standard Version®), copyright © 2001 by Crossway, a publishing ministry of Good News Publishers. Used by permission. All rights reserved.

Scriptures marked KJV are taken from the King James Version of the Bible, public domain.

Printed in the United States of America

Cover design by Scott Schaller

Typesetting by InkSmith Editorial Services

ISBN: 978-1-952599-37-8

Contents

Abbreviations xiii

Introduction.. 1

1. Natural Theology's Dilemma 7

2. Mixing Philosophy with Theology.............................. 35

3. The Natural Theology of Aristotle 53

4. The Natural Theology of Pseudo-Dionysius................... 71

5. The Philosophical Theology of Thomas Aquinas........... 95

6. The Fatal Flaw of Aquinas's Philosophical Theology..... 111

7. The Problems of Divine Immobility 135

8. The Necessity of the Trinity..................................... 151

9. Analogical Language... 175

Appendix 1: Not among the Protestants 195

Appendix 2: Not among the Scholastics: John Owen on
     the Mingling of Philosophy with Theology................. 219

Bibliography.. 237

Index of Names 245

Dedicated to

Dr. James Fetterly

New Studies in Theology

The New Studies in Theology series, edited by Owen Strachan, attempts to bring some of the best contemporary scholarship of the Reformed confessional tradition from the academy to the pew. The goal is to help Christians think deeply and biblically about crucial issues that impact the church.

ABBREVIATIONS

Thomas Aquinas

CJ *Commentary on John*

DDN *Dionysii De Divinis Nominibus*

DT *Commentary on the De Trinitate of Boethius*

EB *On Essence and Being*

OI *On There Being Only One Intellect*

QDP *Quaestiones Disputatae De Potentia Dei*

QDQ *Quaestiones De Quolibet I–XI*

SCG *Summa Contra Gentiles*

ST *Summa Theologica*

TAC *The Aquinas Catechism*

Aristotle

Metaph. *Metaphysics*

Phys. *Physics*

Pseudo-Dionysius

DN *Divine Names*

MT *Mystical Theology*

INTRODUCTION

THOMAS OF AQUINO was a wandering theologian; it's estimated that he trekked over nine thousand miles across Europe.[1] After he turned twenty-three, he never stayed in one place for more than three years. From Naples to Paris to Cologne, he continued to traverse Europe—all on foot—until his untimely death. As a Dominican friar, he had made a vow to never travel on the back of an animal, so he walked everywhere he went.[2]

But even more impressive than the vast number of steps Aquinas logged is the vast number of pages he wrote—almost a hundred books in total.[3] His life was dedicated to writing, and behind a life of writing was a contemplative life of thought. He was often so engrossed in contemplation that he would lose track of his surroundings. Once, forgetting that he was dining with Louis IX, the king of France, he suddenly slammed his fist down on the table and exclaimed, "There is the

---

1 See Thomas O'Meara, *Thomas Aquinas Theologian* (Notre Dame, IN: University of Notre Dame Press, 1997), 34.

2 It should be noted, however, that Jean-Pierre Torrell reports there was such an urgency for Thomas to arrive in Paris in 1268 that his superiors ordered him to travel there by boat from Rome via Civitavecchia to Aigues-Mortes, then up the Rhone. See Jean-Pierre Torrell, *Saint Thomas Aquinas, Vol. 1 The Person and His Work*, trans. Robert Royal (Washington, DC: The Catholic University of America Press, 2005), 181–182.

3 There are over twenty thousand pages in Logos' *Works of Thomas Aquinas*.

1

conclusive argument against the Manichaean heresy!" "'Master,' said the Prior, as he pulled Thomas's sleeve to jar him out of his meditation, 'be careful: you are sitting at the moment at the table of the King of France.'"[4] Another time, while dictating at night, he was so caught up in thought that he didn't notice the candle burning itself out until his fingers were singed.[5] Those who think long and deep on a single subject often have a hard time thinking about anything else, and this was certainly true of Aquinas.

His deep contemplation was motivated by his relentless pursuit of knowledge. He was so dedicated to his studies that he would only take the time to eat one meal a day. And Thomas proved that he loved knowledge more than the riches of this world. In his desire to become a student, he forsook the life of leisure his family's wealth could have provided. He once asserted that the knowledge contained within a particular book he wanted was of greater value than all the wealth of Paris. He said this while beholding the city's panorama, including the newly constructed bell towers of Notre Dame Cathedral.

With such splendor before his eyes, his traveling companion remarked, "How beautiful this city of Paris!"

"Indeed, very beautiful," Thomas replied.

"If only this city were yours!" his friend went on to say.

"In all truth," Aquinas answered, "I should rather have St. Chrysostom's homilies on Matthew."[6]

As a student, Aquinas sought to learn from everyone, even from those with whom he disagreed. He respected his intellectual opponents and presented their arguments in the best possible light—even

4 Jacques Maritain, *St. Thomas Aquinas: Angel of the Schools*, trans. J. F. Scanlan (London: Sheed & Ward, 1948), 12.
5 See Josef Pieper, *The Silence of St. Thomas*, trans. John Murray, S. J., and Daniel O'Connor (South Bend, IN: St. Augustine's Press, 1963), 13.
6 See Martin Grabmann, *Thomas Aquinas: His Personality and Thought* (LaVergne, TN: Kessinger, 2010) 45.

if only to help sharpen his own thinking.[7] When one of his opponents, for instance, sent him a letter objecting to something he wrote, Thomas quickly responded by restating those objections with more clarity and force before he systematically dismantled them.

No doubt, Thomas had a brilliant mind. "When asked," G. K. Chesterton remarked, "[for] what he thanked God most, he answered simply: 'I have understood every page I ever read.'"[8] One of his first biographers, William of Tocco, reported that in all his prayers he would ask God for wisdom.[9]

And though Aquinas didn't make it past his forties, he was able in his abbreviated life to place a permanent stamp on the history of Western thought. The secondary sources on Aquinas are too vast to number, and thousands of commentaries, dissertations, and biographies have been dedicated to analyzing this medieval theologian. The half century that marks the short life of Thomas Aquinas has led to over seven centuries of study on his life and works by laypersons and scholars alike.

After years of studying the life and works of Aquinas, I am awestruck. I am astonished by the rigor, depth, and extent of his thinking. It's inspiring, if not truly astounding, to see what he was able to accomplish in such a short amount of time. When a person of high intelligence like Thomas Aquinas gives himself wholly to a single endeavor, it is remarkable what can be accomplished. Very few even get close to that level of focus and discipline. Truly, Thomas Aquinas was an exceptional thinker and a prolific scholar.

So why critique someone for whom I have such respect? As a Protestant, I am troubled by the resurgence of Thomistic thinking

---

7 This can be seen most vividly in his polemical work *Contra impugnantes Dei cultum et religionem*, where he respectfully refutes the attacks of William of Saint-Amour against the mendicant orders.

8 G. K. Chesterton, *Saint Thomas Aquinas* (Nashville: Sam Torade Book Arts, 2019), 4.

9 See Josef Pieper, *Guide to Thomas Aquinas*, trans. Richard and Clara Winston (New York: Pantheon, 1962), 17–18.

within Protestant Christianity. As a Reformed Baptist, I am increasingly concerned by the newfound attention this Catholic theologian is receiving among many in my own camp. And as pastor, I am deeply disturbed that this revival of Thomism is slowly slipping down from academia into our churches.

Though I greatly respect Aquinas for his intellectual fortitude, depth of learning, and prolific output, I am nevertheless convinced that Aquinas is no friend of Protestantism. Thomas was unorthodox in his soteriology, in part, because he was unorthodox in his ecclesiology. He did not teach the gospel of the apostle Paul—a gospel through grace alone, in the work of Christ alone, received by faith alone. Instead, he taught that salvation is dependent on the Catholic Church and the authority of the pope.[10]

Some would argue that many Protestants are drawn to this Catholic scholar not so much for his soteriology or his ecclesiology but for his theology proper. This may be true. But I am convinced that Aquinas's doctrine of God was wrong as well. More than that, I am persuaded that his doctrine of God is problematic for a proper view of classical theism.

Classical theism is not Thomism. Though classical apologetics is rightly identified with Thomas, classical theism goes much further back than the thirteenth century. And when it came to theology proper, Aquinas in his own day was viewed as an innovator. By introducing Aristotelian concepts into his theology proper, he departed from the established Platonism of Augustine. Many of his contemporaries took up their pen against him. For instance, thirteen articles of Aquinas that relate to his Aristotelianism were condemned by the bishop of Paris, Stephen Tempier, in 1270. And three years to the day after Thomas's death, on March 7, 1277, Pope John XXI, imposed disciplinary sanctions on those who taught the condemned theses of Aquinas.

---

10   See "Appendix: Not among the Protestants."

Thus, to say Thomism is one and the same with classical theism is a vast oversimplification. Classical theism rightly upholds divine aseity, simplicity, and immutability. The confessions of the seventeenth century are right when they say, "God is without body, parts, or passions."[11] Divine aseity, simplicity, and immutability are rooted in the Scriptures, particularly in God's name: "I AM WHO I AM" (Exod 3:14). For God to be independent, all that is in God must be God without separation or mutation.

When Thomas Aquinas introduced Aristotelian concepts into his theology proper, however, he not only departed from the theologians who went before him but he also altered the biblical teaching of God. As this book will seek to demonstrate, Thomas added to God's simple and immutable nature an additional attribute not taught in the Scriptures: *divine immobility*.

Aquinas made the assumption that mobility—the willful exertion of power—is an essential characteristic of imperfection, finiteness, and temporality. Because God can't be any of these things, mobility must not be in God. Yet by Thomas's adding immobility to the list of divine attributes, other attributes of God, such as aseity, simplicity, and immutability, were negatively impacted. Moreover, as we will see, immobility negatively impacts the free and unnecessary acts of God, such as creating and governing the universe. Most importantly, divine immobility is incongruent with the Trinitarian God of the Bible.

The danger of this error does not end with assimilating the immobility of the unmoved mover of Aristotle with the God of the Bible; it ends with a negative impact on the entirety of one's theology. By integrating the philosophical categories of Aristotle into Christianity, Aquinas introduced a hermeneutical framework that shaped his understanding of divine revelation and the language of Scripture. Rather

---

11 See paragraph 1 of chapter 2 in either The Westminster Confession of Faith (1647) or The Second London Confession of Faith (1689).

than using Scripture to interpret Scripture, Aquinas, as we shall see, interpreted the Scriptures through the lens of Aristotelian philosophy.[12]

Because of the similarities between the philosophical god of Aristotle and the God of the Bible (aseity, simplicity, and immutability) and because classical theism is being attacked by process theologians and open theists, some Protestants today are seeking to defend classical theism by appealing to the philosophical writings of Aquinas. This, in my opinion, is an overcorrection and makes the fatal mistake of looking to the wisdom of man—philosophy—rather than to the wisdom of God alone, *sola Scriptura*.

My hope is just that—to drive us to divine revelation in our understanding of the nature of God. What God has revealed in nature and within Scripture is the only sure guide to understanding God. My hope is for us to see that our knowledge of God is utterly dependent on God as the discloser of himself. For he must condescend and manifest himself to us if we are to know anything about God, or otherwise we will be left wondering and groping in the darkness.

Jeffrey D. Johnson
President, Grace Bible Theological Seminary
Conway, Arkansas

---

12   Some, such as J. V. Fesko and Arvin Vos, have argued that Thomas did not subjugate theology to philosophy. See J. V. Fesko, *Reforming Apologetics: Retrieving the Classic Reformed Approach to Defending the Faith* (Grand Rapids: Baker Academic, 2019), 71–96. And Arvin Vos, *Aquinas, Calvin, and Contemporary Protestant Thought: A Critique of Protestant Views on the Thought of Thomas Aquinas* (Grand Rapids: Christian University Press, 1985), 66–75. And more recently, see *Aquinas Among the Protestants*, ed. Manfred Swensson and David VanDrunen (Oxford, UK: Wiley Blackwell, 2018).

I

Natural Theology's Dilemma

THOMAS OF AQUINO sacrificed wealth, power, and honor to become a beggar. At the age of nineteen, when young men are most allured by the enticements and vanities of this world, Thomas turned his back on it all. It is not that he forsook the pursuit of glory as much as he emptied his hands of the glory he already possessed by birth.

Thomas was born into glory because he was born into royalty—pomp and power surrounded him on every side. The Holy Roman Emperor, Frederick II of Germany, was Thomas's cousin. His father, Landulf, was the count of Aquino and a knight of the Kingdom of Sicily. His mother, Theodora, was countess of Teano and likely related to the only king canonized as a saint, Louis IX, king of France.

Because of this, Thomas was born privileged, with the world at his fingertips. He didn't have to climb any mountain to see what the world had to offer him; it was there for him to behold from his birth in 1225.[1] He was born not only at the top of the social ladder but on

---

1 The date of Thomas's birth is determined by counting backward from the date of his death, March 7, 1274. His friend and first biographer, William of Tocco, claimed that Aquinas was forty-nine when he died, which would place his birth in 1225 and seems to be the most common date given for his birth. Confusion came when Tocco later claimed he was not sure if Thomas was in his forty-ninth year or if he had reached his fiftieth year, which

top of a literal mountain—a steep cliff known as Dry Rock. There, in Roccasecca, Italy, he lived in a prominent castle where he was able to gaze over the Apennine Mountains and see the glory of the world that stood beneath his feet.[2]

From this lofty vantage point, Thomas would be given every advantage to become someone notable. At the age of five he was sent to study under his uncle, Sinibald, at the nearby and famed abbey of Monte Cassino.[3] When he was thirteen, Aquinas continued his education at the newly founded university in Naples.[4] All appeared to be moving in the right direction for Thomas. He was destined to be somebody great—that is, until he decided, much to the consternation of his family, to do the unthinkable: join a mendicant order.[5]

At nineteen, Thomas chose poverty over riches and begging over a life of ease. Choosing shame rather than honor, Thomas decided to give up his elevated spot on the mountain to walk in the valley and shadows of obscurity and disgrace.

Such was the frustration of his family that en route to join this newly established order of self-impoverished preachers, the Dominicans, his brothers kidnapped him and locked him away in their father's Castle

---

would then place his birth in 1224. See Pasquale Purro, *Thomas Aquinas: A Historical and Philosophical Profile*, trans. Joseph G. Trabbic and Roger W. Nutt (Washington, DC: The Catholic University of America Press, 2012), 3.

2 When he was a child, Thomas's youngest sister "died in early infancy, struck by lightning while the young Thomas, who was sleeping nearby alongside his nurse, was spared." Jean-Pierre Torrell, *Saint Thomas Aquinas, Vol. 1 The Person and His Work*, trans. Robert Royal (Washington, DC: The Catholic University of America Press, 2005), 4.

3 At this time, Thomas's father, Landulf, donated twenty ounces of gold to the abbey for "the remission of his sins" (see Torrell, *St. Thomas Aquinas*, 5).

4 Founded the same year of Thomas's birth, 1225.

5 His parents were hoping he would follow his uncle, Sinibald, and become the abbot of the renowned Benedictine abbey of Monte Cassino. The abbey is located about eighty miles south of Rome on the border between Hohenstaufen and the papal territory. During the life of Aquinas, the monastery was in its golden age and had a history of producing bishops, cardinals, and even three popes: Stephen IX, Victor III, and Gelasius II.

of San Giovanni, then brought him back to their castle in Roccasecca.[6] For about a year, his family held him captive against his will. To further deter Thomas from throwing his life away, it is reported that his brothers threw a prostitute into his chamber to allure him out of his vow of chastity. Not giving into such a radical deterrent, he drove her away and maintained his resolve.[7] Eventually, his mother, out of compassion, released him, and off the determined young man went to Paris, via Naples, to become a poor and lowly friar.

Arriving in Paris in 1245 at the age of twenty, Thomas went on to study at the University of Paris under the famous Aristotelian and Dionysian scholar, Albert the Great (c. 1200–1280).[8]

Though he was a tall and imposing figure, Thomas was a quiet and bashful student. G. K. Chesterton painted Aquinas as a "huge heavy bull of a man, fat and slow and quiet; very mild and magnanimous but not very sociable; shy, even apart from the humility of holiness."[9] Such a massive man was Thomas that "when he was passing, the peasants in the fields left their labors and came near to look at him, full of admiration for a man of such corpulence and beauty."[10]

And because he was naturally bashful, he was a silent learner. Unlike most people, Thomas spent more time thinking than speaking. His quiet contemplation, however, was misjudged by his brash fellow students. They referred to their large but shy classmate as "the dumb ox."

Nevertheless, Albert, seeing something special in Thomas, defended his star pupil: "You call him the dumb ox, but in his teaching, he will

---

6   Josef Pieper, *The Silence of St. Thomas*, trans. John Murray, S.J. and Daniel O'Connor (South Bend, IN: St. Augustine's Press, 1963), 9.

7   Supposedly, after this event an angel came to Thomas at night and placed a chastity belt on him.

8   See Thomas Schwertner, *St. Albert the Great: The First Universal Doctor* (Post Falls, ID: Mediarix, 2018). Aquinas's first stay in Paris and its purpose is debated by historians. See Torrell, *Saint Thomas Aquinas*, 19–24.

9   G. K. Chesterton, *Saint Thomas Aquinas* (Nashville: Sam Torade Book Arts, 2019), 4.

10   This description of Thomas Aquinas comes from the mother of Thomas's friend and secretary, Reginald, and cited in Jean-Pierre Torrell, *The Person and His Works*, 26.

one day produce such a bellowing that it will be heard throughout the world." Albert's prophecy didn't disappoint. Thomas's bellowing was indeed heard around the world. He would leave his mark on both theology and philosophy. In regard to theology, Thomas became one of the greatest teachers of the Catholic Church. He was declared by Pope Benedict XV (1914–1922) as the official teacher of the Catholic Church. In regard to his philosophy, he is considered one of the foremost philosophers of the Middle Ages.

Natural Theology Is Not Natural Revelation

The focus of Aquinas's theology and philosophy was God. And the branch of philosophy that treats the existence and nature of God is called *natural theology* (i.e., philosophy of religion).

Natural theology is not natural revelation. This is important to stress because natural theology and natural revelation are often conflated together by those seeking to biblically defend the validity of natural theology. For instance, R. C. Sproul made this mistake when he attempted to justify Aquinas's natural theology by appealing to verses in the Bible that affirm natural revelation.[11] J. V. Fesko does this as well in his book *Reforming Apologetics*.[12] James Barr, in his book *Biblical Faith and Natural Theology*, also errs at this point when he, after pointing to the verses about natural revelation, says, "The Bible itself sanctioned, or depended on, or implied, natural theology."[13]

Yet proving the biblical validity of natural *revelation* does not establish the biblical validity of natural *theology*—philosophy. This is because philosophy and revelation are not the same thing. "General revelation differs from natural theology," claims Robert Letham, in that "general

---

11 See R. C. Sproul, *Defending Your Faith: An Introduction to Apologetics* (Wheaton, IL: Crossway, 2009), 85.

12 See J. V. Fesko, *Reforming Apologetics: Retrieving the Classic Reformed Approach to Defending the Faith* (Grand Rapids: Baker Academic, 2019), 1–2.

13 James Barr, *Biblical Faith and Natural Theology: The Gifford Lectures for 1991* (Oxford: Clarendon, 1993), 21.

revelation refers to what God makes known of himself through creation. It is accepted and understood by faith. It proceeds from God and reaches us. On the other hand, natural theology, as it is called, refers to attempts by humans to argue for the existence and nature of God based on what is known or observed in creation and providence. It assumes that we have the capacity to know a great deal about God on the basis of our own powers of reason and observation."[14]

Natural theology is the philosophy of religion, and the philosophy of religion is limited to what can be known about God through reason and our empirical senses. At least Aquinas defined his own natural theology as a "philosophical science" that is "demonstrated" and "built up by human reason."[15]

Natural theology, unlike revealed theology, does not start with God's self-disclosure. Natural theology, at least for Aquinas, begins on the false notion that man is ignorant of God. Rather than starting out with the immediate knowledge and awareness of God, natural theology seeks to construct a knowledge of God through reason and experience. In short, God is the conclusion for natural theology rather than the starting point.

Natural revelation, on the other hand, comes from the heavenly wisdom of an infallible God, while natural theology, like all forms of philosophy, comes from the worldly wisdom of fallible men. The main difference, therefore, between natural revelation and natural theology is the source in which they are derived—one from God and the other from man. Consequently, natural revelation and natural theology have dissimilar starting points.

One may object by saying natural theology is the interpretation of natural revelation. In other words, though natural theology is not the

---

14 Robert Letham, *Systematic Theology* (Wheaton, IL: Crossway, 2019), 55–56.

15 Thomas Aquinas, *Summa Theologica*, trans. Fathers of the English Dominican Province, rev. Daniel J. Sullivan in Robert Maynard Hutchins, gen. ed., *Great Books of the Western World* (New York: Encyclopedia Britannica, 1952), 1.1.1 (hereafter cited in text as *ST*).

same thing as natural revelation, natural theology is built on natural revelation. It is reason built on the light of nature.

But this is not the case at all, at least not the case for Thomas Aquinas. This is another common misunderstanding about the natural theology of Thomas Aquinas. Natural theology for Aquinas is not a philosophical science logically induced or deduced from what is universally communicated in natural revelation (i.e., nature). This is not the case at all, and especially not the case for Thomas Aquinas. Natural revelation does not play any role in Aquinas's natural theology. In fact, as we shall see, Aquinas denied the very existence of natural revelation when he denied its essential attributes. For Aquinas, the knowledge of God is not universally, immediately, and undeniably communicated to man in nature.

As will be shown, rather than natural theology being built on natural revelation, it stands against it. Natural theology denies the efficacy of natural revelation. Rather than bowing the knee to humbly receive what God gives all men freely, men, in their own wisdom, would rather try to climb their way to God. Instead of starting with the knowledge of God as a universal given, the "wise" men of this world would rather pretend their philosophizing is needed to convince themselves and others of the existence of God. In sum, unlike natural revelation, natural theology doesn't begin with the knowledge of God but seeks to end with the knowledge of God.

Yet by starting on the foundation of man rather than God, natural theology will never reach God. If we purposefully, at the start of our inquiry, throw out what we already know to be true, why should we expect to come to the right conclusions about God? As we shall see, natural theology and natural revelation have not only different starting points but also different conclusions. Though the terms *natural theology* and *natural revelation* sound similar, a closer look at their distinct characteristics will reveal that natural theology is actually antithetical to natural revelation.

THE CHARACTERISTICS OF NATURAL REVELATION

Natural revelation is the knowledge of God revealed to us by God in nature. Through natural revelation, we know that God is both absolute and personal. Through the completed works of God (i.e., creation), we know God is above creation; through the ongoing works of God (i.e., providence), we know God is near and cares. Through the law of God written on our consciences, we know that God is both holy (transcendent) and personal (immanent). And this knowledge of God's transcendence and immanence is universally, effectually, immediately, and consistently communicated by the things that are seen (Ps 19:1–3). For this reason, the God who is revealed in natural revelation is the same transcendent and immanent God revealed in special revelation (i.e., the Bible).

Natural Revelation Originates with God

The first attribute of natural revelation is that it originates with God. B. B. Warfield claimed, "The fundamental fact in all revelation is that it is from God."[16] God is the one who is communicating in natural revelation. The medium is not words but His created works. God's completed work—the sun, the stars, the mountains, the streams, the trees, the animals, and every other created thing—testifies of God's glory, power, and creativity. God's ongoing work of providence is designed to manifest his presence (Acts 17:27). The law written on man's conscience testifies of God's displeasure with man (Rom 2:15). God speaks in all these things.

Natural Revelation Is Universal

The second attribute of natural revelation is its universalness. The Bible says, "There is no speech, nor are there words, whose voice is not heard. Their voice goes out through all the earth, and their words to the end

---

16 B. B. Warfield, "Revelation and Inspiration," in *The Works of Benjamin Warfield* (Grand Rapids: Baker, 2003), 1:16.

of the world" (Ps 19:3–4). As the heat of the sun touches everyone, natural revelation speaks to everyone.

Natural Revelation Is Efficacious

The third attribute of natural revelation is its efficacy. God is good at getting his point across. God has revealed himself clearly and persuasively and undeniably to everyone. No one can honestly say that he or she did not understand the message of natural revelation. No one is ignorant, and no one is an honest agnostic or atheist. For this reason, Joel Beeke and Paul Smalley state, "General revelation is not a tool for Christians to convince people of something they do not know, but to convict them of what they do know and fail to live up to."[17]

Natural Revelation Is Immediate

The fourth attribute of natural revelation is its *instantaneousness*. There are no time laps between God speaking and man understanding what God has spoken. All men have an immediate awareness of God. As Beeke and Smalley maintain, "General revelation is not potential revelation, but actual revelation."[18] And John Owen said, "There is no need of traditions, no need of miracles, no need of the authority of any churches, to convince a rational creature that the works of God are his, and his only; and that he is eternal and infinite in power that made them. They carry about with them their own authority. By being what they are, they declare whose they are."[19]

Moreover, no discursive thinking, no syllogism, no inductive or deductive reasoning, no instruction, no argumentation, and no rational proof is needed for man to have an immediate awareness of God in nature. According to Herman Bavinck, man's knowledge of God "arises spontaneously and without coercion, without scientific argumentation

17 Joel R. Beeke and Paul M. Smalley, *Reformed Systematic Theology: Revelation and God* (Wheaton, IL: Crossway, 2019), 1:210.

18 Beeke and Smalley, 1:204.

19 John Owen, "Of the Divine Original, Authority, Self-evidencing Light, and Power of the Scripture," in *The Works of John Owen* (Edinburgh: Banner of Truth, 1968), 16:310–311.

and proof."[20] Creation provides this knowledge to the educated and the uneducated alike. The old and the young and everyone in between are fully aware of God's transcendence and immanence. Herman Bavinck goes on to say, "Knowledge of God never needs to be instilled in people by coercion or violence, nor by logical argumentation or compelling proofs, but belongs to humans by their very nature and arises spontaneously and automatically."[21] And according to Calvin, "there exists in the human mind and indeed by natural instinct, some sense of Deity [*sensus divinitatis*], we hold to be beyond dispute, since God himself, to prevent any man from pretending ignorance, has endued all men with some idea of his Godhead.... This is not a doctrine which is first learned at school, but one as to which every man is, from the womb, his own master; one which nature herself allows no individual to forget."[22]

Natural Revelation Is Continuous

The fifth attribute of natural revelation is its *perpetuality*. Like a constant ringing in the ear, God speaks in every moment of every day and every night. It's ceaseless communication. Creation is a relentless and unending testimony of God. "Day to day pours out speech, and night to night reveals knowledge" (Ps 19:2). Man cannot run or hide from the knowledge of God that is continuously communicated everywhere and in everything. "Wherever you cast your eyes," John Calvin claimed, "there is no spot in the universe wherein you cannot discern at least some sparks of his glory."[23] We may suppress the knowledge of God, but we cannot eliminate the divine communication found everywhere and in everything. As Calvin further remarked, "The whole world is a theater for the display of the divine goodness, wisdom, justice, and power" of God. Therefore, "we cannot open our eyes without

---

20 Herman Bavinck, *Reformed Dogmatics*, trans. John Bolt and John Vriend (Grand Rapids: Baker Academic, 2003), 2:71.

21 Bavinck, 2:73.

22 John Calvin, *Institutes of the Christian Religion*, ed. John T. McNeill, trans. Ford Lewis Battles (Philadelphia: Westminster, 1977). 1.3.1.

23 Calvin, 1.5.1.

being compelled to behold him."[24] "The end of creation," claimed John Owen, "is thus to be another preacher pointing to the Lord."[25]

Natural Revelation Is Infallible

The sixth attribute of natural revelation is *infallibility*. All revelation is infallible. Because revelation comes from the God who cannot err or lie, revelation, in all its forms, cannot be mixed with error or falsehoods. Though natural revelation does not tell us everything about God, what it does tell us about God is infallibly true.

Natural revelation, therefore, extends and is limited to the infallible knowledge of God, which is revealed universally, effectually, immediately, and consistently. Consequently, philosophy and science are not a part of natural revelation. Though all truth is God's truth, not all truth is communicated universally, effectively, immediately, consistently, and infallibly from above.

THE CHARACTERISTICS OF NATURAL THEOLOGY

Philosophy and natural theology, on the other hand, have the opposite characteristics of natural revelation. Natural theology is *not* universally, effectively, immediately, consistently, and infallibly communicated from above. Rather than originating from the mind of God, natural theology originates from the mind of man. Natural theology is man's attempt to discover the truth about God through empirical and rational analysis and philosophical speculation. Consequently, because natural theology is not universally and immediately understood, it doesn't leave everyone without excuse. But above all, natural theology is not infallible.

Natural Theology Does Not Originate with God

The first attribute of natural theology is that it originates with man. Natural theology is not divine revelation but a branch of philosophy.

---

24 Calvin, 1.5.1.
25 John Owen, *Biblical Theology* (Morgan, PA: Soli Deo Gloria, 2002), 40.

Rather than coming from above as a free gift, natural theology comes by way of logical demonstration and human "achievement" (OI, 158). Aquinas called natural theology a "philosophical science" that has to be "demonstrated" and "built up by human reason" (ST, 1.1.1).

This is why John Calvin's theology is a practical rejection of Aquinas's philosophical theology. According to Calvin, natural revelation is not a "philosophical science built up by human reason" but the knowledge of God that all men have immediately communicated to them in nature. Thus, John Owen said, "It is a basic proposition that God can only be known through God."[26] For Calvin, all knowledge begins with an awareness of God. "There is no knowing," Calvin famously claimed, "that does not begin with knowing God." The foundation of the knowledge of God is the starting point upon which all other knowledge is established.

Yet philosophy and natural theology—at least as defined by Aquinas—reject this starting point. "The existence of God," Aquinas argued, "is not self-evident to us . . . [but] can be demonstrated from those of his effects which are known to us" (ST, 1.2.2). In way of explanation, Etienne Gilson states, "Whether we start from the idea of God conceived in the human mind with St. Anselm, or from man and the world with St. Thomas, never, at any rate, do we start from God Himself—He is invariably the goal."[27] Martin Grabmann claims, "The existence of God is . . . not an immediately self-evident, nor an innate truth, but is a truth attained only by means of conclusion from premises."[28]

For Aquinas, the starting point of our inquiring begins with what can be induced from sense experience. "According to the Philosopher [Aristotle]," argued Aquinas, "all our knowledge begins from the

---

26 Owen, 8.

27 Etienne Gilson, *The Spirit of Mediaeval Philosophy* (Notre Dame, IN: University of Notre Dame, 1991), 85.

28 Martin Grabmann, *Thomas Aquinas: His Personality and Thought*, trans. Virgil Michel (New York: Longmans, Green, 1928), 99.

senses. Now [seeing that] God is furthest removed from the senses, . . . we do not know him first, but last."[29]

Therefore, according to Aquinas, to ascertain a knowledge of God, we must start with the study of sensible things: "Now because we do not know the essence of God, the proposition is not self-evident to us; but needs to be demonstrated by things that are more known to us, though less known in their nature—namely, by effects" (ST, 1.2.1). And the knowledge of the creative effects of God begins with the empirical senses: "Now it is natural to man to attain to intellectual truths through sensible objects," Aquinas claimed, "because all our knowledge originates from sense" (ST, 1.1.9).

Thus, the nature of God—that which transcends the physical world—is derived from the study of the physical world. As Aristotle (384 BC–322 BC) before him, Thomas placed his metaphysics after the study of the physical world. This is why Aquinas called his natural theology a physical science that is built up by human reason.

Natural Theology Is Not Universal

Because natural theology is a "philosophical science that is built up by human reason," it is *not* universally understood. According to Aquinas, only extremely dedicated and intelligent people can discover the knowledge of God through this means.

Natural Theology Is Not Efficacious

Unlike natural revelation, natural theology is not efficaciously understood. Agreeing with Moses Maimonides (1135–1204), Aquinas claimed the Bible is needed because not all men are competent philosophers:

If a truth of this nature were left to the sole enquiry of reason,

---

29 *St Thomas Aquinas: Faith, Reason and Theology: Questions I–IV of His Commentary on the De Trinitate of Boethius*, trans. Armand Maurer (Toronto: Institute of Mediaeval Studies, 1987), 1.2 "On the contrary" (hereafter cited in text as *DT*).

three disadvantages would follow. One is that the knowledge of God would be confined to few. The discovery of truth is the fruit of studious enquiry. From this very many are hindered. Some are hindered by a constitutional unfitness, their natures being ill-disposed to the acquisition of knowledge.... Others are hindered by the needs of business and the ties of the management of property. There must be in human society some men devoted to temporal affairs. These could not possibly spend time enough in the learned lessons of speculative enquiry to arrive at the highest point of human enquiry, the knowledge of God. Some again are hindered by sloth. The knowledge of the truths that reason can investigate concerning God presupposes much previous knowledge. Indeed almost the entire study of philosophy is directed to the knowledge of God. Hence, of all parts of philosophy, that part stands over to be learnt last, which consists of metaphysics dealing with points of Divinity. Thus, only with great labour of study is it possible to arrive at the searching out of the aforesaid truth; and this labour few are willing to undergo for sheer love of knowledge. Another disadvantage is that such as did arrive at the knowledge or discovery of the aforesaid truth would take a long time over it, on account of the profundity of such truth, and the many prerequisites to the study, and also because in youth and early manhood, the soul, tossed to and fro on the waves of passion, is not fit for the study of such high truth: only in settled age does the soul become prudent and scientific, as the Philosopher says. Thus, if the only way open to the knowledge of God were the way of reason, the human race would dwell long in thick darkness of ignorance: as the knowledge of God, the best instrument for making men perfect and good, would accrue only to a few, and to those few after a considerable lapse of time. A third disadvantage is that, owing to the infirmity of our judgement and the perturbing force of imagination, there is some admixture of error in most of the investigations of human reason. This would be a reason to many for continuing to doubt even of the most accurate demonstrations, not perceiving the force of the demonstration, and seeing the divers judgements of divers persons who have the name of being wise men.[30]

---

30 Thomas Aquinas, "Summa Contra Gentiles, Book I-II," in Latin/English Edition of the *Works of Thomas Aquinas*, Vol. 11, trans. Fr. Laurence Shapcote (Green Bay, WI: Aquinas

Natural Theology Is Not Immediate

Consequently, the conclusions of natural theology take time to reason through. Syllogisms are a process. The mind doesn't see the conclusion of the syllogism immediately, but it has to connect the dots. Therefore, natural theology is not immediate.

Natural Theology Is Not Continuous

Because God never stops speaking in nature, man cannot honestly deny or forget there is a transcendent and immanent God. Yet natural theology is dependent on the intelligence and memory of the philosopher; consequently, it is not continuous.

Natural Theology Is Not Infallible

In addition, unlike natural revelation, natural theology is fallible. Aquinas admitted that natural theology is subject to error: "Besides, in the midst of much demonstrated truth there is sometimes an element of error, not demonstrated but asserted on the strength of some plausible and sophistic reasoning that is taken for a demonstration" (SCG, 1.1.4).

NATURAL REVELATION IS NOT NATURAL THEOLOGY

For these six reasons, natural theology is not equivalent to natural revelation. R. C. Sproul, therefore, was mistaken when he stated that "natural theology comes by way of God's general revelation in nature. Its origin is divine. Man, being born into this world, does not need to rely on 'unaided reason,' for since the creation of the world, God's 'invisible attributes, namely, his eternal power and divine nature, have been clearly perceived' (Rom 1:20a)."[31] And Fesko was wrong when he said, "Natural theology is drawn from the order of nature, and supernatural theology, which transcends human reason, is drawn from the order of grace. Both forms of knowledge are revealed and are not merely a

---

Institute, 2018), 1.1.4 (hereafter cited in text as *SCG*). Also see Moses Maimonides, *Guide of the Perplexed*, trans. Shlomo Pines (Chicago: University of Chicago Press, 1966), 1.33.

31 Sproul, *Defending Your Faith*, 79.

matter of human discovery."[32] These statements would be fine if they would have replaced *natural theology* with *natural revelation*. But by confusing natural theology with natural revelation, they are sadly using Scripture, which is the wisdom of God, to validate philosophy, which is the wisdom of man.

Understanding the difference between natural revelation and natural theology is vital. Some, such as Sproul and Fesko, falsely view any attack on natural theology as an attack on natural revelation. While others, such as Karl Barth, have rejected natural revelation in their rejection of natural theology.[33] But neither of these options have to be the case if we understand the difference between natural theology and natural revelation.

It is possible to reject natural theology and affirm natural revelation. For example, Max Scheler defended natural revelation in his rejection of natural theology. Unlike Karl Barth, Scheler didn't mistakenly join them together. According to G. C. Berkouwer, "Scheler thinks the basic error of the traditional natural theology is that it tries to conclude to that which is already possessed from a completely different source."[34] In other words, natural theology is not built on natural revelation (on the universal awareness of the absolute and personal God) but dismisses natural revelation altogether. Beeke and Smalley also uphold natural revelation while rejecting natural theology: "We must not attempt a natural theology that sets up human reason as the authority."[35] Consequently, Beeke and Smalley "believe that the best

---

32 Fesko, *Reforming Apologetics*, 2.

33 "One would think," Barth claimed, "that nothing could be simpler or more obvious than the insight that a theology which makes a great show of guaranteeing the knowability of God apart from grace and therefore from faith, or which thinks and promises that it is able to give such a guarantee—in other words, a 'natural' theology—is quite impossible within the Church, and indeed, in such a way that it cannot even be discussed in principle" (*Church Dogmatics*, 2.1).

34 G. C. Berkouwer, *Studies in Dogmatics: General Revelation*, trans. Algemene Openbaring (Grand Rapids: Eerdmans, 1983), 77.

35 Beeke and Smalley, *Reformed Systematic Theology*, 1:241.

approach to these matters is to affirm general revelation and yet avoid natural theology."[36]

In sum, natural theology, like philosophy, places the foundation of knowledge on human experience and reasoning rather than on the foundation of divine revelation. And the Bible makes it clear that wisdom that isn't founded on the fear of God isn't wisdom at all (Prov 9:10). And as Letham stated, "God is the necessary presupposition for human life, so much so that it is the fool who has said in his heart that there is no God (Ps 14:1)."[37]

THE GOD OF NATURAL THEOLOGY

Natural theology seeks to obtain a philosophical knowledge of God by *suppressing* the knowledge of God that comes through natural revelation. Yet, as we shall see, by refusing to begin with the universal awareness of God, natural theology is unable to come to the same God of natural revelation.[38] You can't reject the foundation God has already laid and expect to build a doctrine of God that will stand. Both God's transcendence and immanence, which he has clearly disclosed in natural revelation, are necessary for a proper knowledge of God. And natural theology has no explanation of how God can be transcendent and immanent at the same time.

When revelation is rejected, neither scientists nor philosophers have the ability to explain how God is both transcendent and immanent. Without divine help, there is no human explanation of how God's transcendence and immanence do not cancel each other out. Either God's transcendence will consume God's immanence or God's immanence consumes God's transcendence when man is left to his own wisdom.

---

36 Beeke and Smalley, 1:236.

37 Letham, *Systematic Theology*, 42.

38 Likewise, Letham stated, "The god who is a product of the constructions of human thought and the predication of whose existence depends on human reasoning does not and cannot exist, since in any argument the premises have a higher degree of certainty than the conclusion to which the argument leads" (Letham, 42).

Without the light of God, man is in the dark. The essential problem of natural theology is that, by reason and empiricism and speculation alone, philosophers do not have access to the knowledge needed to resolve the tension between God's absoluteness and his relatability. In every possible construction of natural theology, either God's transcendence or God's immanence is destroyed.

In other words, if divine revelation is rejected, philosophers cease to have access to the knowledge needed to keep God's transcendence and immanence in balance. And without God being both transcendent and immanent, as effectively communicated in natural and special revelation, some form of deism or pan(en)theism emerges.

In denying the transcendent and immanent God of natural revelation, philosophers can't help but reconstruct a new god fashioned after their own likeness (Rom 1:21–23). For instance, if God were entirely transcendent, then it would be impossible for God to be relatable. And an unrelatable God is a deistic being who does not freely govern and interact with the universe. And if God does not govern and interact with the universe, then the universe is left to govern itself without any absolutes. A self-governing universe, moreover, means there is power within the universe that is independent and separate from God. This pantheistic dualism not only destroys God's relatability, it also destroys his absoluteness. For if there is a power that operates independent of God, then God ceases to be absolute. Consequently, if God is totally transcendent, he is neither relatable nor absolute.

Conversely, if God is entirely immanent, then there is no real distinction between God and the universe. And if God and the universe are one, then God not only ceases to be absolute and independent but he also ceases to be personal and relatable.

Because there is a cosmos, for God to be transcendent, he also must be immanent. And for God to be immanent, he has to be transcendent. If he is only one or the other, he can be neither.

Thus, God must be both transcendent and immanent, but there is no way for natural theology to arrive to a transcendent and immanent deity without producing logical contradictions along the way. That is, the precise dilemma facing natural theology (and for that matter, all religions) is the explanation of how *an absolute God can be relatable without losing his independence.* Without borrowing capital from divine revelation, natural theology cannot explain how God can be both (1) independent of the cosmos and (2) the creator and governor of the cosmos.

In particular, natural theology cannot justify unnecessary and free volitional acts in an absolute God. And without God being able to make free and unnecessary decisions, he can be neither absolute nor relatable. In the process, natural theology, in all its various forms, cannot help but destroy either God's independence or his relatability (or destroy both his independence and relatability).

Etienne Gilson explains the dilemma Christian philosophers, like Thomas Aquinas, have in explaining God's relationship with the universe:

> It is a Christian dilemma. I mean a dilemma characteristic of Christian metaphysics, and only arising as a result of rational reflection on the data of revelation. The Greek universe and its interpretation occasioned no such difficulty. For Plato and Aristotle, the world and its gods were given together; neither the one nor the others laid claim to the exclusive possession of being, nothing prevented the latter being posited within the former, and the problem of their composability did not arise. It is quite otherwise in the Christian universe, and may I say that the fact is recognized even by philosophers who regard such an antinomy as insoluble. To balance between affirmation and denial of the necessary being and cause of the world, or to feel constrained to affirm and deny this being simultaneously—these were embarrassments undreamt of by the Greeks, and felt by modern thought only because it lives and moves in a Christian scheme of things.[39]

---

39 Gilson, *Mediaeval Philosophy*, 84–85.

Natural theology's inability to resolve this Christian dilemma is made evident in its twofold method of ascertaining knowledge of God: the *way of negation* and the *way of affirmation*. The way of negation seeks to define the nature of God by identifying how God is not like the cosmos—that is, the way of negation speaks of God's transcendence. Conversely, the way of affirmation seeks to define God by identifying how God is similar or analogous to the cosmos—that is, the way of affirmation speaks of God's immanence.

Both revealed theology and natural theology use the way of negation and the way of affirmation, but only revealed theology can hold these two ways together without one consuming the other. Without the biblical framework that holds the way of negation and the way of affirmation together, natural theology is left to the fallible judgment of individual philosophers to determine the exact relationship between these two seemingly opposing methods of knowing God.

If philosophers say that the way of negation is ultimate, this will naturally push us toward a *totally* unknowable God, leading us into agnosticism or deism or neoplatonic mysticism. If, on the other hand, philosophers say the way of affirmation is ultimate, then this naturally pushes us toward a God that is *totally* one with creation, which leads to process theology, open theism, or pantheism. And those philosophers who seek to hold the two seemingly opposing methods together end up formulating two conceptually different gods—a hidden god and a revealed god. That is, by the way of negation, the hidden god is unrelatable and ineffable ("wholly other"), but by the way of affirmation, the revealed god is relatable, analogous, and knowable ("wholly the same").

All world religions, which are various forms of natural theology, are susceptible to this dualistic approach. As John Hick claims, "Each of the world religions has a dual concept of God as both transcatergorical in the ultimate divine nature and yet religiously available in virtue of qualities analogous to but limitlessly greater than our own."[40]

---

40 John Hick, "Ineffability," in *Religious Studies*, vol. 36, no. 1, 2000, 35–46.

Yet, sadly, through the influence of Greek philosophy (particularly through the influence of Pseudo-Dionysius and Thomas Aquinas), a dualistic conception of God has been introduced into Christianity. On the one hand, the hidden and transcendent god is entirely unknowable (agnosticism), whereas, on the other hand, the revealed and immanent God is essentially a part of creation (panentheism). The influence of Dionysius has led some to claim that the hidden God, which is the real God, remains unknowable, whereas the revealed God is only a symbolic and metaphorical manifestation of the hidden God. This symbolic manifestation of God, moreover, is an imperfect copy of the hidden God. For the sake of accommodation, the hidden and unknowable God *created* an image of himself in the likeness of man for man to be able to conceptualize that which is otherwise ineffable. Only by the unknowable God recasting himself into man's image is man (who is confined to the world of sensible things) able to have any cognitive awareness of an infinite and ineffable God.

How God is both transcendent and immanent (unknowable and knowable) is impossible for natural theology to explain. Even theologians have a hard time systematizing the relationship between God's transcendence and immanence. They have gone back and forth in how to catalog God's attributes as they relate to his transcendence and immanence. It is not uncommon for theologians to classify God's attributes by dividing them into one of the following ways:

- his incommunicable and communicable attributes
- his absolute and relative attributes
- his negative and positive attributes
- his quiescent and operative attributes
- his metaphysical and psychological attributes
- his natural and moral attributes

Yet the tension always comes down to the relationship between God's transcendence and his immanence.

Transcendence	Immanence
absolute	relative
incommunicable	communicable
negative	positive
quiescent	operative
metaphysical	psychological
natural	moral
intransitive	transitive

According to Bavinck, the problem with theologians dividing God's attributes into two classifications is that "they all appear to divide God's being into two halves. They all seem to treat first God's absoluteness, then his personality—first God's being as such, then God in relation to his creatures. They all seem to imply that the first group of terms is obtained apart from the creation, and the second from God's creatures, and that, consequently, there is no unity concord among God's perfections."[41]

For this reason, every attempt to divide God's attributes into two classifications is somewhat misleading. This is because the attributes classified as incommunicable (transcendent) are not completely different from the attributes that exist in men. As Bavinck explained, "If they were totally incommunicable, they would also be totally unknowable and unnamable."[42] And the divine attributes classified as communicable (immanent) are not completely identical to the attributes that exist in men. In reality, there is only one classification of divine attributes. All God's attributes are similar and dissimilar (i.e., analogous) to human attributes. So this means, according to Bavinck, that "all God's attributes are both absolute and relative."[43]

---

41 Bavinck, *Reformed Dogmatics*, 2:133.
42 Bavinck, 2:134.
43 Bavinck, 2:135.

According to Bavinck, there are not two conceptual gods—one hidden and one revealed. God is both transcendent and immanent. God is both absolute and relatable. But how can God be both transcendent and immanent? Both independent and personal? How can God's attributes be both absolute and relatable? How can God both dwell in holiness and inhabit entirety while at the same time dwelling with the one with a contrite spirit (Isa 57:15)?

Natural theology (without borrowing capital from the Scriptures and its Trinitarian solution) simply does not have an answer for this. As philosophy cannot solve the riddle of the "one and the many," natural theology cannot logically reconcile how God is both absolute and relatable. In natural theology, either you have a God who can't create and relate, or you have a God who can't exist without creating and relating. And this is the failure of natural theology. Natural theology has no way of discovering the information needed to explain the free and unnecessary acts in God that allow him to be both independent and personal. According to Bavinck,

> A distinct natural theology, obtained apart from any revelation, merely through observation and study of the universe in which man lives, does not exist. . . . Scripture urges us to behold heaven and earth, birds and ants, flowers and lilies, in order that we may see and recognize God in them. "Lift up your eyes on high, and see who hath created these" (Isa 40:26). Scripture does not reason in the abstract. It does not make God the conclusion of a syllogism, leaving it to us whether we think the argument holds or not. But it speaks with authority. Both theologically and religiously it proceeds from God as the starting point.

> We receive the impression that belief in the existence of God is based entirely upon these proofs. But indeed that would be "a wretched faith, which, before it invokes God, must first prove his existence." The contrary, however, is the truth. There is not a single object the existence of which we hesitate to accept until definite proofs are furnished. Of the existence of self, of the

world round about us, of logical and moral laws, etc., we are so deeply convinced because of the indelible impressions which all these things make upon our consciousness that we need no arguments or demonstration. Spontaneously, altogether involuntarily: without any constraint or coercion, we accept that existence of God. The so-called proofs are by no means the final grounds of our most certain conviction that God exists. This certainty is established only by faith; that is, by the spontaneous testimony which forces itself upon us from every side.[44]

CONCLUSION

The knowledge of God that comes through natural revelation is not the conclusion of a syllogism rooted in science. Rather, it is the immediate awareness of God that comes with the awareness of self and nature. As soon as someone has self-awareness, he or she knows something about the existence and nature of God. "The existence of God," John Brown claimed, "is no less evident than our own."[45] To deny the existence of God is to deny the existence of the universe—which is an act of absurdity. Consequently, natural revelation is not the same thing as natural theology.

The goal of this book is to show the *failure* of natural theology in leading man to a proper knowledge of God. Without divine revelation from above, natural theology (philosophical science) is ill-equipped to resolve the tension between God's transcendence and God's immanence. If we don't start with the God of divine revelation, as Calvin suggested, we will not arrive to the God of divine revelation. If we don't start with the God of divine revelation, our inquiry is destined to end in absurdity.

When God's transcendence and the way of negation consume God's immanence and the way of affirmation, God then loses his relatability and independence. Likewise, when God's immanence and the way of

---

44 Herman Bavinck, *The Doctrine of God* (Grand Rapids: Eerdmans, 1951), 78–79.
45 Brown, *Systematic Theology*, 5.

affirmation consume God's transcendence and the way of negation, God loses his relatability and independence. Either way, God's independence or God's relatability is destroyed by natural theology's attempt to explain the nature of God. Whenever God ceases to be both transcendent and immanent, some version of pan(en)theism begins rearing its ugly head.

As we will expound more fully in the following chapters, natural theology, as it arises from finite and fallible man, does not have the tools to ascend the transcendental wall that separates man from God. "We cannot know," John Owen said, "anything at all of God except as a result of His own intervention in power and grace and the free exercise of His own will and design."[46] Likewise, Calvin remarked, "We lack the natural ability to mount up unto the pure and clear knowledge of God."[47] Like the impossibility of writing a book with only a few letters of the alphabet, natural theology does not have access to the needed data (i.e., the Trinity) to explain the nature of God. Just as the Trinity exceeds the capacity of natural reason, so does the equal ultimacy of God's absoluteness and personal (intra-Trinitarian) relations.

Natural theology may prove there is an "unmoved mover," but this unmoved mover, as it turns out, is not the God of natural or special revelation. Even the most intelligent of men, such as Aristotle, Dionysius, and Aquinas, cannot ascertain a proper knowledge of God through their own wisdom. Calvin was right when he said, "If men were taught only by nature, they would hold to nothing certain or solid or clear-cut, but would be so tied to confused principles as to worship an unknown God."[48] Again, Calvin stated,

> Certainly I do not deny that one can read competent and apt statements about God here and there in the philosophers, but these always show a certain giddy imagination.... But they saw things in such a way that their seeing did not direct them to the

---

46 Owen, *Biblical Theology*, 15.
47 Calvin, *Institutes*, 1.5.15.
48 Calvin, 1.5.12.

truth, much less enable them to attain it! They are like a traveler passing through a field at night who in a momentary lightning flashes far and wide, but the sight vanishes so swiftly that he is plunged again into the darkness of the night before he can take even a step—let alone be directed on his way by its help.[49]

Consequently, Calvin criticized and rejected the Scholastics for this reason. According to William Bouwsma, "His sharpest attacks on philosophy were directed against Scholasticism as the most flagrant example of the attempt of philosophers to storm heaven."[50] "Calvin fundamentally disagreed," claims Bruce Gordon, "with the great medieval Dominican Thomas Aquinas on the nature of theology."[51]

Calvin's friend and fellow Reformer Henry Bullinger leveled the same criticism against natural philosophy. Like Calvin, Bullinger rejected the natural philosophy of Aquinas because Aquinas had rejected revelation as his sole authority:

> There are given many reasons of natural philosophy; but the work of God doth still abide more great and wonderful than that the wit or speech of man is able to comprehend or express it. Let no man therefore, that goeth about to know any certainty of God, descent into himself to search him out with thoughts of his own; neither let him ground his opinion upon men's determinations and weak definitions: for otherwise he shall always worship the invention of his own heart, mere folly, trifles and foolish phantasies. But on the other side again, the man cannot choose but think rightly, judge truly, and speak well of God, that attributeth nothing to himself, deviseth nothing of his own brain, nor followeth the toys of other men's inventing; but in all things giveth ear to the word of God, and followeth always his holy revelation.[52]

---

49 Calvin, 2.2.18.

50 William J. Bouwsma, *John Calvin: A Sixteenth Century Portrait* (New York: Oxford University Press, 1998), 156.

51 Bruce Gordon, *Calvin* (New Haven, CT: Yale University Press, 2009), 62.

52 Henry Bullinger, *The Decades of Henry Bullinger*, ed. Thomas Harding (Grand Rapids: Reformation Heritage Books, 2004), 4.3 (2:125).

The problem, according to Bullinger and Calvin, is that the Schoolmen, such as Thomas Aquinas, did not limit their understanding of God to divine revelation. Rather, they attempted to know more about God than what God was willing to disclose about himself: "God 'does not wish us to be too wise' but to exhibit 'sobriety': we must not seek to know more than it pleases him to teach us. When he 'is our teacher and we hear him speak, he is able to give us prudence and discretion to understand his teaching, and we cannot fail in that; but when our Lord keeps his mouth closed, we must also keep our senses closed and hold them captive.'"[53]

Likewise, Bullinger saw the importance of limiting our understanding of God to what God has chosen to reveal to us: "Therefore," Bullinger claimed, "let this stand as it were for a continual rule, that God cannot be rightly known but by his word; and that God is to be received and believed to be such an one as he revealeth himself unto us in this holy word. For no creature verily can better tell what, and what king of one God is, than God himself.[54]

Moreover, by seeking to reach God outside the boundaries of divine revelation, Calvin believed the Schoolmen perverted what has been revealed in divine revelation. Likewise, John Owen claimed,

> I judge that metaphysical knowledge [dawned from Aristotle and incorporated into theology by the Schoolmen] is quite without use in human life, but rather is harmful to it. If we set apart on the one hand whatever belongs to logic, and on the other what belongs to theology, then whatever remains in the middle ground is but a burdensome, useless hotch-potch of obscure terms, vain ideas, and wordy abstractions which will never make any man better or more learned, more wise or more fitted for his duty to God and his fellow men. Let those who have the greatest reputation for metaphysical studies just open up and review the bookcases of their own hearts, and then declare truly whether any holiness, any uprightness, any wisdom, any pru-

53 Bouwsma, *John Calvin*, 156.
54 Bullinger, *The Decades of Henry Bullinger*, 4.3 (2:125).

dence, any true learning at all has come their way by help and benefit of the study of metaphysics. So what need is there to add to poor students another cross of useless and bewildering ideas when their cry already is that art is long and life but short?[55]

Owen went on to say, "From such sources have sprung all human speculations concerning vice and virtue, and all unaided theories about God and creation. Men who have been trained in the arts of the sophists have cultivated and expanded these studies until they have produced, as it were, a phantom of wisdom while adulterating, and all but fatally damaging, supernatural theology." [56]

This was a mistake that should have never been made, for the apostle Paul made it clear that the speculative reasoning of men cannot lead to a proper knowledge of God: "For after that in the wisdom of God the world by [their own philosophical] wisdom knew not God" (1 Cor 1:21 KJV). As we shall see, if we are going to have a proper knowledge of God, we must humbly receive this knowledge from divine revelation that comes from above. As Calvin went on to say, "It remains for God himself to give witness of himself from heaven."[57] If God does not reveal himself to us, we are unqualified to find him on our own. Without the light of God, we are simply left groping around in the dark.

---

55 Owen, *Biblical Theology*, 95-96.
56 Owen, 96-97.
57 Calvin, *Institutes*, 1.5.13.

2

MIXING PHILOSOPHY WITH THEOLOGY

THOMAS OF AQUINO was a man of his times. The middle of the thirteenth century (1250) marked the middle of the life of Aquinas. It is hard to say if the thirteenth century was made for Aquinas or if Aquinas was made for the thirteenth century. If he were born in any other century, it would be hard to imagine Aquinas being the same philosopher or theologian. He shaped the intellectual thought of the thirteenth century perhaps as much as the thirteenth century had shaped him. The crucial battle during that time would be the same one that would occupy the life and thought of Aquinas: the struggle brought about by the Aristotelian renaissance.

Before the birth of Aquinas, starting around the middle of the twelfth century, the works of Aristotle were being translated into Latin from ancient Greek. Michael Scotus, who was educated at Oxford and had learned Arabic in Toledo, had gathered a team of translators in Naples who were translating all things Aristotle, including the Averroës's unorthodox commentaries on Aristotle.

The Catholic Church did not remain silent. It responded by rejecting Aristotle. According to Jacques Maritain, "Aristotle, who had arrived successively and piecemeal, had for the past half-century been

35

making a fearful inroad into Christianity. It was not merely that he brought in his train a crowd of Jews and Arabs whose commentaries were fraught with danger: the noble treasure of natural wisdom which he imported was full of pagan poisons."[1]

Theology had been the queen of the sciences, and Plato was viewed as the handmaiden of theology. Wisdom for both theology and Platonism was discovered by looking above, to the heavens, not to this world below. The works of Aristotle were viewed as a threat to Christianity because *meta*physics, according to Aristotle, comes not before but *after* physics. Aristotle believed that only by studying the physical world below will we know anything about the invisible God above. In other words, knowledge of God comes through philosophical science rather than from revelation. Thus, because the study of physics and the laws of motion led Aristotle to reject a personal God and a temporal universe, the philosophy of Aristotle was firmly condemned by the church.

By the time Aquinas was born in 1225, the works of Aristotle had been censured for fifteen years. But this didn't deter young Thomas from reading Aristotle. Even prior to studying at the University of Paris under the renowned Aristotelian philosopher Albert the Great, Aquinas had already been introduced to the metaphysics of Aristotle by Peter of Ireland (c. 13th century) at the University of Naples. Because of the local autonomy and independence of the University of Naples, the forbidden fruit of Aristotle was openly dangled in front of potential students. What was banned in other schools could be unreservedly studied and discussed in Naples.

Thus, as a student at the University of Naples, Aquinas became a committed Aristotelian. Like his mentors, Aquinas believed it was possible, with some minor adjustments, to incorporate Aristotle's metaphysics into Christianity. According to Ralph McInerny, "Thomas was convinced of the complementarity of Aristotelian philosophy and

---

1 Jacques Maritain, *St. Thomas Aquinas: Angel of the Schools*, trans. J. F. Scanlan (London: Sheed & Ward, 1948), 16–17.

his Christian faith."[2] He believed there was a way to turn the world's greatest philosopher from foe to friend of Christianity. According to Edward Feser, "Aquinas was determined to show that, when rightly understood, Aristotle's philosophy was not only compatible with Christianity, but the best means of expounding and defending it."[3] "In other words," Etienne Gilson states, "the task to be undertaken [by Aquinas] was to Christianise Aristotle."[4]

By fusing Aristotelianism with Christianity, Aquinas attempted to baptize the pagan philosopher into the church. This, without doubt, was no easy task. Submerging the Aristotelian corpus in a small baptismal font designed for sprinkling babies took all Aquinas's intellectual fortitude. But apparently, that which emerged from the shallow basin was soon afterward absolved of its heresies and confirmed by the pope into the Catholic Church. What had been forbidden at the beginning of Aquinas's life was required reading shortly after his death—essentially due to relentless efforts of Thomas of Aquinas.

THREE DISCIPLINES FOR KNOWING GOD

Aquinas's synthesis of Aristotle's philosophy with Catholic theology does not mean he didn't distinguish philosophy from theology. Far from it. According to Aquinas, natural theology is based on science and reason, whereas revealed theology is based on faith. As stated by Pasquale Purro, "The principles from which philosophy and theology begin are different. In the case of philosophy, these are principles accessible to natural reason, and in the case of theology they are principles held by faith."[5]

---

2   Ralph McInerny, *Aquinas Against the Averroists: On There Being Only One Intellect* (West Lafayette, IN: Purdue University Press, 1993), 1 (hereafter cited in text as OI).

3   Edward Feser, *Aquinas* (London: Oneworld, 2020), 5.

4   Etienne Gilson, *The Philosophy of St. Thomas Aquinas*, ed. G. A. Elrington, trans. Edward Bullough (New York: Dorset, 1948), 17.

5   Pasquale Purro, *Thomas Aquinas: A Historical and Philosophical Profile*, trans. Joseph G. Trabbic and Roger W. Nutt (Washington, DC: The Catholic University of America Press, 2012), xi.

Because philosophy and theology are based on distinct principles (reason and faith), they arrive at their conclusions from different directions. Gilles Emery explains: "Theology and philosophy take inverse routes. Philosophy derives from the consideration of creatures and knows God as the principle of these creatures; whereas Christian doctrine issues from revelation and takes its departure from the study of God, using this to illuminate our knowledge of creatures."[6] Or as stated by Aquinas himself, "In the teaching of philosophy, which considers creatures in themselves and leads us from them to the knowledge of God, the first consideration is about creatures; the last, of God. But in the teaching of faith, which considers creatures only in their relation to God, the consideration of God comes first, that of creatures afterwards" (SCG, 2.4).

In other words, philosophy and theology come to their positions from different principles and dissimilar starting points. Philosophy, through the principle of reason, starts with creation to understand the Creator, whereas theology, through the principle of faith, starts with the Creator to understand the creation. These two distinct departments of knowledge arrive to the knowledge of God from different directions—reason originates from below as a natural achievement, whereas faith initiates from above as a supernatural gift.

Though faith and reason must not be confused, they can be used together for a common end. Like an artist using a hammer and chisel to create a single sculpture, philosophy and theology can both be used to understand God. For these reasons, Aquinas asserted, knowledge of God can be ascertained by three distinct disciplines: (1) natural theology/philosophy—based on reason, (2) theology—based on faith, and (3) philosophical theology—based on faith and reason.

---

6 Gilles Emery, *The Trinitarian Theology of St. Thomas Aquinas*, trans. Francesca Aran Murphy (Oxford: Oxford University Press, 2007), 43.

Philosophy—Based on Science and Reason

Natural theology, according to Aquinas, is a branch of philosophy—a science that depends on the natural light of reason. As he said, it is "a physical science built up by human reason." For Aquinas, only those who can sensibly understand the proofs and rational arguments of philosophy are able to properly accept its logical conclusions. Aquinas believed knowledge ascertained through philosophy was not a gift but an "achievement" (OI, 158). In other words, natural theology is only for the intelligent who have ample time on their hands. Properly speaking, embracing truth claims of divine revelation by faith on the authority of God has nothing to do with philosophy.

Theology—Based on Grace and Faith

Theology, which Aquinas called "sacred doctrine," is the opposite of philosophy. Philosophy relies on the light of reason, is limited to a select few, and is liable to error, whereas theology relies on the light of faith, is open to all who believe, and is inerrant. Aquinas states, "God has provided for the human race another, safe way of knowing, imparting his knowledge to the minds of men through faith" (DT, intro.).[7] Unlike philosophy, the articles of faith, which are the first principles of theology, don't have to be rationally understood before they can be accepted as true (ST, 1.1.8). The truth claims of the Bible can be embraced by faith without understanding, and this is based on the authority of God's Word. Those who believe the Bible is the Word of God have no need for rational proofs. Philosophy is not needed for those who have faith. Believers, even young children, don't have to understand how God created the world out of nothing to believe that God indeed created the world out of nothing. For those who believe, it is enough that God says that he did (Heb 11:6).

Aquinas did believe that some truths, such as the Trinity, could only be accepted by faith. "Those who try to prove the Trinity of persons

7 Thomas Aquinas, *Faith, Reason and Theology*, trans. Armand Maurer (Toronto: Pontifical Institute of Mediaeval Studies, 1997), 3.

by natural powers of reason," stated Thomas, "detract from faith, . . . for the object of faith is invisible realities which are beyond the reach of human reasons" (ST, 1.32.1). Grabmann claims that, according to Aquinas, such truths are "not attainable here below by the mere exercise of our natural power of mind, but rather through revelation and faith, . . . [for] we accept with the conviction of faith, not because we understand them, but because God has revealed them to us."[8] Therefore, as Brian Davies states, "Aquinas recognizes that philosophy can take us so far and no further."[9] And for this reason, Aquinas claimed that "not one of the pre-Christian philosophers could with all his power of thought know so much about God [i.e., Trinity] as a simple woman since the advent of Christ knows through faith."[10]

Philosophical Theology—Based on Reason and Faith

Consequently, Aquinas believed monotheism is the result of natural theology whereas the Trinity is the result of revealed theology. In other words, philosophers can know God's oneness through reason and proof, but believers can know God's threeness *only* by faith without reason or proof.

Nevertheless, though philosophy and theology (like reason and faith or nature and grace) are distinct, they can be brought together to form a third discipline—philosophical theology. Joseph Pieper says, "Thomas . . . made a point of distinguishing between philosophy and theology," not to separate them but to join them together.[11] Thomas argued, for instance, that

> the gifts of grace are added to nature in such a way that they do not destroy it, but rather perfect it. So too the light of faith, which is imparted to us as a gift, does not do away with the light of natural reason given to us by God. And even though the nat-

8 Martin Grabmann, *Thomas Aquinas: His Personality and Thought*, trans. Virgil Michel (New York: Longmans, Green and Co., 1928), 81.

9 Brian Davies, *The Thought of Thomas Aquinas* (Oxford: Clarendon, 1992), 190.

10 Grabmann, *Thomas Aquinas*, 50.

11 Pieper, *Guide to Thomas Aquinas*, 151.

ural light of the human mind is inadequate to make known that is revealed by faith, nevertheless what is divinely taught to us by faith cannot be contrary to what we are endowed with by nature. One or the other would have to be false, and since we have both of them from God, he would be the cause of error, which is impossible. Rather, since what is imperfect bears a resemblance to what is perfect, what we know by natural reason has some likeness to what is taught to us by faith. (DT, 2.3, Reply)

Aquinas alleged that philosophy and theology ought to be united because they can be mutually beneficial. Philosophy can be a hand-maiden to theology by bringing rational understanding to what is accepted by faith, and theology can guide and perfect philosophy. Many doctrines (such as God's oneness) that are "presupposed by faith," Aquinas argued, can be "proved by natural reason" (DT, 2.3, Reply). As Augustine said, "I wanted to see with the intellect what I held by faith."[12] In this sense, Aquinas claimed that "philosophy. . . [is] brought within the bounds of faith," and faith perfects reason (DT, 2.3, Reply). Or, in other words, as Aquinas claimed, "If we resolve the problems posed by faith exclusively by means of authority [revelation], we will of course possess the truth—but in empty hands!"[13]

Explaining Aquinas's proposition, Armand Maurer states, "Since both lights come from the same God, philosophy and theology cannot contradict each other. Rather, they are related like gifts of nature and grace. Grace does not destroy nature, but perfects it. Similarly, the light of faith does not do away with the light of reason, but reveals truths beyond the reach of reason itself."[14]

---

12 *De Trinitate* XV, ch. 28, no. 51.

13 Cited in M. D. Chenu, *Aquinas and His Role in Theology*, trans. Paul Philibert (Collegeville, MN: Liturgical Press, 2002), 26; *Quaestiones Disputatae De Potentia Dei*, trans. English Dominican Fathers (Westminster, MD: The Newman Press, 1952), 4.6 (hereafter cited in text as QDP).

14 Armand Maurer, introduction to *Thomas Aquinas Faith, Reason and Theology: Questions I-IV of His Commentary on the De Trinitate of Boethius*, trans. Armand Maurer (Toronto: Institute of Mediaeval Studies, 1987), xiv.

Though reason cannot prove certain articles of faith, such as the Trinity and the incarnation, it can defend against the arguments opposing the articles of the faith.

In summary, philosophy, according to Aquinas, has three benefits to offer the church:

1. Philosophy can identify certain truths accessible to both natural reason and divine revelation, which he called the "preambles of the faith."
2. Philosophy can provide reason and understanding to what is accepted by faith.
3. Philosophy, though it cannot prove the articles of faith, such as the Trinity and the incarnation, can refute arguments unbelievers use against them.

For these three reasons, though faith and reason are distinct disciplines, they should be brought together for a common objective.

THE USE OF ARISTOTLE IN THEOLOGY

Believing that philosophy and theology are to be united, Aquinas was convinced that the forbidden philosophy of Aristotle could assist theology, and theology could perfect the unorthodox elements of Aristotle's philosophy. By joining faith and reason together, Aquinas was certain he could baptize Aristotle so he could be used as a rational aid for the articles of faith. According to Anton Pegis, "The Christian Aristotelianism of St. Thomas Aquinas is a witness to his belief in the unity of truth, in the completion of reason by faith, indeed in the purification and growth of the very rationality of reason through faith, and in the service of reason to faith as its preamble."[15] Pegis went on to explain:

---

15 Anton Pegis, "General Introduction," in *Saint Thomas Aquinas: On the Truth of the Catholic Faith, Summa Contra Gentiles, Book One: God*, trans. Anton C. Pegis (Garden City, NY: Hanover House, 1955), 23.

We find St. Thomas insisting on how much truth the philosophers professed by Christianity, and how much the Christian
Revelation has clarified their problems, removed their errors,
and completed their search as philosophers. The St. Thomas
who believes that grace perfects nature, also believes that faith
perfects reason, and he is sincerely at pains to show that the philosophy of Aristotle has grown and deepened by living within
the light of revelation.[16]

But according to Armand Maurer, "Not all his contemporaries
shared his appreciation of the value of philosophy, particularly that of
Aristotle, in the work of theology."[17] Thomas O'Meara claims that "because he drew the method of Aristotle into theology, Aquinas was seen
in the turbulent world of Paris as an innovator, as an avid, even risky,
explorer of new ideas, and as an original creator of syntheses for being
and faith."[18] Gilson went as far as to say, "The offence of St. Thomas
Aquinas consisted in following Aristotle and Averroes, a pagan and
his 'wretched commentator,' instead of the perfect representative of the
Christian tradition, St. Augustine."[19]

Bonaventure (1221–1274), for once, believed that mixing the water
of Aristotle with the wine of theology is to turn wine into water. This,
according to Bonaventure, was "the worst of miracles!"[20] Yet Aquinas

---

16 Pegis, 46.

17 Maurer, *Thomas Aquinas*, xiii.

18 Thomas F. O'Meara, *Thomas Aquinas Theologian* (Notre Dame, IN: University of Notre
Dame Press, 1997), 30.

19 Etienne Gilson, *The Spirit of Mediaeval Philosophy* (Notre Dame, IN: University of Notre
Dame, 1991), 15.

20 See Maurer, *Thomas Aquinas*, xv n24. Maurer goes on to say, "Albertus the Great refers
to 'some who in their complete ignorance want to oppose the use of philosophy. This is
especially true among the Dominicans, where no one stands up to contradict them. Like
brute animals they blaspheme against things they do not understand.' Thomas inherited his
teacher's robust confidence in the value of human reason and its achievements in the arts
and philosophy, and he staunchly defended their use in theology. He himself was open to
the influence of Aristotle and his Muslim commentators, as well as the elements in the
Neoplantonic tradition handed down by Augustine, Boethius and the Pseudo-Dionysius.
But when necessary he corrected and modified everything he borrowed from his predecessors
in the creation of his own philosophy" (Maurer, xiii).

maintained the opposite: "Those who use the works of the philosophers in sacred doctrine, by bringing them into the service of faith, do not mix water with wine, but rather change water into wine" (DT, 2.3, obj. 5 and reply).

By mixing philosophy with theology, did Aquinas turn water into wine? Thomistic scholars disagree if Aquinas's philosophical theology is principally rooted in philosophy or principally rooted in theology.[21] And though Aquinas viewed theology as superior to philosophy, Aquinas also believed that philosophy, when done rightly, is consistent with theology. Though revealed theology is required for the knowledge of certain truths that transcend the light of reason (such as the Trinity and the incarnation), the knowledge of God's existence, simplicity, and immutability can be known by either philosophy or theology.

Because Aquinas believed that philosophy and theology overlapped in their doctrine of God's essence, his doctrine of God is not necessarily a two-story structure with the lower level rooted in philosophy and the upper level rooted in Scripture. It's not that simple to say Aquinas was seeking to place theology on the foundation of philosophy. He was not trying to make philosophy a prerequisite for revealed theology.[22] Nor was he saying philosophy did not need the guidance of Scripture. Thomas made this clear when he stated that "one may err because in matters of faith he makes reason precede faith, instead of faith precede reason, as when someone is willing to believe only what he can discover by reason. It should in fact be just the opposite" (DT, 2.1, Reply).

---

21 O'Meara provides a history of the various Thomistic schools in "Traditions, Schools, and Students," in *Thomas Aquinas Theologian*, 152–200. In contrast to Cardinal Cajetan (1469–1534) and many other interpreters of Aquinas, O'Meara advocates that Thomas was principally a theologian rather than a philosopher. Also see Ralph McInerny, *Praeambula Fidei: Thomism and the God of the Phosphors* (Washington, DC: Catholic University of America Press, 2006).

22 See Arvin Vos, *Aquinas, Calvin, and Contemporary Protestant Thought: A Critique of Protestant Views on the Thought of Thomas Aquinas* (Grand Rapids: Christian University Press, 1985), 66–75.

Though Thomas spoke of philosophical theology as the preambles of the faith (*praeambula fidei*), we must bear in mind that he intentionally borrowed capital from the Bible (*articuli fidei*), such as *creatio ex nihilo*, to "guide and perfect" his natural theology.[23] For instance, as claimed by Aquinas, natural reason can't discover that the universe had a beginning. A temporal universe is a biblical truth that must be accepted by faith. Yet, without this particular article of faith, the natural theology of Aristotle is heretical. To rescue his favorite philosopher from unorthodoxy and to construct a more biblical philosophy, Aquinas incorporated a bit of theology into his preambles of the faith. And after using the Bible to guide his preambles of the faith, he then used his preambles as his guide for understanding the Bible.

In other words, Aquinas used the Scriptures to critique the natural theology of his favorite philosopher, Aristotle, then used his own philosophical theology—a mixture of philosophy and theology—as we shall soon see, as his biblical hermeneutic. Thus, it is hard to unravel the amalgamated mixture of Aquinas's theology of God. For this reason, Maurer claimed that "the water of philosophy . . . has been changed into the wine of theology. That is why we cannot extract from the *Summa* its philosophical parts and treat them as pure philosophy. Everything in the *Summa* is shaped and directed to theological ends. It is considered under the formal object of theology, which is divine revelation, and therefore it belongs to the science of theology."[24]

---

23 For instance, Aquinas stated, "The existence of God and other like truths about God, which can be known by natural reason, are not articles of faith, but are preambles to the articles; for faith presupposes natural knowledge, even as grace presupposes nature, and perfection supposes something that can be perfected. Nevertheless, there is nothing to prevent a man, who cannot grasp a proof, accepting, as a matter of faith, something which in itself is capable of being scientifically known and demonstrated" (ST, 1.2.3, ad 1).

24 Maurer, *Thomas Aquinas*, xv.

SHOULD PHILOSOPHY BE MIXED WITH THEOLOGY?

So, the vital question is not if Aquinas's philosophical theology was essentially philosophical or essentially theological but, rather, if philosophy and theology are compatible in the first place.

Of course, natural revelation (what God reveals in nature) and special revelation (what God reveals in the Bible) work together in harmony. Like special revelation, natural revelation is efficacious in all that it communities. And like special revelation, natural revelation is infallible. Even the noetic effects of the fall and man's depravity do not hinder the universal efficacy of natural revelation. In other words, all men everywhere, young and old, know there is a God who created the universe.

It is also fact that all truth is indeed God's truth. Science, when done correctly, will always agree with Scripture, for God is the author of both science and the Bible.

Yet science is not natural revelation. Science is also not the study of metaphysical realities. Other than testifying to the existence of God, how is it possible for science to discover anything that transcends its reach? How is it possible for science to tell us anything about the nature of God? Pan(en)theism is bound to follow when science is used to define the nature of God. But does not the God of the Bible transcend nature by surpassing the reach of the empirical senses? Who is to say that the rules of physics and laws of motion apply to God as they do to us? Who is to say that the physical realm has anything in common with the metaphysical realm? Because physics and metaphysics are not the same thing, how can we trust physics to say anything true about metaphysical realities?

If we want to know anything about God, are we not dependent on God choosing to reveal himself to us? Has not God chosen to reveal himself to us in natural revelation? Doesn't natural revelation provide us with an immediate awareness of God? Does not the Bible say that the knowledge of God is universally communicated to us by nature and without human speculation, argumentation, or rational proofs? Can there be any knowledge of God that does not begin with God's own self-disclosure? Can we trust the opinions of scientists or the speculative reasoning of philosophers when these same men and women refuse to presuppose God as their starting presupposition? Does the Bible affirm Aristotle and Aquinas's claim that all knowledge begins with sense experience?

Protestants who defend the natural theology of Aquinas, such as Arvin Vos and Paul Helm, fail to distinguish natural theology from natural revelation. Natural revelation begins with an immediate and universal awareness of God, whereas natural theology begins, at least for Aquinas, with the denial of the universal awareness of God.[25] Natural theology, according to Aquinas, is not an immediate awareness of God in nature but a "physical science built up by human reason."

Thus, the question before us is not about if natural and special revelation work together in harmony (for I agree that they do), and it's not about if natural man is able to comprehend natural revelation (I also agree that he does). Rather, the question is if natural theology is compatible with special revelation. Or as John Owen asked, "Shall philosophy be suffered to mingle its principles, notions, hypotheses, and conclusions with the teaching of the gospel and bring into it methods

---

25 Paul Helm, for instance, in his attempt to link the metaphysics of Aquinas with the theology of Calvin, failed to see the difference between natural theology and natural revelation. Helm is right when he says, "There is no 'dualism' between nature and grace." ("Nature and Grace," in *Aquinas Among the Protestants*, 243). Yet there is a "dualism" (unreconcilable chasm) between philosophy and theology. But Helm attempted to link Calvin's teaching on *sensus divinitatis*, which is a part of natural revelation, with Aquinas's philosophical theology. "In the *Institutes*," Helm says, "Calvin discusses nature before grace, under the rubric of the twofold knowledge of God and of ourselves, particularly in Book I.3 and I.5. The former discusses the *sensus divinitatis* (or *semen religionis*), the universal awareness that God exists." ("Nature and Grace," 232). Calvin's doctrine of *sensus divinitatis*, however, is not the same thing as the metaphysics of Aristotle. As pointed out in chapter 1, Calvin broke away from the philosophical speculation of the Schoolmen and attempted to subjugate all his theology to divine revelation. Not to mention that Aquinas denied a universal awareness of God within man. Also see Helm's book, *John Calvin's Ideas* (Oxford: Oxford University Press, 2004).

means and conclusions which are subservient to the naked human intellect? Shall philosophers be allowed to employ their reasonings and methodology to the interpretation, declaration, and teaching of the Christian doctrine as they have refined them according to their own discretion and schools of thought?"[26]

Can we begin by rejecting what we already know to be true through natural revelation and expect to come to proper knowledge of God through science and speculative reasoning? And in particular to our evaluation of the natural theology of Thomas Aquinas, does Aristotle need to be corrected, or should he be outright rejected? In short, our objective is to see if Aquinas was able to turn water into wine with his mixture of philosophy with theology. Or did he turn wine into water?

The Sufficiency of Divine Revelation

Aquinas's doctrine of God is not rooted in revelation alone. Because of this, Aquinas's synthesis of the god of Aristotle with the God of the Bible was an inadvertent attack on the sufficiency of divine revelation.

First, Aquinas's fusion of Aristotle's god with the one true God was an attack on the sufficiency of natural revelation. According to the Bible, God's existence, transcendence, and immanence are clearly manifested (without argumentation or logical proof) in natural revelation. But Aquinas denied the efficacy of natural revelation by denying the universal awareness of God (*sensus divinitatis*). Instead of

26 Owen, *Biblical Theology*, 669. Owen answered his own questions by saying, "Biblical truth itself has absolutely nothing in common with secular philosophy." Owen, 670. And in another place he said, "As the Word of God [both natural and special revelation] is enclosed in the Scripture, so the Scripture is our theology, to such an extent that we assign complete authority to every part of it, and to each and every truth contained in it. This declaration is not reached (as in other sciences) by each proposition being built up from another, by application of the rules and conclusions of logic, with human reason adding its consent, but, instead, we receive each revelation or demonstration of truth immediately as it is given with sure confidence because each is Divine revelation—the very thing upon which true theology depends. If follows that any methodology—take for example that which the scholastics call 'discursive,' which draws its roots from several differing standpoints, among which are both divinely revealed truth in Scripture, and natural reason and self-confidence, is simply not admissible by the standard which we have defined." Owen, 17.

building on the foundation of natural revelation, which starts with the knowledge of God, Aquinas built below that foundation by claiming that the knowledge of God needs to be rationally demonstrated from sense experience.

Second, as we shall see more clearly in chapter 9, Aquinas's natural theology was an attack on the sufficiency of special revelation. After integrating philosophical theology with revealed theology, Aquinas used this new philosophical synthesis as an interpretative framework to understand the nature of God and the language of special revelation. Rather than allowing Scripture to be self-sufficient in providing its own rules of interpretation, Aquinas interpreted Scriptures, as we shall see, through the lens of his own philosophical theology. He taught that all knowledge begins with sense experience and all knowledge—even knowledge given by revelation—is confined and limited to concepts gathered from sense experience (DT, 6.3).

Similarities Do Not Mean Agreement

The confusion comes with the apparent similarities between the god of Aristotle and the God of the Bible. For instance, the cosmological argument of Aristotle seems to affirm the biblical doctrines of divine aseity, simplicity, and immutability. As a result of this apparent overlap, Aquinas conflated the god of Aristotle with the simple and immutable God of the Bible. Because of a few similarities, Aquinas thought that philosophy and the Bible taught the same truths about God.

But similarities don't override the vast differences between the "unmoved mover" and the Creator of the universe. The Bible doesn't teach that God is incapable of free and unnecessary acts, and Aristotle wouldn't have recognized the God of the Bible (who can make free and unnecessary decisions) as the unmoved mover. Aristotle believed, as explained in the next chapter, that for the cosmological argument to work, the first cause couldn't have been the efficient (moving) cause of a non-eternal universe. The unmoved mover, by definition, can't create the universe out of nothing, for such an act would involve free and unnecessary movement of the will. For Aristotle, because the cosmological argument does not allow for God to be the moving cause of the universe, the universe must have necessarily existed from eternity. This means that God is not the only necessary being, and this, of course, destroys God's independence as revealed in the Bible.

To better match the god of Aristotle with the God of the Bible, Aquinas turned from his first proof to his other proofs and to the philosophy of Dionysius, or Pseudo-Dionysius, as he has come to be known. For Dionysius, and unlike Aristotle, God is the efficient and moving cause of the universe. Yet, like the god of Aristotle, Dionysius's god, as we shall see in chapter 4, is without differentiation. By merging Aristotle's doctrine of divine simplicity with Dionysius's doctrine of divine simplicity, Aquinas formulated what he thought was a philosophical theology congruent with revealed theology.

But the simplicity of both the unmoved mover and the Neoplatonist god of Dionysius is not identical to the simplicity of the God of the Bible. The biblical doctrine of divine simplicity is rooted in divine independence and derived from the foundation of the Scriptures. For Aristotle, however, divine simplicity is rooted in the concept of divine immobility (a philosophical speculation rooted in science). And Dionysius's concept of divine simplicity is rooted in the numerical oneness of a created manifestation of an unknowable God that transcends "oneness."

But as we shall see, both Aristotle's and Dionysius's understanding of divine simplicity is incompatible with the biblical doctrine of divine simplicity. The simplicity of the divine essence, as revealed in the Bible, does not rule out the free acts of God and the ontological complexity of the three distinct and relatable persons of the Trinity. Nevertheless, what Aquinas thought were overlapping truths about God's nature (as we will explore in more detail in chapter 8), are not so overlapping in reality.

Conclusion

Contradictorily, Aquinas affirmed Aristotle's view of divine immobility when it came to the doctrine of divine simplicity but refused to accept the consequences of Aristotle's divine immobility when it came to the doctrines of creation and providence. Rather than rejecting the natural theology of Aristotle altogether, Aquinas used him as the foundation of his own philosophical theology and only compounded the problem by bringing in the pantheistic philosophy of Dionysius to compensate for the creative inability of Aristotle's god.

Because Aquinas's mistake—embracing divine immobility—was introduced at the foundation of his thinking, it flawed the rest of his doctrine of God. Divine immobility, which is not rooted in the Bible but in Aristotle's cosmological argument, shaped Aquinas's view of divine simplicity, which then formed his interpretive framework of the language of Scripture. In the end, Scripture was interpreted by Aquinas through the lens of Aristotle's god, the unmoved mover. Therefore, I intend to show that Aquinas's theology is principally rooted in philosophical science—that is, he didn't turn water into wine.

Ironically, Aquinas was right when he said, quoting Aristotle, "A small mistake in the beginning is a big one at the end."[27] The fatal flaw introduced by Aquinas at the beginning of his natural theology has led, as this book will seek to demonstrate, to a philosophical theology that is neither in line with Aristotle nor with the Bible.

---

27 Thomas Aquinas, *On Being and Essence*, 2nd ed., trans. Armond Maurer (Toronto: Pontifical Institute of Mediaeval Studies, 1968), 1 (hereafter cited in text as *EB*).

3

The Natural Theology of Aristotle

Thomas of Aquino was brilliant. And his keen intelligence and rigorous dedication to his studies did not go without notice. He was recognized as one of the leading scholars of his day. Bartholomew of Lucca said that Thomas "excels all modern doctors in philosophy and theology"; John of Colonna referred to him as the "incomparable teacher."[1]

His importance only increased over time. Within fifty years of his death, in 1323, he was canonized by Pope John XXII. In 1567, he was declared *doctor communis* (Doctor of the Church) by Pope Pius V. In 1879, Pope Leo XIII claimed Aquinas was "the prince and master of all Scholastic doctors." He is identified by admiring Catholics worldwide as simply "the Angelic Doctor."

All these titles, though a bit grandiose, were bestowed on Aquinas for good reason—his teaching has arguably been the single biggest influence on the theology of the Catholic Church. Aquinas was, according to Pope Pius V, "the most brilliant light of the Church."[2] And "Pius

---

1 Martin Grabmann, *Thomas Aquinas: His Personality and Thought*, trans. Virgil Michel (New York: Longmans, Green and Co., 1928), 28, 62–63.

2 Ronald P. McArthur, "The Popes on St. Thomas," Thomas Aquinas College, accessed October 21, 2019, https://thomasaquinas.edu/a-liberating-education /popes-st-thomas.

XI says of him that the Church testifies in every way that she has made his teaching her own."[3] This reverence for Aquinas has been maintained by the Catholic Church, for in the *Encyclical Studiorum Decem* of June 29, 1923, it declares, "May the instruction of Canon Law be held sacred by all: 'Professors are obliged to form their philosophical and theological studies and the teaching of these subjects according to the method, the teaching of these subjects according to and the basic principles of the Doctor Angelicus: and further, they are to revere the same.' Each one should observe this law in such a way that he is able to call St. Thomas his master."[4]

But not only does Aquinas stand out as one of the greatest minds in the Catholic Church, he is also distinguished as one of the greatest minds in all of Western thought. G. K. Chesterton praised Thomas as "one of the two or three giants; one of the two or three greatest men who ever lived. . . . I should never be surprised if he turned out, quite apart from sanctity, to be the greatest of all."[5] It would be hard to quantify who is the most important philosopher of all time, but along with Plato and Aristotle, the Angelic Doctor would surely make it into every credible top-twenty list.

Though Thomas was brilliant, his intelligence did not prevent his natural theology, at the foundational level, from being gravely flawed. Thomas agreed with Aristotle's presupposition that all knowledge begins with sense experience. Though Aquinas claims to have prioritized the Scriptures (which he viewed as infallible) over the writings of Aristotle (which he viewed as fallible), the cornerstone of Aquinas's

---

3 Josef Pieper, *The Silence of St. Thomas*, trans. John Murray, S. J., and Daniel O'Connor (South Bend, IN: St. Augustine's Press, 1963), 36.

4 Pieper, 116–117. "Can anything express more clearly the high opinion of the Church for this Doctor, than the fact that the Tridentine Fathers determined that during all of their secession only two books should be reverently placed before them on the altar, namely, the Holy Scriptures and the *Summa Theologica*?" Pieper, 116–117.

5 G. K. Chesterton, "St. Thomas Aquinas," The Society of Gilbert Keith Chesterton, accessed March 30, 2020, at https://www.chesterton.org/st-thomas-aquinas.

doctrine of God, as we shall see in chapter 5, is the cosmological argument of Aristotle that is based in empiricism.[6]

With that said, the most important stone in any infrastructure is the cornerstone. As goes the cornerstone, so goes the building. According to Aristotle, since all things in motion have an external cause, there must be something without motion that is the first cause, and this static, stationary, and immobile first cause Aristotle defined as *actus purus*. Aquinas constructed his rationale for both the *existence* and the *nature* of God on the foundation of Aristotle's cosmological argument. But is this foundation capable of holding the infrastructure of Aquinas's natural theology? Can God's existence and, more importantly, God's nature be logically and consistently induced from a philosophical assumption derived from causal relationships between things in motion? Can a right view of God's nature be induced from the notion that all things in motion have an external cause? It certainly seems like a tall task.

ROOTED IN THE STUDY OF MOTION

As for Aristotle, he disagreed with his teacher, Plato, who believed that the idea of God (i.e., the Form of the Good) was already pre-stored in man's mind prior to any sense experiences. Rather than starting with *a priori* knowledge of God's existence, Aristotle claimed the opposite—all knowledge, including knowledge of God, is *a posteriori*. Though the English empiricists—John Locke, George Berkeley, and David Hume—would not arrive on the scene until the seventeenth century, Aristotle set the stage for them by building his natural theology on empirical reasoning. Aristotle believed that we cannot explain the existence of the cosmos by starting with the knowledge of God; rather, we must start with the knowledge of the cosmos to explain the existence of God.

---

6 This is made evident in the first few chapters of part 1 of the *Summa Theologica* and the constant references back to the cosmological argument throughout the rest of part 1.

Consequently, according to Aristotle, we are all born agnostics. Without divine communication from above or innate knowledge from within, man is left to try to uncover the knowledge of God for himself. Man is the source of all his knowledge. For this reason, and in this sense, Aristotle claimed to agree with Protagoras, who said, "Man is the measure of all things."[7]

Since all knowledge begins with sense experience, theology must begin with the empirical study of the cosmos. Like Plato and Heraclitus before him, Aristotle observed that everything in the cosmos is in motion. As water moves from the raindrop to the river to the ocean, a seed turns into a sprout and then into a tree, and the process starts over again. The cosmos is ever changing as time is forever moving from one moment to the next. So, for Aristotle, the study of the cosmos is the study of motion. "Nature has been defined," Aristotle claimed, "as a 'principle of motion and change.'"[8] And at the heart of Aristotle's metaphysics is the philosophical assumption that "everything that is in motion must be moved by something" (*Phys.* 3.5).

But how did Aristotle come to this philosophical assumption? How did he conclude that everything in motion must have an external cause? He arrived there by studying motion in the physical universe. According to Aristotle, there are four types of motion: (1) locomotion, motion from one place to another; (2) qualitative motion, the motion that leads to an alteration (e.g., a leaf changing from green to brown); (3) quantitative motion, the motion that leads to an increase or decrease; and (4) substantial motion, the motion that is coming to be or passing away. In these four types of motion, Aristotle sought to identify the attributes of all moving objects.

---

7 Aristotle, *The Metaphysics: Books X–XIV*, in Loeb Classical Library, vol. 287, trans. Hugh Tredennick (Cambridge, MA: Harvard University Press, 1997), 10.1.20 (hereafter cited in text as *Metaph.*).

8 Aristotle, *Physics*, in "Great Books of the Western World," gen. ed., Robert Maynard Hutchins, trans. R. P. Hardie and R. K. Gaye (New York: Encyclopedia Britannica, 1952), 3.1 (hereafter cited in text as *Phys.*).

Objects in Motion Are Finite

Motion, first of all, requires something, such as an object, to be moved. As Aristotle stated, "If there is motion there is also something which is moved" (*Metaph.*, 11.6.9). Yet all objects in the cosmos are in motion. As Aristotle claimed, "There is no motion apart from things, for change is always in accordance with the categories of Being" (*Metaph.*, 11.8.12). Thus, everything that is in motion is finite.

Objects in Motion Are Temporal

Objects in motion are temporal because they all move successively through time. There must be a *before* and an *after* for movement to exist. For this reason, Aristotle's definition of time came from his study of motion: "Time is so called on account of motion" (*Metaph.*, 11.10.15).

Objects in Motion Are Composite

Motion takes place, according to Aristotle, when *form* and *matter* come together. Form, such as the shape and dimensions of a statue, is nothing (non-being) without matter. Matter, such as the bronze that makes up the statue, is also nothing (non-being) without form. Thus, neither form nor matter is a movable object because neither is an existing object in and of itself. Yet, when form and matter come together as a composite entity, they actualize into a real, moving object that has existence. Consequently, all moving objects are composite substances.

Objects in Motion Are Mutable

Movement requires at least two points for the object to travel between. The runner moves from the starting line to the finish line. Temperature moves from hot to cold or from cold to hot. Knowledge moves from ignorance to higher degrees of understanding. A sapling starts from a seed and grows into a tree. Moreover, movement not only takes place between two points but between opposite points. Temperature moves from cold to the opposite of cold, hot. Growth moves from something small to something big. The various stages and degrees of change always take place between two antithetical points. "Evidently," Aristotle claimed, "one thing cannot have more than one contrary." And it is only between these two contrary points that movement occurs. Things do not move from, for example, cold to light but from dark to light or from cold to hot. As explained by the philosopher, "Change is not found in all things but only between contraries and intermediates and contradictories" (*Metaph.*, 11.11.3).

Consequently, if the movement is between two contrary and antithetical points, movement involves a change from one thing into its opposite. "Everything," Aristotle stated, "is moved from something and into something" (*Metaph.*, 11.6.9). Aristotle agreed with Heraclitus, who years earlier famously stated, "No man ever steps in the same river twice, for it is not the same river and he's not the same man." Thus, moving from one state of being to another requires mutability within the objects being moved. Again, Aristotle claimed, "Every motion is a change from one thing into something else" (*Metaph.*, 11.12.4).

Objects in Motion Are Deficient

Since movement requires change and mutability, it requires privation or imperfection within the object that is moved. The table in the process of being built is moving from a state of incompleteness to a state of completeness. It begins with the construction of a few pieces, but it is not finished until all the parts are properly fitted together. Things move either for the better or for the worse. But either way, things that remain in motion remain in a state of imperfection or incompleteness. Thus, wherever movement occurs, deficiency and privation and imperfection exist in the objects being moved.

Aristotle defined movement, therefore, as the process of things going from something that has potentiality (incompleteness) to something that has actuality (completeness). "Now since every kind of thing is divided into the potential and the real [actuality]," Aristotle claimed, "I call the actualization of the potential as such, motion" (*Metaph.*, 11.9.2). And as long as motion continues, complete actualization is never reached. As Aristotle maintained, "Motion is considered to be kind of actualization, but incomplete; the reason for this is that the potential, of which it is the actualization" (*Metaph.*, 11.9.11). In this way, all moving objects are deficient and will always remain deficient as long as they are in a state of movement. Therefore, for Aristotle, movement equals mutability, and mutability equals imperfection.

Objects in Motion Are Contingent and Dependent

Most importantly, Aristotle noticed that moving objects have been placed in motion by something else. Nothing, Aristotle reasonably assumed, is the cause of its own movement. "Everything that is in motion," he stated, "must be moved by something. For if it has not the source of its motion in itself, it is evident that it is moved by something other than itself" (*Phys.* 7.1). And this philosophical assumption—*everything in motion must have an external cause*—became the foundation of Aristotle's natural theology.

And it was from this philosophical assumption that Aristotle derived the existence and nature of God. Every moving object, as stated by Aristotle, must have been moved by something. If moving objects were set in motion by something already in motion, then those objects in motion must have yet another object that placed *them* in motion. Though, according to Aristotle, this chain of causes and effects cannot logically go back indefinitely without having a first uncaused cause, all moving objects are dependent on something outside themselves.

Objects in Motion Are Eternal

Though motion must have a first cause, Aristotle nevertheless believed that objects in motion are eternal. Nothing in the cosmos is the cause of its own existence. Aristotle agreed with Parmenides, who famously stated, "Nothing comes from nothing." In the same way it is illogical for an effect to be its own cause (for that thing would have to exist prior to it coming into existence), it is illogical for existence to come out of nonexistence. For this reason, as per Aristotle, motion and time must have always existed: "But motion cannot be either generated or destroyed, for it always existed; nor can time, because there can be no priority [before] or posteriority [after] if there is no time. Hence as time is continuous, so too is motion; for time is either identical with motion or an affection of it" (*Metaph.*, 12.6.1–2). Therefore, Aristotle supposed, motion is best defined as either the eternal process of becoming or the endless process of actualization of a potentiality.

In short, the study of God starts with the study of the cosmos, and the study of the cosmos is the study of motion. And by studying physical objects in motion, Aristotle moved from physics into metaphysics. He did this, moreover, by making the philosophical assumptions that movement is only found in finite, composite, and mutable objects.

ARISTOTLE'S PROOF FOR GOD'S EXISTENCE

In all of this, Aristotle was forced to reconcile two opposing ideas: (1) the idea that motion and the material universe are eternal (seeing that nothing comes out of nothing), and (2) the idea that motion and the material universe have a first cause (seeing that it is logically impossible for there to be an infinite chain of causes). How can both ideas be true? How is there a first cause for something eternal—such as the universe?

Aristotle believed the answer was found in his cosmological argument, in which these two seemingly opposing ideas—(1) the first cause of (2) an eternal cosmos—are brought together to form a third idea: the unmoved mover. But does this truly resolve the conundrum? British philosopher and logician Bertrand Russell explains that as a young man he came upon this statement in *The Autobiography of John Stuart Mill*: "My father taught me that the question 'Who made me?' cannot be answered since it immediately suggests the further question 'Who made God?'" Reading this led Bertrand Russell to reject the cosmological argument for the existence of God. In the words of Russell, "If everything must have a cause, then God must have a cause. If there can be anything without a cause, it may just as well be the world as God, so that there cannot be any validity in that argument."[9]

But for Aristotle, nothing caused God because God is without motion, for that is what Aristotle meant by claiming God is the unmoved mover. God doesn't need an external cause because God is without cause because God is without motion. Based on his study of physics, Aristotle assumed that God was the opposite of all the attributes associated with physical things in motion. Because the study of physics indicates that motion requires an *external* cause, and because of the impossibility of endless chain of external causes, God must be the motionless first cause of the universe.

Yet how did an inactive and motionless God set the universe in motion? In other words, if God can't move, how did he set the universe in motion? The answer, at least according to Aristotle, is that God did not set the universe in motion. To put something in motion would require motion in God, and such motion in God would prevent him from being the *unmoved* mover. As Aristotle claimed, "The instrument of motion [the efficient cause] must both move something else and be itself in motion" (*Phys.* 8.5).

Thus, God cannot be the instrumental cause (efficient/moving cause) of the universe because God would cease to be God (*actus purus*) if he exerted any free acts of power. That is to say that God couldn't have placed the universe in motion even if he wanted. If God exerted any power or force or energy on the cosmos, even in the slighted degree, he would cease to be immobile.

The Four Causes of Motion

But how, then, does an immobile God, who can't move himself, move the universe? How can there be such a thing as an *unmoved* mover? Well, for Aristotle, there is more than one way to move something.

---

9 Bertrand Russell, *Why I Am Not a Christian* (New York: Simon & Schuster, 1957), 6–7.

In fact, he believed there are four causes of motion: (1) the formal cause, (2) the material cause, (3) the efficient cause, and (4) the final cause. As an illustration, think of the different things that go into bringing a table into existence. First, we would need some idea of what the table should look like—a mental blueprint of the shape and dimensions of the table. This, according to the philosopher, is known as the formal cause of a table. Second, we would need some material—wood, glue, and nails. This is considered the material cause of the table. Third, we need to roll up our sleeves or call a carpenter to build the table for us. This is the efficient cause of the table, also known as the motor cause. This efficient cause is the moving cause or the agent that generates the power and energy behind the object set in motion. And finally, for Aristotle, there is one more cause for the table's existence—the final cause. This is the purpose for which the table came into existence—such as a place to eat dinner with the family. The final cause, therefore, is the objective and purpose the other three causes are trying to fulfill or bring about.[10]

The First Cause Is the Final Cause

But this brings us back to our question on how the unmoved mover moves the cosmos when he doesn't even move himself. For Aristotle, God is not the formal cause or the material cause; God is not even the efficient cause. He exerted no power or energy. Rather, he is the final cause of the cosmos. Aristotle imagined that the final cause is the ultimate good to which all things aspire and desire, the ultimate purpose behind the existence of everything. Why is the universe in motion? What is the motivation behind all the endless energy moving things from one state of being to other states of beings? It is the final cause— God—a perfect being without change or actualization.

---

10 According to Aristotle, the formal cause (the mental blueprints) of a table has no real existence in and of itself. Likewise, the material cause and the efficient cause have no real existence in and of themselves. A table only comes into existence when the formal cause and the maternal cause come together with the efficient cause. When this happens—presto!—we have a real table that comes into existence.

To understand why Aristotle identified pure actuality (*actus purus*) with the ideal "goodness" or with "perfection,"[11] we must remember that in his physics, all material objects are in motion and all objects in motion are finite, temporal, and mutable. In other words, movement, which he defined as the actualization of potentiality, exists only in things that are imperfect or lacking in goodness/being. Pure being, on the other hand, is perfect goodness. Thus, in short, for Aristotle, pure actuality is synonymous with that being which is perfectly motionless, while all things in motion (as observed in the physical universe) are in various states of incompleteness and unactualized being. This would imply, as the Gnostics would latter claim, that physical matter is bad.

Nevertheless, not only did Aristotle associate ultimate goodness with immobility, he also defined ultimate goodness as the ultimate *object of desire*. Rather than goodness being defined as charity (something that gives of itself to others), ultimate goodness (the unmoved mover) gives nothing of itself. For Aristotle, God is the ultimate good because he is perfect, and God is perfect because he is without motion. And because God is immobile, he desires nothing outside himself. God cannot be jealous because he lacks and needs nothing. He is his own ultimate object of desire. He alone is perfect, content, and at rest. Thus, he alone is motionless. Because he alone is pure actuality, he alone is perfect goodness.

Consequently, for Aristotle, good (perfection) is that which is without motion, and bad (imperfection) is that which is in motion. And because the unmoved mover is the ultimate good, he is the ultimate object of desire, not only for himself but for everything else. God is without motion because he already has everything he needs. He lacks and wants nothing. Yet everything outside God is in motion because everything outside God is missing something they need. In other words, things in motion are in motion because they desire to be like God. All things in motion are in motion because they are aspiring to *become* something they are not. This aspiration to be like God, to be

---

11 For Aristotle, "pure actuality," "pure being," and "actus purus" all speak of the same thing.

perfect, to be pure actuality, to be motionless, constantly moves them. That is, it is in the nature of all finite things to desire pure actualization.

Aristotle believed that in all things desiring their own actuality, they are (even if they are unaware of it) desiring God. The inherent desire of all moving objects is *actus purus*.

This brings us to how the unmoved mover can move things without moving himself. Like the pull of a magnet, the unmoved mover (actus purus) remains completely passive and unaware that he is exciting objects to move after him. Simply put, God incites movement by being the ultimate object of desire. In this way, without moving himself, God is the final cause of all movement. Aristotle explained it this way: "The first principle and primary reality [God] is immovable, both essentially and accidentally, but it excites the primary form of motion, which is one and eternal. Now since that which is moved must be moved by something, and the prime mover must be essentially immovable, and eternal motion must be excited by something eternal, and one motion by some one thing" (*Metaph.*, 12.8.3-4).

Aristotle further stated that "[God] causes motion as being an object of love" (*Metaph.*, 12.7.4). This means that things in motion cannot help but love God, but God cannot love things in motion. Nevertheless, in this way, God moves things without moving at all: "Now it [God] moves in the following manner. The object of desire and the object of thought move without being moved" (*Metaph.*, 12.7.2).

But because the cosmos never obtains perfection, it will forever remain in a state of ceaseless motion. Ever aspiring to be like God but never reaching pure actuality, the universe is stuck in an eternal state of perpetual motion.

In the end, God is the first cause because he is the final cause that moves everything without being able or even desirous to move himself or anything outside himself. In this way, Aristotle believed God is the unmoved mover.

ARISTOTLE'S GOD

Aristotle's natural theology not only includes a rationale for God's existence, it also includes an explanation of the nature of God. By studying the various finite, composite, temporal, mutable, and dependent objects in motion in the physical realm, Aristotle concluded that God (who transcends the physical realm) must be the precise opposite of all these deficient objects in motion. That is, because God cannot be in motion, he cannot have the attributes of motion. Instead of being a composite being, God must be an indivisible and simple being; he must be infinite rather than finite, immutable rather than mutable, and most importantly, immobile instead of mobile. By studying the attributes of things in motion, Aristotle thought it was possible to define God as the unmoved mover or, in other words, as actus purus.

The Way of Negation

This jump from the study of the cosmos (physics) to the study of God (metaphysics) is based on a single, unfounded premise—that what is true concerning finite objects in motion in the physical realm must be true concerning motion (if mobility were possible) for God in the metaphysical realm. Based on this assumption that motion in God (if it did exist) would function the same as it functions in the cosmos, Aristotle formulated his view of the nature of God *via negativa* (the way of negation).

The Way of Affirmation

Though at first Aristotle defined God's nature by the way of negation (how God is transcendent), he later explained God's nature by the way of affirmation (how God is immanent). How is God similar to observable things in the universe? Though a vast difference exists between the unmoving God and the ever-moving eternal objects in the universe, they have at least one thing in common: being. They are both eternal and share in the state of being. God is pure being, whereas everything else that exists has partial being (potentiality). As everything in motion

is moving from potentiality to actuality, everything in motion participates in various states of being or becoming.

Hence, there is an analogous chain of being that descends from pure
actuality (perfect being) down to the various moving objects that share
in the process of actualization. God is pure being because he is without motion, whereas everything else in motion is in various degrees
of being. God, as actus purus, is the highest form of goodness, but all
moving objects share in various degrees of goodness and imperfection.

Actus Purus Is Not the God of the Bible

On the foundation that "things in motion must have been placed in
motion by something else in motion," Aristotle used the way of negation and the way of affirmation to affirm the existence and nature of
God.

Yet, as we shall see, the cosmological argument does not lead to the
God of the Bible. Though there is some overlap between the god of
Aristotle and the God of the Bible (e.g., divine simplicity and immutability), the unmoved mover of Aristotle comes short of being the personal and relatable God of the Bible who willfully and actively created
the world out of nothing.

Aristotle turned everything upside down. The unmoved mover
can do nothing but remain in a single, timeless, and necessary act of
self-contemplation. God, for Aristotle, cannot be the efficient cause of
the universe. Aristotle's god can neither create nor destroy. The exertion of creative and governing power is not in God. He can't even have
knowledge of the universe. He is powerless to do anything other than
timelessly think about himself. The unmoved mover can only do what
he has always done.

This means that the efficient cause of motion exists within the
universe itself, and things propagate and deteriorate without the

involvement of God. Thus, the cosmos has more freedom to will, to act, and to do than the unmoved mover, who is perfect actuality.

Actus Purus Is Oblivious and Unconcerned

Like the God of the Bible, Aristotle's god is an immaterially simple being—without body or parts. Yet, unlike the simple God of the Bible, Aristotle's god is both *immobile* and *undifferentiated* (non-Trinitarian) in its simplicity. For Aristotle, an immobile and undifferentiated simple God cannot contemplate anything other than that which is also immobile and undifferentiated. Actus purus can only think of himself in a single and eternal act of undifferentiated thought. Aristotle gives three reasons for this:

1. Actus purus is undifferentiated in its simplicity. This means that actus purus is identical to his thoughts. Everything that is in God, even the concepts and thoughts in the mind of God, is God. As Aristotle stated, "Thought and the object of thought are the same" in God (*Metaph.*, 12.7.8). Again, he said, "Since thought and the object of thought are not different in the case of things which contain no matter, they will be the same, and the act of thinking will be one with the object of thought" (*Metaph.*, 12.9.5). For Aristotle, there is no distinction between the pure and simple essence of God and the knowledge of God. And if God could think about something other than himself, then those additional thoughts would become essential to the very essence of God. Of course, this would undermine God's pure actuality, as it would make his essence dependent on thoughts of things outside himself.

2. Because actus purus is undifferentiated in his simplicity, he cannot make any distinctions within himself. He is his thought, and thus, his thought must be indivisible and undifferentiated for him to remain indivisible and undifferentiated (*Metaph.*, 12.9.6). This not only rules out any thoughts

about anything outside himself, but it also rules out any differentiated thoughts about himself. For God to think about anything other than his simple, undifferentiated self, he would cease to be undifferentiated in his simplicity. Thus, actus purus is pure self-contemplation. Anything less would lead to a distinction within the mind and essence of God.

3. Because actus purus is immobile in his simplicity, he cannot process any divisible thought without there being a movement within the act of thinking. Composite ideas, according to Aristotle, include movement or "change in passing from one part of the whole to another" (*Metaph.*, 12.9.6). Therefore, claimed Aristotle, "surely it would be absurd of [God] to think about some subjects" (*Metaph.*, 12.9.3) because divine thought must be "indivisible" (*Metaph.*, 12.9.6).

Hence, the god of Aristotle, according to B. A. G. Fuller, "knows only himself with a knowledge in which there is distinction neither of self from not-self, nor of the activity of thought as such from its content."[12] "All God's life and thought," Fuller went on to explain, "are locked up. He knows nothing but it, nothing but himself."[13] With such a god as this, Aristotle turns things backward. The cosmos somehow can aspire after God, but God knows nothing of the cosmos. Aristotle's god is oblivious and unconcerned about the affairs of men. Though this deistic god may be simple, it is not the personal and relatable God of the Bible.

Actus Purus Cannot Create

According to the logic, actus purus can't be the efficient cause of the universe because an efficient cause requires movement, which is impossible for the unmoved mover. The biblical account of creation requires free and unnecessary acts of power in God. But if Aristotle's

---

12 B. A. G. Fuller, "The Theory of God in Book Λ of Aristotle's Metaphysics," *The Philosophical Review* 16, no. 2 (March 1907), 173.

13 Fuller, 175.

god cannot move, how will he actively move anything inside or outside himself?

Actus Purus Does Not Have a Free Will

Actus purus can neither have any unnecessary nor free acts of the will. Not only would this require movement in the mind and the will of God, but it would also require a division within the mind of God between what is essential and nonessential to his thinking. According to Brian Davies, "The God of Aristotle is like a great, transcendent magnet. There is a sense in which he causes or explains motion or change. But he does not preside over it as doing what he wants to do. He does not act voluntarily to get things done. He does not exercise will."[14]

Actus Purus Is Impersonal

In all this, actus purus is not the personal and relatable God of the Bible. It is impossible to have a personal relationship with a god who is not even aware of us. Because actus purus does not love us, it is hard to imagine any rational creature being motivated to love this type of god in return. Is actus purus, who is cold, static, apathetic, indifferent, unaware, and impersonal, the perfect being? Aristotle may have thought so, but I am glad that divine revelation gives us a different definition of God.

A DEISTIC/PANTHEISTIC GOD

Thus, according to Aristotle, God is somewhat deistic in that he is oblivious to the universe. Yet, in another way, Aristotle's god is somewhat pantheistic. Because the unmoved mover cannot be the instrumental or moving cause of the universe, the universe could not have had a beginning. The world must be eternal. The moving cause of the universe must be something in a continuous state of motion: "The instrument of motion must both move something else and be itself in motion (for it changes together with the moved, with which it is in

---

14 Brian Davies, *The Thought of Thomas Aquinas* (Cambridge: Clarendon, 1993), 140.

contact and continuous)" (*Phys.* 8.5). Consequently, two things are logically necessary and coeternal: (1) eternal motionlessness (i.e., God) and (2) eternal motion (i.e., the universe). According to Aristotle, both the existence of the unmoved mover and the existence of ceaseless motion, an eternal universe, are both needed to explain why there is something rather than nothing; thus, "the non-existence of motion is an impossibility" (*Phys.* 8.5). Because the universe could not have had a beginning, the universe has to be coeternal and co-necessary with the unmoved mover—hence, a form of pantheism.

CONCLUSION

The god of Aristotle may be simple. Yet unlike the simplicity of the Trinitarian God of the Bible, Aristotle's god is immobile and undifferentiated. And, unlike the Trinitarian God of the Bible, *actus purus* cannot create, know, or relate to us. Moreover, for Aristotle, the universe is eternal and necessary. As a result, the natural theology of Aristotle, which is built on the philosophical assumption that nothing has the power to move itself, does not lead to the God of natural and special revelation.

4

The Natural Theology
of Pseudo-Dionysius

THOMAS OF AQUINO and Bonaventure (1221–1274) were friends. In many ways, the lives of these scholastic scholars paralleled each other. Aquinas was born just a few years after Bonaventure. As young boys, they were both extremely gifted and dedicated to their studies. They were equally committed to the church and joined mendicant orders in the same year; Aquinas became a Dominican friar, while Bonaventure became a Franciscan friar. They were classmates, co-graduates, and eventually, through a papal order, became teachers on the same day at the University of Paris.[1] They were both commissioned by the pope to defend the validity of the mendicant orders. They died prematurely in the same year within months of each other; Aquinas died on his way to the Second Council of Lyon, and Bonaventure died after arriving at the Second Council of Lyon. And both of these notable men have been recognized by the Catholic Church as universal teachers and doctors of the church.

---

1 See Josef Pieper, *The Silence of St. Thomas*, trans. John Murray, S. J., and Daniel O'Connor (South Bend, IN: St. Augustine's Press, 1963), 12.

Yet unlike his friend, Bonaventure saw Aristotle as a threat to Christian orthodoxy. Like Augustine before him, Bonaventure was a committed Christian and Platonist. Both Plato and the Bible, according to Bonaventure, were being challenged by the newly discovered writings of Aristotle. The new Latin translation of Averroes's commentaries on Aristotle were causing certain clerics to embrace the unorthodox views of Aristotle.

What was the main problem with Aristotle? Etienne Gilson writes that, for Bonaventure, "the fundamental error of Aristotle consists in his rejection of the Platonic doctrine of ideas. Since, according to Aristotle, God does not possess in himself, like so many models, the ideas of all things, it follows that God knows only himself and is ignorant of the particular."[2] And this, Bonaventure held, was not only an attack on Plato but also on the biblical doctrine of divine providence, as Gilson states: "From this first error springs the second, namely, that God, ignorant of all things, possesses no prescience and exercises no providence in regard to things."[3]

Bonaventure was concerned that Aristotelianism would undermine Christianity. Such a concern was warranted. Professors at the University of Paris, such as Boethius of Dacia (c. 13th century) and Siger of Brabant (c. 1240–1280s), were using Aristotle to affirm an eternal universe and to deny the biblical doctrines of creation and providence.[4]

Being influenced by the Arabic and Aristotelian philosopher Averroes (1126–1198), these men became known as the Latin Averroists.[5] These Averroists believed it was important to follow the

---

2 Etienne Gilson, *The Philosophy of St. Thomas Aquinas*, ed. G. A. Elrington, trans. Edward Bullough (New York: Dorset, 1948), 14.

3 Gilson, 14.

4 Just within a forty-year period, the University of Paris changed its stance on Aristotle. It went from, in 1212 and 1215, officially prohibiting the reading of Aristotle to, in 1252 and 1255, making him required reading.

5 Averroes believed there was only one intellect in all men and that the world was eternal. He also denied the concept of free will.

argument wherever it leads, regardless of if the conclusions contradicted the faith. And according to Thomas, at least one of the Latin Averroists held to the "double truth" or "two-truth" theory—philosophy and theology can both be true though they contradict each other. In his book against the Latin Averroists, Thomas cited (without mentioning by name) one of the supposed Averroists who said, "Through reason I conclude necessarily that intellect is numerically one, but I firmly hold the opposite by faith" (OI, 123).[6]

Obviously, the double-truth theory is irrational. Somewhat mockingly, Chesterton highlighted its absurdity: "While we are being naturalists, we can suppose that Christianity is all nonsense; but then, when we remember that we are Christians, we must admit that Christianity is true even if it is nonsense."[7]

Because of this new war on orthodoxy, something needed to be done, and Aquinas found himself somewhere in the middle. While some sought to suppress the study of Aristotle altogether, Aquinas, following the lead of Boethius (c. 477–524) in the early sixth century and his own teacher, Albert the Great, advocated for a more moderate solution.[8] On the one hand, Thomas couldn't deny the significance of Aristotle's physics. Much of Aristotle's philosophy was too compelling for Aquinas to reject. On the other hand, Aquinas knew it was impossible to fully embrace Aristotle's metaphysics without undermining the foundation of the Christian faith. Aquinas was a committed theologian as well as a committed philosopher. So rather than fully rejecting or embracing Aristotle, Aquinas was convinced it was possible, with a little adjustment, to unite what others deemed irreconcilable.

---

6   In his polemic against the Averroists, Aquinas quotes someone he does not mention by name who seems to be saying that philosophical and religious truth don't have to agree. Etienne Gilson says that neither Siger of Brabant nor Boethius of Dacia held to the "double truth" theory and denied that anyone actually held to it. Ralph McInerny, trusting that Aquinas wouldn't have fabricated this quote, believed that there must have been at least one person holding to this theory (OI, 112–113).

7   G. K. Chesterton, *Saint Thomas Aquinas* (Nashville: Sam Torade Book Arts, 2019), 46.

8   Boethius, in his book *The Consolation of Philosophy*, first attempted to reconcile Plato with Aristotle, then afterward attempted to reconcile philosophy with Christianity.

To reconcile Aristotle with Christianity, Aquinas had to use Catholic orthodoxy to "correct" Aristotle. That is, "Aristotelian philosophy," according to Grabmann, "[needed to be] judged, purged, and corrected on the basis of the teaching of the Church."[9] There would be no way of synthesizing the unmoved mover with the God of the Bible as long as the unmoved mover is unable to create and govern a temporal universe. In other words, as long as the concept of goodness is identical to the concept of motionlessness, and as long as a motionless God is unable to create and give of himself, Aristotelianism is incompatible with Christianity.

To help make the needed adjustment to Aristotle, Aquinas turned to his second-most trusted philosopher: the Neoplatonist Pseudo-Dionysius (fl. c. 650–c. 725). According to Pseudo-Dionysius, God is the *efficient* cause of the universe. This was the one thing Aquinas needed to bring Aristotle in line with the Bible. He believed that if Aristotle and Dionysius could be reconciled, then Aristotle and the Bible could be unified in the process. With just a little assistance from one of Plato's disciples, Aquinas thought he could rescue Aristotle from his unorthodoxy.

PSEUDO-DIONYSIUS

But who was Pseudo-Dionysius? As his name implies, Pseudo-Dionysius was not who he claimed to be. Like the nature of the Dark Ages in general and mysticism in particular, the author of the Dionysian corpus is surrounded by darkness and mystery.

The real Dionysius lived in the apostolic times (as mentioned in Acts 17) and was one of Paul's first converts in Athens. Tradition claims that he became the first bishop of the church of Athens and suffered martyrdom under the persecution of Domitian. Dionysius was known as the Aeropagite, likely because he was a former member

---

9 Martin Grabmann, *Thomas Aquinas: His Personality and Thought.* Translated by Virgil Michel (New York: Longmans, Green and Co., 1928), 10–11.

of the Areopagus council that convened on Mars Hill ("Mars Hill" is translated from the Greek, *Areopagos*).

It would appear that Pseudo-Dionysius was seeking to add weight and credibility to his philosophical/religious writings by claiming to be Dionysius the Areopagite of Acts 17—a man who presumably was first schooled in the philosophy of Athens and then in the doctrine of the apostle Paul. It is no wonder that Pseudo-Dionysius, in his attempt to mix Athens with Jerusalem, chose the name Dionysius the Areopagite to be his own.

Regardless, because of the author's unwillingness to be open and truthful about his real name, not much is known about his life. [10] For hundreds of years, his books were passed on and generally believed to be the writings of an earlier age. Because of this, his Neoplatonic ideas had a huge influence on the church in the Middle Ages. It was not until the Florentine humanist scholar Lorenzo Valla (c. 1407–1457) challenged the date of the Dionysius corpus in the mid-fifteenth century that the author Dionysius became known as *Pseudo*-Dionysius, for the earliest reference to the Dionysian corpus was by Severus in 553 at the council of Constantinople in defense of monophysitism. [11] Because Pseudo-Dionysius was certainly a disciple of Plotinus (c. 205–270), he must have lived sometime between the late third and early sixth centuries.

THE PLATONISM OF PLOTINUS

Plotinus was an Egyptian who studied philosophy in Alexandria at the feet of Ammonius Saccas (c. 175–242). [12] Although Plotinus didn't leave behind any writings, he, above all others, had the largest influence

---

10   "Everything that we know about him," Bernhard Blankenborn stated, "comes from his corpus." Bernhard Blankenhorn, *The Mystery of Union with God: Dionysian Mysticism in* tia*Albert the Great and Thomas Aquinas* (Washington DC: The Catholic University Press, 2015), 4.

11   Monophysitism asserts that Christ's human nature was absorbed by his divinity.

12   Origen was also one of his students.

in re-popularizing Platonic thought. Though it was Saccas who introduced the writings of Plato to Plotinus, it was Plotinus who ushered Platonism into the Greco-Roman world.

According to Plotinus, there are three principal modes of being, or *hypostases*, which are different degrees or levels of being. The first hypostasis is called the *One*. The One is the very ground of existence, the principal and prime source of all being. The second mode of being is the *Nous* (mind). The Nous is the realm where Plato's *forms* exist, all the archetypal ideas or prototypes. The third mode of being is the *World Soul*.

How does all this fit together? According to Plotinus, the Nous and the World Soul emanated and flowed out of the One (the very ground of all being), each hypostasis weakening the further it was removed from the One. Last of all is *matter*, which proceeded from the World Soul. Matter, being the furthest away from the One, is the weakest stage of the cosmos and the antithesis of the One.

In other words, as light emanates from the sun, the Nous emanated from the One, and the World Soul from the Nous. The farther light travels away from the sun, the dimmer it becomes. Although the Nous has emanated from the One, the brightness and strength of its being does not shine as strong. The World Soul, having proceeded from the Nous, is even dimmer. Eventually, light, when traveling far enough away from its origin, dissipates altogether—being engulfed by the surrounding darkness. When this occurs, light ceases to be light at all. Likewise, matter, although having its origin from the One (via the Nous and the World Soul), has traveled so far away from the One that it ceases to have any relationship or similarities with the One. Like beams of light that begin to dim and slowly dissipate, turning into their opposite (darkness), matter has turned into its opposite: non-being. The One is absolute being; the Nous is somewhat diluted in its being; the World Soul is very weak in its level of being; and matter is the antithesis of being.

Neoplatonism, therefore, is a sort of paradoxical panentheism. Panentheism claims that God is in everything and everything is God. In other words, God and creation cannot be separated. Even matter is considered to be a part of God. Neoplatonism, however, claims that though everything has emanated from God, some things no longer remain a part of God. The physical world, for instance, with all its particulars, has traveled so far away from God, pure unity, that it is on the verge of losing its connection with God.

Nevertheless, the goal is for things to be reunited with God—that which has flowed out of God needs to find a way back into God. *Henosis*, like nirvana of Buddhism, is the process of being stripped of all individual identity, escaping the material cage of the body, and being absorbed back into the original source of being, ending ultimately in an unconscious blank slate of the divine oneness.

How does henosis take place for Neoplatonism? According to Plotinus, the World Soul consists of two parts: (1) a celestial part, that which contemplates the divine Nous, and (2) a terrestrial part, that which generates the material world based on the blueprints, "forms," or archetypal models contained within the Nous. In this sense, the World Soul can move closer or further from the divine Nous—closer by meditating on the Nous, or further by generating the material world of the particulars.

Likewise, individual souls, which have proceeded from the divine mind, can move in two directions. By being preoccupied with this physical world, our souls will slide further away from the divine mind. But by meditating on the forms of the divine mind (Nous), our souls will slowly be absorbed back into the Nous from whence they came.

Even though Plotinus taught (in a positive way) that all forms of existence have emanated from the One, and that the One is the ultimate source of all existence, he was still agnostic. Plotinus believed that nothing for certain can be known about God. He believed that because God is absolutely transcendent, he cannot be contemplated at all. The lower forms of being, the Nous, can be contemplated, but the One transcends all thoughts or ideas.[13]

The Platonism of Porphyry

The next major influence on Dionysius was the teaching of Porphyry (c. 233–c. 305). Porphyry was the student of Plotinus. What is interesting about Porphyry is that, unlike Dionysius, who tried to synthesize Christianity with Neoplatonism, Porphyry attempted to use Neoplatonism as a means to criticize and undermine Christianity. He authored fifteen books attacking Christianity and was considered in his day as the greatest enemy of the Christian faith.

The Platonism of Proclus

After Porphyry came Proclus (c. 412–485). Proclus was considered to be the last of the great philosophers of the Greek tradition. According to Armstrong, "Neo-Platonism reached its Greco-Roman apogee in the Athenian School under the administration of Proclus."[14] Proclus had such an influence on Pseudo-Dionysius that some textual critics have speculated Proclus and Pseudo-Dionysius were one and the same. Though this is not likely, Proclus was certainly a major influence on Dionysius.

The Neoplatonism of Pseudo-Dionysius

The outflow and inflow of all things from and back into God is the heart of Neoplatonic thought. Dionysius sought to synthesize Neoplatonism with Christianity by inserting biblical terms into this divine outflow and inflow framework.

---

13   See Allan Armstrong, *Dionysius the Areopagite on the Divine Names and The Mystical Theology* (Berwick, ME: Ibis, 2004), vii–xx.
14   Armstrong, ix.

The highest degree of being, according to Dionysius, is God. God is the One—the very ground of all being—because he is simple and without differentiation. The second degree of being is the Trinity. This is because the Trinity has two opposing streams eternally flowing out of the Godhead and back into the Godhead. The stream of unity (the divine essence) is the universals and the stream of diversity (the three divine persons) is the particulars. And from the universals and particulars flowing out of and back into the Trinity emanates the cosmos with all its universals and particulars. And finally, flowing out from the cosmos, moving further and further away from the ultimate ground of being, is non-being, which Dionysius labeled as *sin*.

Salvation, for Dionysius, is the process of being reunified and absorbed back into God—a blank slate of unconsciousness. As we have emanated from God in various stages, the steps back into God take place in stages. Reunification begins with meditating on the murky image of God through his reflection stamped in the particular things of the universe. Seeing that all things have emanated out of God, all things maintain a bit of God within them. As long as our mind focuses on the divine within the particulars, our thoughts will be pushed upward away from the particulars of this world until we can behold God a little clearer in the universals. Seeing the universals, our attention is pointed away from the world of the particulars. But we will not be reunited with God, who is beyond all the universals, until we take a mystical leap into the unknowable darkness and lose consciousness altogether.

THE TRIPLEX VIA

Reunification with God begins with thinking about God. According to Dionysius, there are two main ways of arriving to a knowledge of the unknowable God—the *way of affirmation* and the *way of negation*—both coming by the *way of causation*. Unlike Aristotle, Dionysius believed God was the efficient cause of the universe. Seeing that creation has flowed out of God, we can know God by knowing creation.

And thus, we can know God by three ways (*triplex via*): the way of causation, negation, and affirmation.

The Way of Causation

Dionysius held that though we cannot know God's essence, we can know something about God by knowing those things that have emanated from God:

> It may be true to say that we know God not from his own nature—for this is unknown and transcends all reason and intellect—but that from the order of beings, which, having been established through him bears certain images and similarities of his divine exemplars, we ascend with method and order, insofar as possible according to our capacity, to him who is beyond all things, both by removing all things from him [the way of negation] and affirming them superlatively [the way of affirmation], and through the causality of all things [the way of causality]."[15]

Thus, from the way of causation, the way of negation and affirmation are established.

The Way of Negation

According to Dionysius, the undifferentiated simple God, who is completely transcendent, is entirely unknowable. Dionysius claimed that God transcends all thought and is beyond any human comparisons: "For if all the branches of knowledge belong to things that have being, and if their limits have reference to the existing world, then that which is beyond all Being must also be transcendent above all knowledge" (DN, 1.4). Therefore, nothing positive can be said about God at all: "We must not then dare to speak, or indeed to form any conception, of the hidden super-essential Godhead" (DN, 1.1). Again, he said, "The One which is beyond thought surpasses the apprehension of thought,

---

15 Dionysius, "The Divine Names," In *Dionysius the Areopagite on the Divine Names and The Mystical Theology*, trans. C. E. Rolt (Berwick, MI: Ibis, 2004), 4.2 (hereafter cited in text as *DN*).

and the Good which is beyond utterance surpasses the reach of words" (DN, 1.1).

Since God cannot be described using any meaningful language, God is best understood by the things which he is not (*via negativa*). In this, Dionysius agreed with Plotinus, as summarized by Herman Bavinck:

> According to Plotinus nothing can be said of God which is not negative. God is an absolute unity, raised above all plurality. Accordingly, he cannot be defined in terms of thought, goodness, or being, for all these descriptive terms imply a certain plurality. God, as pure unity, is indeed the cause of thought, being, and goodness, etc., but is himself distinct from any of these and transcends them all. He is unlimited, infinite, without form, and so entirely different from every creature that even activity, life, thought, consciousness, and being cannot be ascribed to him. Our thought and language cannot attain to him. We cannot say what he is, but we can only say what he is not.[16]

What is God not? First, God is not a person. Man is personal because he can be distinguished from other persons. Personhood is something that is separate from the whole, something that is distinguishable. God, however, is simple and absolute, something that transcends all forms of separation. God is beyond all relations. According to Dionysius, God is "Unity." Thus, God is beyond personhood; he is "Super-Personal," or as Dionysius often stated, God is "Super-Essential."

Second, God is not even a conscious being. Why? Because consciousness implies a state of thinking and thinking implies self-awareness. Self-awareness cannot happen without a thinking object making a distinction between his thoughts and that which is being thought on. Thus, there is a separation, at least in the mind, between the thinking subject and the object of thought. With the Super-Essential, however, there can be no distinction or divisions.

16　Herman Bavinck, *The Doctrine of God* (Grand Rapids: Eerdmans, 1951), 20.

Third, God does not even exist—at least he transcends the concept of existence. As stated by Dionysius, "He neither was, nor will be, nor hath entered the life-process, nor is doing so, nor ever will, or rather he doeth not even exist" (DN, 4.5). This is because, according to Dionysius, the word *existence* implies a distinction between that which exists and that which does not exist. And God, being purely simple, is beyond all distinctions.

Finally, Dionysius went so far as to undermine the foundation of his whole argument. The reason why God is not a person, a conscious being, or even a being that exists is because he is absolute unity. God is absolute unity because God is one. Because God is simple, God is without differentiation. Yet, according to Dionysius, even the word *unity* comes infinitely short in defining God. Although it might be the best human term to help push our minds off into unknowable darkness, it remains inadequate in bringing us to any true knowledge of the unknowable. The term *unity* fails in that it implies a distinction and separation from that which is plural or divided. God is neither *one* nor *many*; he transcends them both. Thus, Dionysius's god is not even unity—he is, as Dionysius claimed, "Super-Unity."

For Dionysius, God is beyond consciousness, life, unity, essence, existence, and every other cognitive concept. God is beyond all these things, even beyond the word *transcendence*. What is left? Nothing. That is, nothing that is knowable:

> It [that is, God] is not soul, or mind, or endowed with the faculty of imagination, conjecture, reason, or understanding; nor is It any act of reason, or understanding; nor can It be described by the reason or perceived by the understanding, since It is not number, or order, or greatness, or littleness, or equality, or inequality, and since It is not immovable nor in motion, or at rest, and has no power, and it not power or light, and does not live, and is not life; nor is It personal essence, or eternity, or time; nor can It be grasped by the understanding, since It is not knowledge or truth; nor is It kingship or wisdom; nor is It one, nor

is It unity, nor is It Godhead or Goodness; nor is It a Spirit, as we understand the term, since It is not Sonship or Fatherhood; nor is It any other thing such as we or any other being can have knowledge of; nor does It belong to the category of non-existence or to that of existence; nor do existent beings know It as it actually is.[17]

Dionysius built his natural theology on negation. But even the way of negation, he claimed, was a faulty means of knowing God: "We apply not unto It [God] either affirmation or negation," claimed Dionysius, "inasmuch as It transcends all affirmation by being the perfect and unique Cause of all things, and transcends all negation by the pre-eminence of Its simple and absolute nature-free from every limitation and beyond them all" (MT, 5). The way of negation is a dead end. Though it can push our minds in the right direction, it can only take us so far—and no further.

The Way of Affirmation

The way of affirmation, like the way of negation, is based on the way of causation. Because all things flow from the goodness of God—the first cause—all things share in his goodness. Thus, both the way of negation and the way of affirmation understand the nature of God by understanding the nature of the cosmos. The way of negation says God is like the cosmos but without all the imperfections, while the way of affirmation says God is like the cosmos in its perfections.

With this said, how is God the efficient cause of the world? How can something come out of nothing by a God who transcends existence? How could Dionysius say that "It [God] is the Universal Cause of existence while Itself existing not" (DN, 1.1), and in another place, "It [God] is the Cause of all things and yet Itself is nothing" (DN, 1.5). Moreover, how does an unconscious God reveal himself to creation? What motivation do we have to seek God when he is completely

---

17 Dionysius. "The Mystical Theology," In *Dionysius the Areopagite on the Divine Names and The Mystical Theology*, trans. C. E. Rolt (Berwick, MI: Ibis, 2004), 5 (hereafter cited in text as *MT*).

unknowable and nowhere to be found? Rather than attempting to reconcile these statements, Dionysius seemed to revel in the inherent tension of his position: "How these things are so we cannot say, nor yet conceive" (DN, 2.7).

To understand why Dionysius gloried in these paradoxes, we must understand his doctrine of "unification and differentiation." According to Dionysius, two antithetical poles exist in God—unity and diversity. There is a transcendent and hidden God and an immanent and revealed God. The revealed Trinitarian God flows out of the hidden non-Trinitarian God. And from unity and diversity within the Trinity flows the unity and diversity in creation, in the souls of men, and in everything else that exists. Therefore, Dionysius believed there are two sides to all existing things: unity and diversity, oneness and divisions, universals and particulars, and the one and the many. Unification and differentiation are the sole ingredients to all existing things, and their source flows out of the hidden God that transcends both unity and diversity.

Thus, Dionysius goes from a God who does not exist to a God who emanates out of his own being two separate streams—unity and diversity. In this way, God is the sole source of all universals and particulars. These two streams flow from God and at the same time remain in God. As Dionysius often stated, "The Super-essence actually passes outside of Itself even while It remains all the time wholly within Itself."[18] Nevertheless, although God transcends unity and diversity, God still is somehow (in a mystical way) both unity and diversity and thus the source of all universals and particulars that exist in the universe.

These two streams of unity and diversity are invisible emanations that eternally proceed out from and back into God. From a timeless and ongoing eternal act, these two streams forever flow out of his being and back into his being. The stream running out of God is diversity, whereas the stream rushing continuously back to God is unity.

---

18   Armstrong, *Dionysius the Areopagite*, 15.

Diversity proceeds out of God as light emanates from the sun, and unity proceeds back into God as raindrops merge with the ocean. The closer something is to God, the more unified it is with God, as light beams are brighter the closer they are to their source. Conversely, the further something is removed from its source, the more diverse and different it becomes. Since God's diversity is running (or emanating) continuously out from God, it grows weaker in its being. Conversely, since the stream of unity is traveling back into God, its level of being continues to strengthen.

In this sense, Plato's ideas or universals have more in common with God than the individual and diverse objects of creation. "Universals," because they are closer to God, reflect the image of God a little more clearly than the particular objects of creation. Yet because individual objects are copies of their universal prototypes, they still have a small yet murky imprint of God upon them. In a word, the two streams of unity and diversity emanating out from and back into God are only manifestations of the ineffable and inexpressible God. The stream of unity, however, is a little clearer manifestation than the stream of diversity.

The Trinity

The "unification and differentiation" doctrine, according to Dionysius, can be seen most clearly in the Trinity. The essence of the triune God is unity. Yet without division or disturbance to this unity, the Trinity is at the same time diverse in that the Trinity includes three separate persons. Not only is the Trinity both unity and diversity but it is also both without compromise. In way of explanation, Dionysius stated,

> Even so do we see, when there are many lamps in a house, how that the light of them all are unified into one undifferentiated light, so that there shineth forth from them one indivisible brightness; and no one, methinks, could separate the light of one particular lamp from the others, in isolation from the air which embraces them all. . . . Yea, if any one takes out of the

dwelling one of the burning lamps, all its own particular light will therewith depart from the place without either carrying off in itself ought to the other lights or bequeathing any of its own brightness to the rest (DN, 2.4).

The Godhead is diverse, seeing that the three persons are emanations that have flowed out of God. Yet, the three persons are one in unity, in that they continually flow back into God. Although diversity flows out of God, God never ceases to be God since he remains unified in his essence.

Though Dionysius taught that the Trinity is God, he often backpedaled by claiming that the Trinity is only an emblematic representation of God. As Armstrong states, "The Trinity because They have been revealed . . . must belong to the sphere of Manifestation or They could not be revealed."[19] In other words, the doctrine of the Trinity is not something that defines the ontological essence of God. The Trinity, therefore, exists only as an outward and visible manifestation of the invisible and unknowable Godhead, who is beyond differentiations and relations.

Creation

What is more troubling about Dionysius's doctrine of the Trinity is that his view of creation is not much different. Dionysius never identified creation with God per se, but it appears that the Trinity has more in common with creation than it does with the ineffable and nonexistent God. No matter how Dionysius tried to explain it, the Trinity and creation are both symbolic manifestations of the two emanating streams of God's unity and diversity. Creation just happens to have traveled a little further down the river of emanations than the Trinity. It seems, therefore, that either the Trinity is a part of creation or creation is a part of God, thus the pan(en)theism.

---

19 Armstrong, 8.

For instance, the emanating stream of unity consists of the "universal ideas" or blueprints in which every particular item in the universe is made. This stream of unity, due to its natural desire to be reunified with God, continues to flow back into God, seeking to reemerge into the blank slate of "nothingness." Whereas the stream of diversity is always seeking to travel away from God and become something entirely the opposite. It seeks to become more diverse and different.

Nevertheless, creation occurred when these two invisible streams of unity and diversity happen to cross paths, and out of the emanations of God came everything. The stream of diversity emanating out of God found the needed blueprints in the stream of unity (universals) flowing back into God. The result was a unified and diverse universe. Thus, a God who transcends existence created an existing world. Yet this non-existing God did not create the world out of nothing (*ex nihilo*) but out of his own emanations. As stated by Dionysius himself:

> For bestowing upon all things and supernaturally infusing [his] Communications unto the goodly Universe, [God] becomes differentiated without loss of Undifference; and multiplied without loss of Unity; from [his] Oneness [he] becomes manifold while yet remaining within [himself]. For example, since God is super-essentially Existent and bestows existence upon all things that are, and brings the world into being, that single Existence of his is said to become manifold through bringing forth the many existences from [himself], while yet he remains One in the act of Self-Multiplication; Undifferenced throughout the process of Differentiation; Super-Essentially transcending the Being of all things, and guiding the whole world onwards by an indivisible act, and pouring forth without diminution his indefectible bounties. (DN, 2.11)[20]

If unity is that which is most like God, then diversity, although emanating from God, is that which is most unlike God. In fact, according to Dionysius, if something travels far enough away from God,

---

20 Words for God have been changed within the brackets from *It* and *Itself* to *God, his, he,* and *himself* (DN, 2.11).

if something becomes so diverse, it will turn into its opposite: nonbeing. If God is the source of all existence and being, then that which is completely different to God is something that is completely without existence and being altogether.

Therefore, every object in the universe (depending on its nearness to God) must be viewed as ranging somewhere in the ascending scale between union with the One (ultimate being) and a self-annihilated state of nonbeing. As Dionysius stated, "The various kinds of existences being now created in the world of time, we can regard them as ranged in an ascending scale between Nothingness and the Super-Essence."[21] The strength of existence is determined by its closeness to God, for in him everything moves and has its being.

Sin

Since everything in the universe derives its existence from the existence of a good God, everything that exists is good. In this way, Dionysius equated existence with goodness.

Unlike Aristotle, who defined goodness as the object of desire, Dionysius, following Plato, defined goodness as charity. Goodness is that which gives of itself. Because God is perfect in his goodness, God is the efficient cause of all that shares in the state of goodness. Because God is love, he cannot help but eternally give of himself through the timeless and eternal act of creation. Thus, all that flows out from a good God is good. But all that flows from God also begins to weaken its goodness. It will continue to weaken until it ceases to be good at all.

In this sense, evil is not something God created any more than darkness is created by light. What is evil then? According to Dionysius, "Evil is weakness and deficiency of Good" (DN, 4.30). Evil, consequently, is not something positive or an active force but a passive and powerless nonentity: "For that which is altogether destitute of Good is nothing and hath no power" (DN, 4.32). Evil in the strictest sense

---

21 Armstrong, *Dionysius the Areopagite*, 19.

is nonexistence (nonbeing). "For evil hath no being at all," claimed Dionysius, "except when mingled with the Good. And no thing in the world is without a share in the Good, and evil is the deficiency of Good and no thing in the world is utterly destitute of Good" (DN, 4.33).

Because devils and sinners exist, they are not completely evil and devoid of all good. Evil cannot exist without some form of deprivation of being. In the same way, light dissipates as it moves away from its source; evil arises only as existence begins to weaken and fade away. The level of goodness of something is measured consequently by how close it participates in God. Since God is the absolute source of all goodness and existence, nothing can exist or share in his goodness outside of being in union with God. Sin is that which moves away from "being." Consequently, when something finally becomes completely separate from the source of all existence and goodness, it self-dissolves into nonexistence. Only when something ceases to exist is there pure sin. Thus, pure sin is nonbeing. Hence, pure sin cannot exist at all.

According to Dionysius, both God and sin, in their purest form, do not exist. Consequently, Dionysius concluded that sin is the desire to get back to a blank state of nothingness the wrong way. That is, sin is the attempt to become divine by traveling in the opposite direction. And if this is the case, then salvation is the process of being reunified with God the right way.

The Scriptures

Dionysius, in his attempt to reconcile Neoplatonism with Christianity, claimed that he did not want to add or take away anything from the Scriptures. Concerning the Scriptures, he asserted, "We strive to preserve its treasure in ourselves without addition, diminution, or distortion" (DN. 2.3). Nevertheless, he completely undermined the objectivity and sufficiency of Scripture by reducing divine revelation to an analogical language that is essentially and completely symbolic: "[The Scriptures] enwrapped spiritual truths in terms drawn from the world

of sense, and super-essential truths in terms drawn from Being, cloth-
ing with shapes and forms things which are shapeless and formless,
and by a variety of separable symbols, fashioning manifold attributes
of the imageless and supernatural Simplicity" (DN. 1.4).

For instance, because God transcends all *a priori* knowledge and
goes beyond all sense perception, God has chosen to reveal himself
through earthly and human symbols and types. What are these symbols? Since he cannot speak to us in his own ineffable language, he
chose to use things from our created universe to depict himself. He
chose to use symbols and metaphors that correspond to the concepts
and language we understand.

Symbolic Language

Because no one thing in the universe fully depicts God, many symbols
are utilized in the Bible to describe him. Since all things have emanated from God, all things, in various degrees, depict something about
God. Light explains something about God, yet it falls short in giving
us a full understanding of his nature. God is also depicted as a lamb,
yet this poor animal also fails to explain the fullness of the Godhead.

The Bible uses hundreds of things and names and attributes to help
our limited minds contemplate the ineffable Godhead that transcends
every biblical concept of God. This is why Dionysius often stated God
was without a name (*anonymous*) yet has many names (*polyonymous*).
He is anonymous because he is ineffable; he is polyonymous because
he is known through multiple symbols taken from the created universe.

But not all symbols recorded in the Scriptures are of equal value. The
term *door*, when applied to the Lord, implies something about God,
but it does not compare to the words *infinite*, *absolute*, or *immutable*.
Dionysius stated that "the more anything participates in the One in-
finitely-bountiful God the more is it brought near to Him and made
diviner than the rest" (DN, 5.3). Therefore, he stated that "the more
universal a Title is, the more truly it is applicable to God."[22] Universal

---
22 Armstrong, 134.

ideas such as *life, wisdom, truth,* and *goodness* express more truth about God than words that are drawn from the created visible world, such as *shepherd, lamb,* and *door.* Herman Bavinck would explain Dionysius's position almost fourteen hundred years later: "All knowledge of God is analogical; this analogy is more clearly evident in one group of creatures than in another, and more manifest in the universe of invisible reality than in the world of visible things."[23]

Yet what good are these "variety of separable symbols" if they do not communicate actual realities? What good is even the more universal terms, such as *simplicity,* if God's essence transcends the very concept of simplicity? What good is the term *trinity* if God transcends all personal relations? According to Dionysius, the terms, names, and attributes of God recorded in the Scriptures are valuable not because they give any true knowledge of God but because they jump-start our minds by pushing our thoughts upward in the right direction. Although the metaphorical and symbolic language of the Scriptures cannot take us to a real knowledge of God, it can at least point us in the right direction.

Therefore, according to Fran O'Rourke, "While Dionysius gives the way of positive affirmation a real value, it is nevertheless evident that he attaches even greater significance to the path of negative knowledge."[24] And thus, for Dionysius, the way of negation and affirmation are both dead ends. As Herman Bavinck concluded, "Even negative theology fails to furnish us any knowledge of God's being, for in the final analysis, God surpasses both all negation and all affirmation, all assertion and all denial."[25]

---

23 Bavinck, *The Doctrine of God,* 179.
24 Fran O'Rourke, *Pseudo-Dionysius and the Metaphysics of Aquinas* (Notre Dame, IN: University of Notre Dame Press, 2010), 16.
25 Bavinck, *Reformed Dogmatics,* 2:38.

Mysticism

According to Dionysius, the Scriptures point us to God via symbols. Though these symbols don't reveal God's essence, they assist us in our salvation by helping us in our reunification with the divine. How does one go about being reunited with the divine? The answer is found in Dionysius's teaching on mystical theology.

The aim of the mystic is something more important than ascertaining a concrete knowledge of God. It is experiencing God through divine unification. The ultimate goal is to become one with God—to become divine. First, the mystic begins this quest by meditating on the diverse symbols of the created universe, starting at the base level of the physical universe. Second, to ascend the ladder to God, the mystic must eventually leave behind those rudimentary symbols. Meditating on physical things must cease. The mystic is called to push his thoughts upward and see God as existing more fully in the realm of the universals. Yet, to climb higher and be fully merged into the Divine, the seeker must go beyond what is written (lay his Bible down) and leave off all contemplation.

Because God is ineffable, the mystic must close his mind altogether and plunge himself into the darkness where God exists. The mystic must free himself from all that is physical, all that is tangible, all that is bodily, and all that would hold him back from the knowledge of an unknowable God. Finally, the mystic must rid himself of all cognitive thought; he must renounce all former knowledge of the Divine, for it is only when he can see nothing that he can see a God who is ineffable. Only when a person can see the ineffable essence of God can he become one with God and, thus, become divine. Only when this happens, according to Dionysius, does "that which contemplates become that which is contemplated" (DN, X). Dionysius summarized the process in his book, *Mystical Theology*:

Dear Timothy, I counsel that, in the earnest exercise of mystic contemplation, thou leave the sense and the activities of the intellect and all things that the senses or the intellect can perceive, and all things in this world of nothingness, or in that world of being, and that, thine understanding being laid to rest, thou strain towards a union with Him whom neither being nor understanding can contain. For, by the unceasing and absolute renunciation of thyself and all things, thou shalt in pureness cast all things aside, and be releases from all, and so shalt be led upwards to the Ray of that divine Darkness which exceedeth all existence (MT, 1.1).

In another place he stated, "Darkness of Unknowing wherein he renounces all the apprehensions of his understanding and is enwrapped in that which is wholly intangible and invisible, belonging wholly to Him that is beyond all things . . . and being through the passive stillness of all his reasoning powers united by his highest faculty to Him that is Unknowable, of whom thus by a rejection of all knowledge he possesses a knowledge that exceeds his understanding" (MT, 1.1).

Commenting on the mysticism of Dionysius, O'Rourke stated, "Entering the 'darkness of unknowing,' the soul renounces all cognitive apprehension and encounters that which is intangible and indivisible, belonging neither to itself nor to any other but to him who is beyond all things."[26]

In short, for us to reach God, we must begin our journey by seeing God through the dark spectacles of the created world of diversity. As we march upward, we must view God as transcending all diversity and existing in the realm of the universals as recorded in the symbolic language of the Scriptures. Finally, to reach God, we must remove our glasses, close the eyes of our understanding altogether, and be willing to step into the irrational abyss of the unknowable darkness. To get to God, we must close our Bibles. Then and only then is there any hope of us seeing the invisible and ineffable God who does not exist.

---

26 O'Rourke, *Pseudo-Dionysius*, 20.

Conclusion

The natural theology of Dionysius, either by the way of negation or by the way of affirmation, does not lead to the God of the Bible. Like Aristotle before him, the way of negation (based on an undifferentiated simplicity) ends up consuming the way of affirmation. For Dionysius, even God as Trinity gets swallowed up in God's transcendence. Whatever diverse things, names, and attributes that can be used to define God are ultimately undermined and made void by the undifferentiated nature of God's oneness. God, as he is in himself, remains locked behind the transcendental wall.

The way of affirmation can bring us to the edge of the wall, but it can take us no further. Because the way of affirmation is only able to describe God by sensible signs found within the cosmos, the way of affirmation leads to the pantheistic notion of a chain of being—such a notion that destroys the Creator-creature distinction. And once that is compromised, God's interdependence is compromised as well. Regardless, Dionysius's natural theology leads neither to an absolute God nor to a personal God who created the world out of nothing.

5

THE PHILOSOPHICAL THEOLOGY
OF THOMAS AQUINAS

THOMAS OF AQUINO was not an innovator. Assimilating philosophy with theology was nothing novel. Many of the church fathers, principally Origen, Boethius, and Dionysius, had attempted to synthesize Greek philosophy with Christianity. The early Schoolmen, such as Anselm (c. 1033–1109) and Peter Abelard (c. 1079–1142), incorporated philosophy into their theology. Aquinas was not even attempting something completely new by fusing Aristotelianism with Christianity. Though at that time the metaphysics of Aristotle were being rejected by the Catholic Church, others, such as Thomas's teachers, were doing their best to show how Aristotelianism was compatible with Catholic orthodoxy.

Aquinas's first contact with Aristotle likely came when he was a young teenager at the University of Naples.[1] There he studied under the Aristotelian philosopher Peter of Ireland (Ibernia). Aquinas would go on to be thoroughly immersed in the metaphysics of Aristotle at the University of Paris. There he would be taught by the most important

---

1 Pasquale Porro, *Thomas Aquinas: A Historical and Philosophical Profile*, trans. Joseph G. Trabbic and Roger W. Nutt (Washington, DC: The Catholic University of America Press, 2012), 4.

Aristotelian commentator of his day, Albert the Great. It's highly probable that Aquinas was introduced to Pseudo-Dionysius at this time, for Albert was not only an Aristotelian but a Neoplatonist who wrote commentaries on the works of Dionysius.[2] And like Boethius, who sought to reconcile Aristotle, Plato, and Christ, Albert believed that wherever truth is found, either in Aristotle or in Plato, it ought to be assimilated into Christianity.

Under the influences of Peter of Ireland and Albert the Great, Aquinas formed his philosophical theology. Thomas went on to give his life to reconciling natural theology with revealed theology. And like his mentors, Thomas principally leaned on the writings of Aristotle, Augustine, Boethius, and Dionysius.[3]

ARISTOTLE AND THE WAY OF NEGATION

Though Thomas sought to reconcile Aristotle with Plato and Augustine, he sided with Aristotle's empiricism over Plato's notion of innate ideas and Augustine's belief in the universal awareness of God. Following Aristotle, Aquinas believed that all knowledge, including knowledge of God, originates with sense experience. "The natural gaze of the human mind," Thomas claimed, "cannot fix itself in the first light of truth, by which everything can be easily known. As a consequence, human reason in the development of its natural knowledge must advance from things that are posterior to those that are prior, and from creatures to God" (DT, intro.).[4]

---

2 See Bernhard Blankenhorn, *The Mystery of Union with God: Dionysian Mysticism in* etf*Albert the Great and Thomas Aquinas* (Washington DC: The Catholic University Press, 2015), iv.

3 Along with his commentaries on Aristotle, Aquinas wrote favorable commentaries on the writings of Boethius and Dionysius. After Aristotle, Aquinas cited Dionysius more than any other philosopher (over 1,700 times, and 607 times in *Summa Theologica*), with the apostle Paul receiving less than 120 references. Aquinas cites Augustine 3,156 times, Aristotle 2,095 times, and Dionysius 1,700 times. In his commentary on Peter Lombard's *Sentences*, Aquinas quotes Aristotle over 2,000 times, Augustine over 1,000 times, and Dionysius over 500 times.

4 Thomas Aquinas, *Faith, Reason and Theology*, trans. Armand Maurer (Toronto: Pontifical Institute of Mediaeval Studies, 1997), 3.

This is where Aquinas turned to Aristotle's cosmological argument, which he used as a bridge connecting our sense experience to the existence of God, who transcends sense experience. "Aristotle proceeds," Aquinas noted, "to prove the existence of God from the consideration of motion" (SCG, 1.1.13). And from the study of finite objects in motion, Aquinas (via Aristotle) concluded there must be a first cause that is without motion:

> Therefore, whatever is in motion must be put in motion by another. If that by which it is put in motion be itself put in motion, then this also must needs be put in motion by another, and that by another again. But this cannot go on to infinity, because then there would be no first mover, and, consequently, no other mover; seeing that subsequent movers move only inasmuch as they are put in motion by the first mover; as the staff moves only because it is put in motion by the hand. Therefore it is necessary to arrive at a first mover, put in motion by no other; and this everyone understands to be God. (ST, 1.2.3)

By attempting to prove the existence of a non-physical God through the study of motion in the physical universe, Aquinas was attempting to say something about the essence of this non-physical God: "God is altogether without motion," Thomas claimed (SCG, 1.1.15). If everything in motion has a cause, and if God is first cause, then God must be immobile. According to Edward Feser, the idea of immobile God is the very heart of Aquinas's conception of God: "Actus purus or act utterly unmixed with any potentiality is . . . the core of Scholastic philosophy's conception of God. Everything else is act in some way mixed with potency."[5] Likewise, the Dominican Reginal Garrigou-Lagrange claimed that "the definition of potency [i.e., motion] determines the Thomistic synthesis."[6]

---

5   Edward Feser, *Scholastic Metaphysics: A Contemporary Introduction* (Lancaster, UK: Editiones Scholaticae, 2014), 40.
6   Reginald Garrigou-Lagrange, *Reality: A Synthesis of Thomistic Thought*, trans. Patrick Cummins (St. Louis: Herder, 1950), 37.

"Following Aristotle," Robert Barron remarks, "Thomas takes the term 'motion' in the very broad sense of transition or change, in his words, the 'reduction of a thing from potency to act,' from non-being to being. Whatever is in the process of changing must be in potency."[7] For Thomas, God is without potency because God is without motion.

Thus, *immobility* is at the heart of Aquinas's doctrine of God. By establishing divine immobility (that actus purus is without potentiality) through Aristotle's cosmological argument, Aquinas laid the foundation for the rest of his knowledge of God's nature. Unlike all physical objects in motion, God is simple, atemporal, immutable, impassible, infinite, and so forth.

The deduction of these attributes comes by the way of negation. "Now, because we cannot know what God is," claimed Aquinas, "but rather what he is not, we have no means for considering how God is, but rather show what he is not" (ST, 1.3.0). And seeing that God is not able to move, then he must not have any of the attributes of motion. As stated by Aquinas, "Now it can be shown how God is not by denying of him whatever is opposed to the idea of him—viz., composition, motion, and the like" (ST, 1.3.0).

And, for Aquinas, the first attribute deduced from divine immovability is divine simplicity. Seeing that God is not in motion, God must be without composition. "In everything which is moved, there is some kind of composition to be found," claimed Aquinas (ST, 1.9.1). This also means that God must be without body or parts: "It is absolutely true that God is not a body. . . . First, because no body is in motion unless it be put in motion, as is evident from induction. Now it has been already proved . . . that God is the First Mover, and is himself unmoved. Therefore it is clear that God is not a body. Secondly, because the first being must of necessity be in act, and in no way in potentiality" (ST, 1.3.1).

---

7   Robert Barron, *Thomas Aquinas: Spiritual Master* (New York: Crossroad, 1996), 64.

Aquinas explained this in more detail when he said, "In every compound there must be actuality and potentiality. For a plurality of things cannot become one thing, unless there be actuality and potentiality" (SCG, 1.1.18). From this he asserted that God is altogether without composition: "For there is neither composition of quantitative parts in God, since He is not a body; nor composition of form and matter; nor does His nature differ from His *suppositum*; nor His essence from His existence; neither is there in Him composition of genus and difference, nor of subject and accident. Therefore, it is clear that God is nowise composite, but is altogether simple" (SCG, 1.3.7).

After Aquinas deduced divine simplicity from divine immobility, he went on to deduce divine atemporality:

> We attain to the knowledge of simple things by way of compound things, so must we reach to the knowledge of eternity by means of time, which is nothing but the numbering of movement by "before" and "after." For since succession occurs in every movement, and one part comes after another, the fact that we reckon before and after in movement, makes us apprehend time, which is nothing else but the measure of before and after in movement. Now in a thing bereft of movement, which is always the same, there is no before or after. As therefore the idea of time consists in the numbering of before and after in movement; so likewise in the apprehension of the uniformity of what is outside of movement, consists the idea of eternity. (ST, 1.10.1)

From the way of negation, which is rooted in divine immobility, Aquinas deduced many other divine attributes, such as immutability, impassibility, and so forth.

In all this, however, Aquinas had yet to say anything positive about God. All these terms—immobility, indivisibility, immutability, and impassibility—at best only explain what God is not. It's like giving directions to your home by telling a few of the places where you don't live. Though this may be true knowledge, it is not sufficient for someone to find your home. So, for Aquinas, the way of negation only tells us what God is not.

DIONYSIUS AND THE TRIPLEX VIA

The way of negation tells us that God is transcendent, but it is incapable of saying much about God's immanence. For this, Aquinas turned to his second proof (the efficient cause) and to the way of causation as expressed in the mystical writings of Pseudo-Dionysius. For Dionysius, the way of negation and the way of affirmation are the result of the way of causation. O'Rourke explains: "The *triplex via* is rather a threefold variation of the dominant and underlying theme of causality: the variants reveal how we may approach a knowledge of God by three paths which merely reflect differing moments of the causal relation between God and creatures."[8] Following Dionysius, Aquinas made his position clear when he said,

> Our intellect cannot be led by sense so far as to see the essence of God; because sensible creatures are effects of God which do not equal the power of God, their cause. Hence from the knowledge of sensible things the whole power of God cannot be known; nor therefore can his essence be seen. But because they are his effect and depend on their cause, we can be led from them so far as to know of God that he exists and that he has whatever must belong to the first cause of all things which is beyond all that is caused. Thus we know about his relation to creatures; that he is the cause of all things; also that creatures differ from him since he is none of the things which are caused by him; and that these are removed from him not through any defect, but because he transcends them. (ST, 1.12.12)

Therefore, "Aquinas appropriates from Dionysius the entire method of his natural philosophy of God, of knowing and not-knowing."[9] And

---

8   Fran O'Rourke, *Pseudo-Dionysius and the Metaphysics of Aquinas* (Notre Dame, IN: University of Notre Dame Press, 2010), 32.
9   O'Rourke, 3.

it seems that Aquinas turned to Dionysius because Aristotle did not believe the unmoved mover could be the efficient cause of the universe. In other words, Aquinas needed Dionysius if he was going baptize Aristotle's god, who is unable to be the efficient and moving cause of the cosmos:

> We perceive a series of efficient causes of things in the world. Nothing exists prior to itself. Therefore nothing [in the world of things we perceive] is the efficient cause of itself. If a previous efficient cause does not exist, neither does the thing that results (the effect). Therefore if the first thing in a series does not exist, nothing in the series exists. If the series of efficient causes extends ad infinitum into the past, then there would be no things existing now. That is plainly false (i.e., there are things existing now that came about through efficient causes). Therefore efficient causes do not extend ad infinitum into the past. Therefore it is necessary to admit a first efficient cause, to which everyone gives the name of God. (ST, 1.2.3)

Without any immediate explanation of how the second proof is congruent with the first proof, Aquinas claimed that God is both the *unmoved* mover and the *moving* cause of objects in motion.

The Way of Causation

Nevertheless, in his second proof, Aquinas sought to establish a path to knowing God by the way of causation. Though the knowledge of God's essence will always remain beyond the range of our categories of thought, we can at least know something about the unknowable God by knowing something about what God created. As Aquinas stated, "Now because we do not know the essence of God, the proposition is not self-evident to us; but needs to be demonstrated by things that are more known to us, though less known in their nature—namely, by effects" (ST, 1.2.1). And by studying the works and the effects of God, we can come to the knowledge that there is a God. "We can demonstrate the existence of God," Aquinas affirmed, "from his effects; though from them we cannot perfectly know God as he is in his essence" (ST, 1.2.2).

Therefore, by studying effects we learn something about their causes, and by studying created things, we learn something about the Creator. For "every effect," says Aquinas, "in some degree represents its cause, but diversely" (ST, 1.45.7). And again, he said, "All created things, so far as they are beings, are like God as the first and universal principle of all being" (ST, 1.4.3). Aquinas explained this analogous relationship in more detail:

> Effects disproportionate to their causes do not agree with them in name and essence. And yet some likeness must be found between such effects and their causes: for it is of the nature of an agent to do something like itself. Thus also God gives to creatures all their perfections; and thereby he has with all creatures a likeness, and an unlikeness at the same time. For this point of likeness, however, it is more proper to say that the creature is like God than that God is like the creature. (SCG, 1.1.29)

The Way of Affirmation

The way of causation leads to the way of affirmation. Aquinas held that because every effect resembles its cause, there is a type of participation (or analogous relationship) between God and all created things. For we must remember that Aristotle claimed that motion only exists between polar opposites—things move from cold to hot or from hot to cold. Thus, all created things in motion have traces of their original cause of motion. As explained by Aquinas,

> God is in all things; not, indeed, as part of their essence, nor as an accident, but as an agent is present to that upon which it works. For an agent must be joined to that wherein it acts immediately and touch it by its power; hence it is proved in Phys. vii that the thing moved and the mover must be joined together. Now since God is very being by his own essence, created being must be his proper effect; as to ignite is the proper effect of fire.

Now God causes this effect in things not only when they first begin to be, but as long as they are preserved in being; as light is caused in the air by the sun as long as the air remains illuminated. Therefore as long as a thing has being, God must be present to it, according to its mode of being. But being is innermost in each thing and most fundamentally inherent in all things since it is formal in respect of everything found in a thing. . . . Hence it must be that God is in all things, and innermostly. (ST, 1.8.1)

The Way of Affirmation Is the Way of Immanence

In the act of creating, God has painted a symbolic picture of himself. For Aquinas, God is immanent not because he steps over the transcendental wall and enters our world of time and space but because he, as the moving cause, is represented in every effect. That is, by observing the effects we can learn a bit about the nature of the efficient cause. "Since we cannot know him naturally except by reaching him from his effects, it follows that the terms by which we denote his perfection must be diverse, as also are the perfections which we find in things" (SCG, 1.31).

The Way of Affirmation Is the Way of Analogy

Because God is the efficient cause of all created things, all created things reveal God in some way. This means every name or word assigned to created things also has something to say about God. "Transforming his similitude in some manner to all things," Thomas stated, "he may thus be named from the names of creatures."[10] For this reason, Aquinas agreed with Dionysius that the hidden God is anonymous (nameless) whereas the revealed God is polyonymous. According to

---

10   Thomas Aquinas, *Expositio super librum Dionysii De divinis nominibus* (Commentary on Pseudo-Dionysius' *De divinis nominibus*), 1265-1268, translation: Marsh, Harry C., trans. "A Translation of Thomas Aquinas' *In Librum beati Dionysii de divinis nominibus expositio*." In his "Cosmic Structure and the Knowledge of God: Thomas Aquinas' *In Librum beati Dionysii de divinis nominibus expositio*," 265–549. PhD diss. (Vanderbilt University, 1994), 1.1.30 (hereafter cited in text as *DDN*).

O'Rourke, Aquinas "adopts from Dionysius" the idea that "all names designating effects in creatures belong to the Divine Essence."[11]

In the way of negation, God is entirely inexpressible and ineffable. Yet by the way of affirmation, God is knowable through a variety of names associated with sensible things:

> [God's] names signify the divine substance and are predicated substantially of God, although they fall short of a full representation of him. Which is proved thus. For these names express God, so far as our intellects know him. Now since our intellect knows God from creatures, it knows him as far as creatures represent him. . . . Hence every creature represents him, and is like him so far as it possesses some perfection; yet it represents him not as something of the same species or genus, but as the excelling principle of whose form the effects fall short, although they derive some kind of likeness thereto, even as the forms of inferior bodies represent the power of the sun. . . . Therefore the aforesaid names signify the divine substance, but in an imperfect manner, even as creatures represent it imperfectly. So when we say, "God is good," the meaning is not, "God is the cause of goodness," or "God is not evil"; but the meaning is, "Whatever good we attribute to creatures, pre-exists in God," and in a more excellent and higher way. Hence it does not follow that God is good, because he causes goodness; but rather, on the contrary, he causes goodness in things because he is good. (ST, 1.13.3)

And though every effect in nature communicates something about God, not every effect communicates something about God equally. "The nearer a thing is to its cause," Thomas said, "the greater share it has in the effect" (SCG, 3.64). The hotter something is, for instance, the more it resembles fire.

The Way of Affirmation Is the Way of Symbolism

Yet because of this, our knowledge of God remains tied to temporal concepts and terms. As Aquinas stated, "Our natural knowledge be-

---

11 O'Rourke, *Pseudo-Dionysius*, 42.

gins from sense. Hence our natural knowledge can go as far as it can be led by sensible things" (ST, 1.12.12). Consequently, even the way of affirmation does not lead to knowing anything truly about God as God knows himself. What knowledge we can know about God, we can only know metaphorically. As stated by Aquinas,

> Whatever names denote properties that are caused in things by their proper specific principles, cannot be predicated of God otherwise than metaphorically. But the names that express such perfections with that mode of supereminent excellence in which they appertain to God, are predicated of God alone, as for instance, 'Sovereign Good,' 'First Being,' and the like. . . . 'Goodness' denotes something as not subsisting by itself: 'good,' something as concrete and composite. In this respect, then, no name befits God suitably except in respect of that which the name is imposed to signify. Such names therefore may be both affirmed and denied of God, affirmed on account of the meaning of the name, denied on account of the mode of signification. But the mode of supereminence, whereby the said perfections are found in God, cannot be signified by the names imposed by us, except either by negation, as when we call God 'eternal' or 'infinite,' or by reference or comparison of him to other things, as when he is called the 'First Cause' or the 'Sovereign Good.' For we cannot take in (*capere*) of God what he is, but what he is not, and how other beings stand related to him. (SCG, 1.1.30)

The meaning of words we use to describe God are better suited to describe the world of sensible things than they are in describing the God who transcends all conceptual categories of thought. This means that human terms or names cannot truly picture God. "Now it is evident," Aquinas claimed, "that the Divine essence cannot be known through the nature of material things. For . . . the knowledge of God by means of any created similitude is not the vision of his essence" (ST, 1.12.11).

Any possible conception of God will have more in common with the cosmos than it will have with the God who transcends the cosmos.

Thus, our knowledge of God at best is only a symbolic representation of God. In this sense, man cannot rise above Plato's cave of shadows that enslaves him. As Aquinas stated, "Things known are in the knower according to the mode of the knower" (ST, 1.8.3).

The Way of Negation

The way of causation leads to the way of affirmation, but even the way of affirmation leads back to the way of negation, for every effect and every name says something positive and something negative about God. As Aquinas stated, "Such names may therefore, as Dionysius teaches, be both affirmed and denied of God; affirmed indeed due to the meaning of the name; denied, however, due to its mode of signification" (SCG, 1:30). Thus, everything reveals and conceals the divine. In this way, God is both immanent and transcendent in all things. Though God has many names, none of his names say anything true about God as God knows himself.

Consequently, "Negative theology . . . assumes for Aquinas," according to O'Rourke, "a greatly superior role in understanding God."[12] As Aquinas himself stated, "The most perfect to which we can attain in this life in our knowledge of God, is that he transcends all that can be conceived by us" (DDN, 1.1.30). O'Rourke goes on to explain that, for Aquinas, "negations are absolutely true while affirmations, although not false, are only relatively true"—that is, "affirmations are true of God only under qualification."[13]

In Aquinas's reality, then, we don't know anything about God's essence. Aquinas stated, "Thus, according to the reasoning of Dionysius, it is fitting to say that God is both incomprehensible to all intellects and incontemplatable to us in his essence, in that our intellect has been bound to created things, namely to things which are similar nature to us."[14] What knowledge we can have of God is not a knowledge of

12 O'Rourke, *Pseudo-Dionysius*, 48.
13 O'Rourke, *Pseudo-Dionysius*, 51.
14 "Prologue and Book I, Lecture 1.," *Aquinas' Exposition of "On Divine Names"* (blog), September 1, 2013, https://in-librum-dionysii.blogspot.com/2013/09/

God's nature as God knows himself but a symbolic knowledge. At best, we can only know the created representation of God painted by sensible and empirical signs taken from this world of sense experience. As Thomas explained, "We cannot know the essence of God in this life, as he really is in himself; but we know him according as he is represented in the perfections of creatures" (ST, 1.13.2). In other words, we can only know the revealed God of symbols and not the hidden God of reality.

THE SCRIPTURES

This applies to the language of Scripture as well. God can only manifest himself by using symbols and metaphors taken from the things he has created. As Thomas stated, "Although through Revelation we can become capable of knowing things which we otherwise would not know [such as the Trinity], we do not know them in any other way than through the senses" (DT, 6.3). This means that we cannot have any direct knowledge of God. Our relationship with God is based on knowledge, and this, based on a creative picture. It doesn't matter if God can speak to us or not; we cannot rise above the cave that enslaves us. As O'Rourke concludes, "In whatever way we use the term, our language is always bound to our experience of the finite world."[15] "Thomas asserted," claims Josef Pieper, "that all our knowledge, including the spiritual, and also our knowledge of God, took its starting point (and therefore always remained somehow dependent upon) sense perception."[16] As Aquinas himself claimed,

> The human understanding cannot go so far of its natural power as to grasp his substance, since under the conditions of the present life the knowledge of our understanding commences with sense; and therefore objects beyond sense cannot be grasped by

prologue-and-book-i-lecture-1.html.

15   O'Rourke, *Pseudo-Dionysius*, 69.
16   Josef Pieper, *The Silence of St. Thomas*, trans. John Murray, S. J., and Daniel O'Connor (South Bend, IN: St. Augustine's Press, 1963), 29.

human understanding except so far as knowledge is gathered of them through the senses. But things of sense cannot lead our understanding to read in them the essence of the Divine Substance, inasmuch as they are effects inadequate to the power that caused them. Nevertheless our understanding is thereby led to some knowledge of God, namely, of his existence and of other attributes that must necessarily be attributed to the First Cause. (SCG, 1.1.3)

MYSTICISM

Hence, all that we can know about God is that we don't know God at all. "Man reaches the highest point of his knowledge about God," claimed Aquinas, "when he knows that he knows him not, inasmuch as he knows that that which is God transcends whatsoever he conceives of him" (DT, 7.5. ad 14). This is why, in the end, like Dionysius, Aquinas was a mystic who claimed that God, as he really is, is unknowable: "And this is the ultimate and most perfect limit of our knowledge in this life, as Dionysius says in the Mystical Theology, 'We are united with God as the unknown.' Indeed, this is the situation, for, while we know of God what he is not, what he is remains wholly unknown" (SCG, 3.49).

PHILOSOPHY INTERPRETS THEOLOGY

Thus, the empirical foundation of Aristotle (or more precisely, the physical assumption that *nothing in motion placed itself in motion*) and the mysticism of Dionysius shaped Aquinas's hermeneutical understanding of the language of Scripture. First, Aquinas, by applying the empiricism of Aristotle to Scripture, claimed that "it is befitting Holy Writ to put forward divine and spiritual truths by means of comparisons with material things. God provides for everything according to the capacity of its nature. Now it is natural to man to attain to intellectual truths through sensible objects because all our knowledge originates from sense" (ST, 1.1.9). Second, Aquinas went on to appeal to the mysticism of Dionysius: "Hence in Holy Writ, spiritual truths are fittingly taught under the likeness of material things. This is what Dionysius says, 'We cannot be enlightened by the divine rays except they be hidden by the covering of many sacred veils'" (ST, 1.1.9).

By incorporating Aristotle's empiricism and Dionysius's way of causality, Aquinas didn't just mix philosophy with theology, he subjugated theology (and the interpretation of the Scriptures) to philosophy. For instance, Pieper explains,

> In St. Thomas' opinion theology is, to be sure, the higher form of wisdom, being the interpretation of revelation. But in order to practice its own trade it needs the tools of science and philosophy. *Propter defectum intellectus nostril,* because of the failings of our own intellect—and the theologian must also fall back upon human intellect when he engages in theology—because of this weakness, theology requires the independently obtained information of natural knowledge; theology "makes use" of it, "presupposes it," listens to it, takes note of it, and learns from it.[17]

How Aquinas's theology depended on his philosophy can be seen in Aquinas's mysticism. Though Scripture speaks of God as having certain positive names and attributes, as per Aquinas, we learn through philosophy that these positive names and attributes are merely an earthly and creative reflection of the unknowable and transcendent God. Philosophy teaches us we cannot know God in reality. In this, we need philosophy to rightly understand that all Scripture is not just analogical in nature but also symbolical. We need philosophy to know that Scripture can't tell us anything about the true nature of God.

Conclusion

Aquinas's doctrine of God is principally guided and shaped by the philosophical assumption of the impossibility of a self-moving object. Though Scripture still has an important role to play in Aquinas's epis-

---

17 Pieper, *Guide to Thomas Aquinas*, 157.

temology, the foundation of it is the metaphysics of Aristotle as guided by the mysticism of Dionysius. Both the way of negation and the way of affirmation claim that the knowledge of God's essence remains above the knowable realm of cognition. Scripture defines God using human language, but such language is inherently ineffective in revealing God as he truly is. In the end, philosophy informs us, according to Aquinas, that biblical language is not sufficient in getting us past the transcendental wall that separates us from the ineffable God.

6

The Fatal Flaw of Aquinas's Philosophical Theology

Thomas of Aquino had reasons to feel confident about his ability to baptize Aristotle into the church. As a young student at the University of Paris, he captured the attention of one of the most respected teachers of his day—the great Albertus. Ulrich of Strasburg (c. 1225–1277) identified Albertus (i.e., Albert the Great) as "the miracle and wonder of our time."[1] And this great "miracle and wonder" of the thirteenth century must have seen something special in his young apprentice. Not only did Albert defend Thomas before others, he also esteemed his pupil enough to make him his teaching assistant. In the same year, 1248, that the foundation stone for Cologne Cathedral was laid, Albert was called by the Dominicans to start a *studium generale* in Cologne. Albert brought the twenty-three-year-old Thomas with him.[2] Just four years later, in 1252, through the recommendation of Albert, the Dominicans

---

1 See Kevin Vost, *St. Albert the Great: Champion of Faith and Reason* (Charlotte, NC: Tan Books, 2011).

2 Pasquale Purro, *Thomas Aquinas: A Historical and Philosophical Profile*, trans. Joseph G. Trabbic and Roger W. Nutt (Washington, DC: The Catholic University of America Press, 2012), 5.

called Aquinas back to Paris to lecture on Peter Lombard's *Book of Sentences*.[3]

Thomas had won not only the respect of his renowned teacher but also the pope. In 1256, Thomas was officially appointed, by Pope Alexander IV's intervention, to regent master in theology at the University of Paris. No longer a student, he was a teacher in one of the most prestigious universities in the world. Thomas had firmly established himself as one of the elite intellectuals of his day at the relatively young age of thirty-one.

According to his first biographer, William of Tocco, Thomas had gained the respect and favor of the king of France, Louis IX.[4] His fame had grown quickly, and students had begun to crowd into his classroom. As another one of his early biographers, Peter Calo, reported, "When Thomas had taken up his work as teacher, and had begun the disputation and lectures, such a multitude of pupils flocked to his school, that the lecture room could hardly contain all who were attracted by the word of so renowned a master."[5]

His confidence would only grow stronger as he became an accomplished author. At thirty-one, he had already written his commentary on Lombard's *Sentences* and *On Being and Essence* as well as a few other books. But the bulk of his writings and his chief works lay ahead of him. He would have only eighteen years before his untimely death (in 1274) to write most of his works. Both *Summas*, his commentaries on Boethius, Dionysius, and Aristotle, and many other works would be published at an astonishing rate. He wrote no less than two books a year and up to fourteen in one year, with an average of four books

---

3 Jean-Pierre Torrell, *St. Thomas Aquinas, The Person and His Works*, trans. Robert Royal (Washington, DC: The Catholic University of America Press, 2005), 1:24.

4 See Romanus Cassario, O.P. "St Thomas Aquinas on Satisfaction, Indulgence, and Crusades" in *Medieval Philosophy and Theology*, ed. Mark D. Jordan (Notre Dame, IN: University of Nota Dame, 1992), 2:81.

5 Quoted in Martin Grabmann, *Thomas Aquinas: His Personality and Thought*, trans. Virgil Michel (New York: Longmans, Green and Co., 1928), 60.

a year, between 1257 and 1274—all while he continued to traverse Europe on foot as a mendicant beggar.

Such confidence remained with him throughout his life. Though some changes can be detected in the development of Aquinas's thinking, as noted by one of the first commentators of Thomas, John Capreolus (1380–1444), the basic consistency of Aquinas's earlier books with his more mature books is striking. Of course, the *Summa Theologica*, written at the end of Thomas's life, is the most developed representation of his philosophical theology, but like John Calvin who would come after him, Aquinas never experienced any radical shifts in his thinking.

From the start, following the influence of Albert the Great, Aquinas was fully committed throughout his life to reconciling philosophy with theology. He knew what he wanted to do, and he did not divert from it. With such confidence, he dared his opponents to try to refute him: "If anyone glorying [boasting] in what is falsely named a science wishes to say anything to reply to what we have written, let him not speak in corners nor to boys who cannot judge of such arduous matters, but reply to this in writing, if he dares" (OI, 124).

This confidence was not grounded so much in himself as much as in his firm commitment that all truth, wherever it is found, had to be compatible with the truths of the Bible. Chesterton identified the source of Thomas's confidence when he said, "St. Thomas was willing to allow the one truth [about God] to be approached by two paths, precisely *because* he was sure there was only one truth."[6] "Those things," Aquinas claimed, "which are received by faith from divine revelation cannot be contrary to our natural knowledge" (SCG, 1.7). It was with this unyielding commitment that Thomas gave his life to reconciling Aristotle with Christianity.

---

6 G. K. Chesterton, *Saint Thomas Aquinas* (Nashville: Sam Torade Book Arts, 2019), 46.

Is Aristotelianism Compatible with the Bible?

Of course, truth is truth wherever it's found. The Bible is not the only source of truth, and facts discovered in the secular world, such as in science or history, will be congruent with the truths revealed within the Bible. But this is not the issue. The issue is whether the scope of philosophy ("philosophical science derived by human reason") can reach a proper knowledge of God. Is philosophy—without the aid of revelation—even capable of leading rational people to the same God of natural and supernatural revelation?

The Fatal Flaw

Was Thomas Aquinas able to turn water into wine? Turning water into wine is a miracle indeed, but such a miracle would be easier to perform than the Christianization of a philosophy that is antithetical to Christianity. As it is impossible to reconcile darkness with light, it is impossible to reconcile the philosophical worldview of Aristotle with the theological worldview of the Bible. If premise A is logically incompatible with premise B, it does not matter how tightly premises C, D, E, and F are argued. As long as premise B remains a contradiction to premise A, the argument is fatally flawed.

The tension with Aquinas's philosophical theology lies at the beginning of his merger. In other words, the fatal flaw of the philosophical theology of Thomas Aquinas is the foundation of his natural theology—divine immobility, the idea that God cannot move himself.[7] The God of the Bible cannot be the unmoved mover. This is the basic problem even the confident Angelic Doctor could not overcome. Divine immobility cannot be reconciled with the God of the Bible because it is inherently incongruent with the God of the Bible.

---

7 To be more precise, I would say that the fatal flaw lies in Aquinas's unbiblical commitment that all knowledge begins and is confined to sense experience.

Yet for Aquinas, divine immobility is what connects philosophy with theology. It is what joins the knowledge of God's *existence* with the analogical knowledge of God's *essence*. Aristotle's cosmological argument not only proves God's existence, so Aquinas thought, it also proves God is immobile. And from the single attribute, other divine attributes are deduced. Seeing God is motionless, he is not like material, complex, finite, and changing objects in motion. Divine immobility, therefore, is not one of many concepts within Aquinas's philosophy and theology but, rather, is the heart of both. This means, however, that if divine immobility falls, Thomas's philosophical theology falls with it.

No matter how hard Aquinas tried, he could not change the fact that divine immobility is incompatible with the God of the Bible. Divine immobility is neither taught in the Scriptures, nor is it consistent within Aquinas's natural theology—and this for three reasons:

1. Divine immobility is not a necessary conclusion of Aquinas's first proof, which is based on God being the *final cause* of the universe.
2. Divine immobility is not consistent with Aquinas's second proof, which is based on God being the *efficient cause* of the universe.
3. Divine immobility is not consistent with Aquinas's fifth proof, which is based on God being the governor of the universe.

In this chapter, we will see how divine immobility is inconsistent with Aquinas's natural theology, and in the following chapter, we will observe how divine immobility is inconsistent with revealed theology—the Bible.

Divine Immobility Is Not a
Necessary Conclusion of the First Proof

What Aristotle assumed, Aquinas treated as a fact. Though it was a reasonable assumption, it was not a necessary conclusion of Aristotle's cosmological argument. Aristotle presumed that what was true concerning motion in the observable realm would be true concerning motion (if it existed) in the unobservable realm. He assumed that the laws of physics operate the same with God as they do with the physical universe in which the laws are derived. In the realm of sense experience, finite things cannot be the cause of their own motion. This is a fact that everything in motion in the physical universe needs an external cause. But from this fact, Aristotle supposed that a first cause without motion exists in the metaphysical realm.

But is this a necessary conclusion? Is it a necessary conclusion that the first cause of the universe be immobile? It does seem reasonable, or otherwise there would be an eternal regression of causes, which is impossible. Yet is there not another option? Could not God be self-moving? Aristotle believed that motionlessness and motion must both be eternal. Does not the law of inertia, Newton's first law of motion (i.e., objects in motion will remain in motion unless acted upon by an outside force) at least make it theoretically possible for motion to be eternal? And let's not forget that Aristotle thought motion was eternal.

But who is to say both non-motion and motion couldn't exist in the Trinity? Seeing that God is triune, could not his essence be without cause, while motion eternally exists within the relationship of the three persons as they eternally communicate their love toward one another? Is it not possible that this internal (*ad intra*) movement within the Godhead could allow for the three persons to work together (*ad extra*) as the moving cause of the universe? Of course, nothing in the cosmos has the power to move itself, but does this empirical fact rule out the possibility of a transcendent and triune God being self-moving?

Aristotle assumed that motion would apply the same to an autonomous being as it applies to contingent beings; Aquinas made this assumption as well. Because nothing in the observable realm can move itself, Aquinas concluded that it would be impossible for God to be able to move himself: "Now it is not possible that the same thing should be at once in actuality and potentiality in the same respect, but only in different respects. For what is actually hot cannot simultaneously be potentially hot; but it is simultaneously potentially cold. It is therefore impossible that in the same respect and in the same way a thing should be both mover and moved, i.e. that it should move itself" (ST, 1.2.3).

Though this may be the case concerning physical and contingent objects in motion, according to Gilson, it is not necessarily the case concerning a non-physical and independent God: "It does not follow from the fact that there is a first Mover, unmoved from outside, that there exists a first Mover who is absolutely immobile. Hence Aristotle points out that the expression 'a first Mover, not set in motion' is ambiguous. It can, in the first place, mean an absolutely immobile first Mover; in that case our conclusion holds. But it can also mean that this first Mover receives no movement from outside, while conceding that it may move itself."[8]

Of course, this does not prove that God moves himself. It just means that we cannot know for certain, based on Aquinas's first proof, if God moves himself or not. Herman Bavinck placed his finger on the problem when he stated, "We have no right . . . to apply the law of causality to such a first cause, and that we therefore cannot say anything specific about it."[9] The cosmological argument collapses because it jumps from physics to metaphysics, from science to philosophy, without having any epistemological warrant for such a leap. It may appear that God's nature can be derived from sense experience, from natural science, but such a conclusion is only a philosophical assumption. Even one of the leading Thomistic scholars of our day, Edward Feser, admits to this: "I

---

8   Gilson, *The Philosophy of St. Thomas Aquinas*, 75.
9   Bavinck, *Reformed Dogmatics*, 2:82.

do deny that arguments grounded in natural science alone can get you to classical theism."[10]

This is the breaking point. This is where the natural theology of Thomas Aquinas *fails*. There is no certainty, one way or another, if the attributes associated to contingent things in motion correspond positively or negatively to a non-contingent being. Just because all contingent things in motion require an external cause does not mean that motion in God, if motion exists in God, requires an external cause. This may be true in the realm in which we live, but who is to say this correlates to the supernatural being who transcends our natural abilities to comprehend?

The point is that natural theology has no way of knowing if God is immobile or self-moving. Just as natural theology has no way of knowing if God is a trinity of persons (as Aquinas admitted) and does not rule out the possibility of God being a trinity of persons, natural theology has no way of knowing if this trinity of persons allows for God to be both independent and free to move, create, and govern an unnecessary universe without the aid of anything outside himself. Natural theology must conclude that it is dependent on divine revelation to go any further than the knowledge of God's existence.

Therefore, if the concept of the unmoved mover is not a necessary conclusion of Aquinas's first proof, we should not look to divine immobility as the foundation of our doctrine of God as Aristotle and Aquinas did. Most importantly, the entire foundation on which the notion of divine immobility rests completely collapses.

Divine Immobility Is
Inconsistent with the Second Proof

By appealing to Aristotle in the first proof, Aquinas sought to establish divine immobility; by appealing to Dionysius in the second proof,

---

10 Feser, *Essays*, 62.

Aquinas sought to establish God as the moving cause of the universe. This, of course, was something Aristotle deemed impossible. God can't be the moving cause of the universe because God can't even move himself. But by holding to the first and second proofs together, Aquinas taught that somehow God is both without motion and the moving cause of the universe.

To baptize Aristotle, both proofs must be true at the same time. But how is it possible for something that can't move to be the moving cause of things that do move? It appears it was for this reason Gilson claimed that "one of the most difficult problems the classical metaphysicians had to face was the determination of the relation of being to its causal activity."[11]

Immobility and the Efficient Cause

For Aquinas, the immobile God is *actus purus*—without any unrealized potentiality. This does not mean that God does not do anything; it just means that whatever God does, he is doing in an undifferentiated, single, necessary, timeless, and ever-present act. God will never do anything more than what he has always been doing from all eternity. In other words, there is no passive potency in God. God is what he does; he always is what he always has been doing.

Of course, Aquinas was faced with the unorthodox implication of such a conclusion. If God's essence is identical to his creative acts, then creation is necessary for God to be God. Or as Charles Hodge framed it, if the "knowledge and power in God are identical," then "to know a thing is, and to will it, are the same undivided and perpetual act. From this it would seem to follow, that as God knows from eternity He creates from eternity; and that 'all He knows is.' We are thus led, by these speculations, into pantheistical views of the nature of God and of his relation to the world."[12]

---

11 Etienne Gilson, *The Spirit of Mediaeval Philosophy* (Notre Dame, IN: University of Notre Dame, 1991), 86.

12 Charles Hodge, *Systematic Theology* (Grand Rapids: Eerdmans, 1981), 1:395.

Though Aquinas did his best to deny such a conclusion, he maintained the divine immobility that logically leads to this conclusion. It must be kept in mind that, for Aquinas, divine immutability (which the Bible teaches) means the same thing as divine immobility (which the Bible does not teach). Aquinas taught that God is not just immutable in his character but also in his actions (i.e., immobile). Any new actions would be a change from potency to actuality—which is impossible for God who is *actus purus*.

Like Aristotle, by constructing a theology from the physical laws of motion, Aquinas deemed movement as something inherently bad, and motionlessness as something inherently good. Consequently, any new action would be an imperfection in God because it would entail some form of motion (change) in God. God is immobile, according to Aquinas, because God is perfect. For Aquinas, as with Aristotle, immobility is one of the attributes of perfection. That which is perfect cannot move from potency to actuality, for only deficient things seek actuality. This led, at least for Aristotle, to the impossibility of God being the efficient cause of the universe.

Edward Feser reminds us that, even for Aquinas, "an efficient cause is that which brings something into being or changes it in some way. An efficient cause thus actualizes a potency, and it does so by exercising its own active potencies or powers."[13] And so we must ask, How does God exercise his "own active potencies" if he does not have any potencies?

Aquinas held that immobility doesn't just mean the lack of potencies, but it also means undifferentiated simplicity. All movement, according to Aristotle, is from passive potency to actuality. But with God, there is no movement because there are no differentiated points within him for him to move between. No differentiation is present between God's nature and God's actions. Everything in God is identical

---

13   Edward Feser, *Scholastic Metaphysics: A Contemporary Introduction* (Lancaster, UK: Editiones Scholaticae, 2014), 42.

to God, meaning that God's nature and his actions are one and the same thing. More than that, there is no differentiation between the mind, will, and acts of God. He is what he does, and he does what he is—and this takes place in a single, undifferentiated, timeless, ever-present action.

Consequently, if God is good, perfect, immutable, and simple because he is immobile, then how is it possible for pure act (i.e., God) to will anything other than his undifferentiated self? And this is why, at least for Aristotle, there can be no free and unnecessary acts in God.

So Aquinas, who sought to integrate the unmoved mover of Aristotle with the God of the Bible, had to explain how the unmoved mover can be the moving cause of the universe. This leads to a host of questions, such as these:

1. How can the unmoved mover create anything new?
2. How can motion have a beginning?
3. If God created the universe, how is the universe not eternal?
4. If the universe is an eternal act, how is the universe not necessary?
5. If God is identical to his acts, how is God not one with his act of creating the universe?
6. How does this not lead to pantheism?

Of course, Aquinas rejected pantheism by claiming, as an article of faith, that the universe was created out of nothing. But, as we shall see, it was not easy for him to reconcile this article of faith with the philosophy of Aristotle. The difficulty is that the first and the second proofs don't appear to be compatible. It is not as if the second proof is illogical; it just doesn't seem to be congruent with the first proof. Yet by joining the two proofs, Aquinas was faced with various dilemmas.

Immobility and a Temporal Universe

The first dilemma that arises from joining the first and second proofs is the problem of a temporal universe. For Aquinas, not only is the knowledge and mind of God undifferentiated, the mind, will, and acts of God are undifferentiated. And because of this, Aquinas explained that the eternal and timeless act of willing the nonessential creation is identical to the eternal and timeless act of God willing his own essential essence: "God in willing himself wills all the things which are in himself; but all things in a certain manner pre-exist in God by their types. God, therefore, in willing himself wills other things" (SCG, 1.75). But if this is the case, how does willing himself and creation in the same eternal, single, and undifferentiated act not make creation coeternal with God?

According to C. S. Harris, the Aristotelian concept of the relation of form to matter embraced by Aquinas is simply incompatible with a temporal universe:

> Thomas accepts the Aristotelian conception of the relation of form to matter, and is then forced to spend a vast amount of ingenuity in attempting to escape its awkward consequences. He adopts the peripatetic theory of form and matter as correlatives, form standing to matter as act to potency, or determinant to determinable. Matter is pure potency having no *esse* of its own; it cannot exist without form, it is unknowable *per se* and does not even possess a representative idea in the divine mind; (though somehow God knows it); it is ingenerable and incorruptible, being the *subjectum* of substantial change. So far pure Aristotle; but now difficulties begin to arise. For in the Aristotelian cosmos, matter and form are metaphysical constituent of an eternal world which consists of a hierarchical series of substances stretched as it were between the two opposite poles of pure matter, which has no existence or actuality, pure form, *i.e.*, God; and while each of the constituents form and matter are eternal, the compounds of the two, the concrete substances of the physical world, are alone generable and corruptible in time, the world process being a perpetual and eternal repeated effort of the various forms to realize themselves in a matter which is forever, as it were, eluding their grasp, according to an immanent but unconscious teleology. For God, the form of forms, moves the universe as end or final cause,

being himself unmoved, and there is nothing to show that He is aware that a world exists at all. Such a theory could not, of course, commend itself to the Christian consciousness; it has therefore to be mutilated and mangled in order to be fitted into the theological frame. Form and matter are no longer coeval principles of an eternal world; matter is itself a product of divine creation (though how it can be so seeing that it has no actuality of its own, it is impossible to conceive), and the forms which are realized in it are also created, being imitations or ectypes of the eternal ideas in the divine mind, conceived somewhat after the manner of the λογόι of Plotinus. Thus the whole significance of the peripatetic theory is quietly ignored, and an Aristotelian cosmos suspended from a neo-platonist deity. But the worst is not yet. For besides the pure actuality or form of forms, there are the pure intelligence or Angels, *substantiae separatae*, which have somehow to be fitted into the scheme. These contain no matter, they are pure forms, yet they are neither εἴδη in the Platonic sense, nor are they eternal, but created. But a "Form" is as such abstracted from time, and all forms exist eternally in the mind of God, and are of their very nature simple. A new mode of composition has therefore to be introduced, a dualism between essence and existence, the latter being to the former as act to potency, in order to safeguard the creature-hood of these immaterial spirits. Creationism and Angelology thus make havoc of the whole Aristotelian scheme, and while the Aristotelian terminology is retrained, the meaning of the underlying ideas has been distorted almost beyond recognition. Finally, the whole question of creation is left philosophically doubtful, for it is in the last resort impossible to prove that the world has not existed *ab eterno*, and though the contrary is actually the fact, it is a fact which can be known only by revelation.[14]

Aquinas knew that an eternal universe could not be affirmed without compromising Christian orthodoxy. An eternal universe creates all kinds of problems for the Christian faith. Mainly, creation has to be temporal to uphold God's independence. Yet Aquinas admitted that a

---

14   C. R. S. Harris, "Duns Scotus and His Relation to Thomas Aquinas," *Proceedings of the Aristotelian Society, New Series* 25 (1924): 219–46, Accessed July 23, 2021, http://www.jstor.org/stable/4544081.

temporal universe could not be proven by reason, for a temporal universe, he believed, is one of the articles of faith made known only by divine revelation:

> The articles of faith cannot be proved demonstratively, because faith is of things "that appear not" (Heb. 11:1). But that God is the Creator of the world: hence that the world began, is an article of faith; for we say, "I believe in one God," etc. And again, Gregory says (Hom. i in Ezech.), that Moses prophesied of the past, saying, "In the beginning God created heaven and earth": in which words the newness of the world is stated. Therefore the newness of the world is known only by revelation; and therefore it cannot be proved demonstratively. (ST, 1.46.2)

Again, in another place, Aquinas stated,

> By faith alone do we hold, and by no demonstration can it be proved, that the world did not always exist, as was said above of the mystery of the Trinity. . . . The reason for this is that the newness of the world cannot be demonstrated on the part of the world itself. For the principle of demonstration is the essence of a thing. Now everything according to its species is abstracted from "here" and "now"; whence it is said that universals are everywhere and always. Hence it cannot be demonstrated that man, or heaven, or a stone were not always. Likewise neither can it be demonstrated on the part of the efficient cause, which acts by will. For the will of God cannot be investigated by reason, except as regards those things which God must will of necessity; and what he wills about creatures is not among these. . . . But the divine will can be manifested by revelation, on which faith rests. Hence that the world began to exist is an object of faith, but not of demonstration or science. (ST, 1.46.2)

This is where Aquinas's natural theology breaks down. For his second proof to correlate with his first, Aquinas admittedly had to borrow capital from the Scriptures. But once revealed theology is used to adjust natural theology, natural theology ceases to be natural theology. Aristotelian metaphysics on its own merit cannot establish a temporal universe. And without a temporal universe, God ceases to be absolute. Seeing that this is the case, why would one trust Aristotle at all?

Immobility and Free Acts of the Will

This is not where the problems end for Aquinas. Not only does an eternal universe appear to be the logical consequence of an immobile creator, but a necessary universe appears to naturally follow as well. If God's essence is equal to his act(ions), then it seems natural that the world exists by necessity. That is, if God wills the existence of the universe in the very same undifferentiated act as he wills his own necessary existence, as claimed by Aquinas, then it would seem that the existence of the universe is just as necessary as the existence of God.

Of course, Aquinas, the theologian, could not accept this philosophical conclusion. Aristotle's god needed to be adjusted by Thomas, for Aristotle believed it was impossible for the unmoved mover to have free acts of the will because the unmoved mover cannot share or give of himself while remaining in a motionless state. Because the unmoved mover is perfectly good, according to Aristotle, the unmoved mover needs and desires nothing. Hence, God can only desire himself in a timeless act of self-contemplation. Though every moving object desires God, God is content in his perfect goodness to remain in an eternal state of perfected motionlessness. God is good, according to Aristotle, because he is altogether desirable.

To adjust the unmoved mover's inability to give of himself, Aquinas turned to Dionysius for help. Dionysius, following Plato, defined *goodness* a little differently. For Dionysius, two concepts are included in the idea of goodness: *desirability* and *charity*. Like Aristotle, Dionysius believed God was good because he is altogether desirable, but unlike Aristotle, Dionysius also believed God's goodness included the concept of charity. Charity consists of giving of oneself. For Dionysius, though God is perfect and needs nothing, he nevertheless in his goodness gives of himself in the creation of all things.

By combining these two ideas, desirability and generosity, Aquinas sought to make room for unnecessary and free acts within God. Aquinas claimed that contained within the goodness of God is (1) the final and (2) the moving cause of the universe. Aquinas agreed with Aristotle that the final cause of the universe is God's own perfect goodness, which moves all things to aspire after him. Aquinas claimed that "the divine goodness is the end of all things" (ST, 1.44.4). God moves the universe by not moving himself. And at the same time, Aquinas also agreed with Dionysius that the efficient cause of the universe is God willing for his own sake, his own goodness, which moves him to give of himself in the creation of all things after the likeness of his own goodness.

For Aquinas, God's love that motivated him to give of himself did not come by looking outside himself. His love of himself moved him to reproduce himself, but because it is impossible to create another God, he created the universe after his own similitude. And since not one thing could perfectly capture his essence, he created multiple things that reflect his likeness.

Thus, being moved by necessity to will his own goodness, God somehow freely chose to create the universe that depicts his goodness. As Aquinas sought to explain: "God, by willing his own goodness, wills other things to be, inasmuch as they partake of his goodness. Now, since God's goodness is infinite, it can be participated in an infinite number of ways, and in other ways besides those in which it is participated by those creatures which now are" (SCG, 1.81.4).

Yet, though God wills himself by necessity, he does not will creation out of necessity, as Gilson stated: "God wills himself necessarily but does not will anything other than Himself necessarily, and all that He does will He wills with respect to Himself."[15]

But why not? How is it possible for God to will his own existence by the same undifferentiated and timeless act of willing the universe

---

15   Gilson, *The Spirit of Mediaeval Philosophy*, 93.

without the universe being eternal and necessary? In his attempt to answer this dilemma, Aquinas claimed, "If, then, through willing his own goodness, he willed of necessity the things which participate in it, then it would follow that he wills an infinite number of creatures partaking of his goodness in an infinite number of ways. But this is clearly false: for if he willed it, they would exist, since his will is the source of being to things. . . . Therefore, he does not necessarily also will those things that are not" (SCG, 1.81.4). In other words, seeing that there were an infinite number of universes God could have chosen to create, he must have created this one out of freedom and not necessity.

Yet, this solution only compounds Aquinas's dilemma. How is it possible for the unmoved mover to have an infinite number of options to choose from if his thoughts are undifferentiated? Not only does this argument not solve Aquinas's dilemma, it highlights another problem. For, according to Thomas, actions, such as the act of creating, takes place either by the intellect moving the will or by the will moving the intellect in accordance with God's own goodness: "A thing is said to move in two ways: First, as an end; for instance, when we say that the end moves the agent. In this way the intellect moves the will, because the good understood is the object of the will, and moves it as an end. Secondly, a thing is said to move as an agent, as what alters moves what is altered, and what impels moves what is impelled. In this way the will moves the intellect and all the powers of the soul" (ST, 1.82.4).

Such an explanation, however, can't apply to the undifferentiated unmoved mover. This is for two reasons: (1) the will cannot *move* the intellect in God because there is simply no movement in God, and (2) the reason there is no movement in God is that there is no differentiation in God. God's intellect and God's will are identical with God's simple essence: "The essence of God is his intellect and will, from the fact of his acting by his essence" (ST, 1.19.4). Again, Aquinas said,

> The act of God's intellect is his substance. For if his act of understanding were other than his substance, then something else,

as the Philosopher says (Metaph. xii), would be the act and perfection of the divine substance, to which the divine substance
would be related, as potentiality is to act, which is altogether
impossible. . . . Now in God there is no form which is something
other than his existence. . . . Hence as his essence itself is also
his intelligible species, it necessarily follows that his act of understanding must be his essence and his existence. (ST, 1.14.4)

So, regardless of if the works of God are moved by the intellect or
by the will of God, the intellect and will of God are both identical
with each other and identical with the essence of God. And seeing
that God's essence is immobile, it would seem that whatever God does
must be identical to who God is. Furthermore, if there is no movement
in God because there is no differentiation in God, how is there any
difference between the final and moving cause of the universe? Again,
does this not make the creation necessary?

Of course, Aquinas's commitment to the Scriptures would not allow
him to accept such a conclusion. Nevertheless, Aquinas was fully aware
of this dilemma. For in his book on disputed questions, *Quaestiones
Disputatae De Potentia Dei*, Aquinas attempted to face this dilemma
head on.[16] In question 3, article 15, he asked, "Did things proceed from
God of natural necessity or by the decree of his will?" Aquinas went
on to articulate the dilemma in various ways. "In God nature and will
are the same," he stated. "Consequently, if he produces things willingly
it would seem that he produces them naturally"[17] (QDP, 3.15, Obj. 6).
Another way he stated the problem was to say, "God's operation is his
essence: and his essence is natural to him. Therefore whatever he does
he does naturally" (QDP, 3.15, Obj. 8). Again, he stated,

It cannot be said that in God anything is potential or contingent: since this argues mutability according to the Philosopher

---

16 Or, *Disputed Questions on the Power of God*

17 Thomas Aquinas, *Quaestiones Disputatae De Potentia Dei*, trans. English Dominican
Fathers (Westminster, MD: The Newman Press, 1952), 3.15, Obj. 6 (hereafter cited in text
as QDP).

(*Metaph.* xi, 5), because what is contingent may happen not to be. Again, nothing in God is necessary by coercion because in him nothing is violent or contrary to nature (*Metaph.* v, 5). Nor is there anything necessary by supposition, because this depends on certain things being presupposed, and God is not dependent on anything. It remains then that all in God is absolutely necessary, and it would seem consequently that he produced things necessarily (QDP, 3.15, Obj. 11).

So, it is evident that Aquinas understood the problem facing his philosophical theology. But his answers to the problem seem less than satisfactory: "Although will, and nature are identically the same in God, they differ logically, in so far as they express respect to creatures in different ways: thus nature denotes a respect to some one thing determinately, whereas will does not" (QDP, 3.15, Reply 6). Again, he repeated himself when he stated, "Although God's operation belongs to him naturally seeing that it is his very nature or essence, the created effect follows the operation of his nature which, in our way of understanding, is considered as the principle of his will, even as the effect that is heating follows according to the mode of the heat" (QDP, 3.15, Reply 8). And once more he stated, "As regards the things which are in God himself, nothing can be described as potential: all is naturally and absolutely necessary. But in respect of creatures we can call certain things potential not in regard to passive potentiality, but in regard to an active power which is not limited to one effect" (QDP, 3.15, Reply 11).

In other words, from our human perspective, we must distinguish between God's will and God's intellect, otherwise God ceases to be able to have free and unnecessary acts of the will. But how does making a cognitive distinction in our minds change the fact that there are no real distinctions within God? In the end, Aquinas affirms that the acts of God's will are identical to his existence and essence. In speaking of the passage where Aquinas says, "In willing himself primarily, he wills all other things" (SCG, 1.75), Arthur Lovejoy identifies the inconsistency of Aquinas: "Now this, as a recent Roman Catholic commentator on the *Summa contra Gentiles* obverses, 'taken by itself might seem to argue that God wills the existence of all things that He understands as possible, and that He necessarily wills the existence of things outside himself, and so necessarily creates them.' Not only might the passage mean this; it can, in consistency with assumptions which Aquinas elsewhere accepts, mean nothing else."[18]

Josef Pieper claims that "the *Quaestiones disputatae* frequently comes to an end like the Platonic dialogues; they make no claim to offering comprehensive answers, but throw open the gates to an infinitude of further seeking."[19] Aquinas did his best to save Aristotle from unorthodoxy, but it does not appear that he was able to do so. Though he may have sprinkled a few drops of water on the Aristotelian corpus, full immersion proved to be too difficult.

Thomas could have saved himself a lot of trouble if he would have just abandoned Aristotle's god—the unmoved mover—altogether. Because the philosophical concept of the unmoved mover is incompatible with the Trinitarian God of the Bible, it was impossible for the Angelic Doctor—no matter how clever he may have been—to reconcile the tension between his first and second proofs.

DIVINE IMMOBILITY IS INCONSISTENT WITH THE FIFTH PROOF

But even if we skip over these difficulties and grant that God is the immobile moving cause of the universe, Aquinas still has another dilemma to reconcile: How does a motionless God govern and interact with the ever-moving universe? According to Aquinas's first proof, God is immobile. According to his second proof, God is the moving cause of the universe. And according to Thomas's fifth proof, God is the governor of all moving things in the universe, as he is directing all things to

---

18 Arthur O. Lovejoy, *The Great Chain of Being: A Study of the History of an Idea* (Cambridge, MA: Harvard University Press, 1976), 74.
19 Pieper, *Guide to Thomas Aquinas*, 99.

their proper end. The Bible affirms divine providence, but the question is this: How does the immobile god of Aristotle know, love, relate, and interact with the temporal affairs of men?

Immobility and Knowledge of the Universe

Yet if God is going to govern the universe, he must be aware of the universe. If God and his thoughts are without any differentiation, then how can God think of things outside himself?

For Aristotle, the unmoved mover cannot think about anything other than himself. First, God is only aware of himself because that which is undifferentiated can only contemplate that which is also undifferentiated. Second, God cannot think of anything but himself because he is identical to that which he contemplates. Thus, the only thing God can think about is himself. Unlike Aristotle, however, Aquinas claimed God does know things other than himself. For the unmoved mover to be the God of the Bible, he must be aware of every particular thing in the universe. God must be able to distinguish between himself and all the particulars in the created universe. This is a matter of Christian orthodoxy.

But seeing that God is undifferentiated in his simplicity and identical to concepts in his mind, would not such knowledge of particular things be impossible for God? First, if God's knowledge is undifferentiated, how can God know the difference between his undifferentiated self (*ad intra*) and all the particular and differentiated things outside of himself (*ad extra*)? Second, if God's essence is identical to his knowledge, how does the knowledge of the existing universe not make God's essence dependent on the existing universe?

Though this seems impossible, Aquinas attempted to reconcile the difficulty by claiming that God knows differentiated and particular things by knowing his own undifferentiated self. As we know the simplicity of God by knowing the particulars, Aquinas claimed, God knows the particulars by knowing himself. So Aquinas claimed that, on the one hand, God knows all particular things outside of himself, but, on the other hand, God only knows the particulars by knowing himself (*ad intra*) in a simple act of self-awareness.

Though it is hard to determine if Aquinas actually believed God can distinguish between things or not, I can understand the difficulty of trying to reconcile these two contrary concepts. If God can distinguish between particular things outside of himself, then he is no longer undifferentiated in his simplicity. For if he knows, at least in his mind, that there is a difference between the knowledge of himself and the knowledge of things outside himself, then God ceases to be undifferentiated in his thinking. But once there is a differentiation in the mind of God, God can no longer be said to be undifferentiated in his simplicity. Once the content of God's knowledge is not identical to God's simple essence, the logic of Aristotle breaks down.

Immobility and Providence

Knowledge of the universe is not the only problem for an immobile God. Even if we accept that the unmoved mover knows everything outside himself in a single, undifferentiated act of self-awareness, the problem remains of how God can govern all the particular things.

It appears that, for Aquinas, all God's eternal acts are performed *ad intra*. In the single act of willing himself, all God's acts of knowing, creating, governing, and destroying are carried out. But admittedly, according to Thomas, this rules out any new relationships with God (QDP, 7.9), for God is like a stone column that does not relate to the dog circling it. Though the ever-moving dog enters into a new relationship with the column, the column remains completely unmoved. Though God somehow is able to govern the universe from a single and timeless act of willing himself, he does not enter into any new relationships, which, according to Matthew McWhorter, seems like a major inconsistency: "Aquinas consistently teaches throughout his career that God creates, knows, and loves the world, yet, at the same time, that there is no real relation between God and the world. Taken together, these doctrines seem to contradict one another. How can God know and love that with which he has no real relation?"[20]

THE LAWS OF PHYSICS DON'T APPLY TO GOD

All these conflicts are a result of Aquinas not being willing to give up his desire to baptize Aristotle. Aristotle's mistake was the assumption that the laws of motion would operate the same way with God as they do with finite things within the cosmos. He assumed that the metaphysical realm could be understood by the study of the physical realm. But because God is triune, he is unlike anything in the cosmos. What applies to finite and contingent things doesn't necessarily have to apply to the infinite and independent God. It may just be possible for God to be the only being that is self-moving. It may just be possible that the Trinitarian God is without an external cause for his own necessary existence and the external moving cause of an unnecessary universe.

Aquinas knew that his philosophical theology was filled with tension. In *Disputed Questions on the Power of God*, Aquinas cataloged the various difficulties—chiefly the difficulty of a temporal and unnecessary universe that is created out of nothing. When it came to Aristotle's belief that something cannot come from nothing, Aquinas responded by saying the rules of motion don't apply to God: "The Philosopher says that it is a common axiom or opinion of the physicists that from nothing nothing is made, because the natural agent, which was the object of their researches, does not act except by movement. Consequently there must needs be a subject of movement or change which, as we have stated, is not required for a supernatural agent" (QDP, 2, Reply to 1).

Aquinas repeatedly asserted that the rules that apply to finite things in motion do not apply to the unmoved mover (see QDP, 2 and 3), which is true. But Aquinas was not consistent in applying this principle. Why not apply this principle at the beginning of his philosophical

20 Matthew R. McWhorter, "Aquinas on God's Relation to the World," *New Blackfriars*, vol. 94, no. 1049, 2013, 3–19, 3.

theology by rejecting Aristotle's cosmological argument altogether? It sure would've made his job much easier.

But somehow, Aquinas believed that we could learn that God is the unmoved mover by studying the principles of motion, but when these same principles make it impossible for the unmoved mover to be the creator of an unnecessary and temporal universe, they are no longer useful in telling us anything more about God. And for this reason, according to Aquinas, a temporal and unnecessary universe is not the logical conclusion of natural theology but, like the doctrine of the Trinity, is an article of faith that can only be received by divine authority. In other words, a non-eternal universe "cannot be proved by demonstration" (ST, 1.46.1).

CONCLUSION

Because Aquinas was committed to rescuing Aristotle from unorthodoxy, he was committed to maintaining Aristotle's notion of divine immobility regardless of the vast number of unreserved difficulties it introduced into his philosophical theology. Josef Pieper recognizes the considerable amount of tension in Aquinas's doctrine of God: "His endeavor was fraught with a multitude of potential conflicts; that it would be a source of virtually incalculable difficulties and discords which could scarily ever be brought to a final 'harmony.'"[21] In the end, though Aquinas may have been confident that he could baptize Aristotle, it does not appear that the pagan philosopher wanted to get wet.

---

21 Pieper, *Guide to Thomas Aquinas*, 118.

7

THE PROBLEMS OF DIVINE IMMOBILITY

THOMAS OF AQUINO was a traveling professor. At the age of twenty-eight, he left the side of his mentor and friend, Albert the Great, and journeyed from Cologne to his first teaching post at the Dominican Priory of St. Jacques in Paris. Just a few years later, in 1256, he became regent master in theology at the University of Paris. And just after three years of teaching there, he was called, in 1259, by Pope Alexander IV to serve in the papal court, located at that time in Viterbo, about fifty miles north of Rome. So he left Paris and its recently constructed Cathedral of Notre Dame to move back to Italy.[1] After the death of Urban IV, Aquinas moved from Viterbo to Rome with the assignment of establishing three new colleges for the Dominican order.[2] But within two short years, the newly elected pope, Clement IV, called Thomas to return to the papal court. Thomas would only serve two years in Viterbo before being recalled for the second time at the University of Paris. Once more, he lasted three years in Paris before he was summoned, in 1272, back to where he started, Naples. In Naples, he was asked to start a new college for his own Dominican order.

---

1 The west façade of Notre Dame Cathedral, with its two famous bell towers, was completed in 1250.
2 See Joseph Pieper, *The Silence of St. Thomas*, 12–13.

He traveled the length and breadth of Europe, teaching here and there, only to return to where he began—three stays in Paris, three stays in Naples, two stays in Viterbo, and one stay in Cologne. And though his location was always changing, the basic content of his teaching remained the same. Thomas, though not committed to a location, was committed to Christianizing Aristotle. Whether he was in France or Germany or Italy, Aquinas was intent on teaching that Aristotelian philosophy was in harmony with Christian dogma.

And it must be kept in mind that Aquinas's unification of Aristotle and the Bible did not end with his apologetics. Because Aquinas was convinced that philosophy and theology arrive at the same truths about God's nature, his theology was philosophical, and his philosophy was theological. He was not only a theologian but also an Aristotelian and a Platonist.[3] For instance, his Platonic hermeneutic shaped his understanding of divine revelation. And the influence of Aristotle in particular can be detected in almost every line of Aquinas's dogmatic theology. His commentaries on the Bible include hundreds of citations from Aristotle, and his commentaries on Aristotle include hundreds of citations from the Bible. In other words, Aquinas's philosophy permeated his theology, and his theology permeated his philosophy.

To be more precise, because of his commitment to the metaphysics of Aristotle, Aquinas added an attribute to God's nature that is not revealed in the Scriptures—divine immobility. This additional attribute, as we have already stated, influenced the rest of Aquinas's theology. His theology proper, anthropology, soteriology, and Bibliology were all shaped in part by his philosophical devotion to the notion that God is the unmoved mover. But not only is the concept of divine immobility not compatible with apologetics, it is also incompatible with theology.

---

3 See Pieper, *Guide to Thomas Aquinas*, 22.

DIVINE IMMOBILITY AND THEOLOGY PROPER

According to Thomas, divine simplicity, immutability, and impassibility are taught by both Aristotle and the Bible. Yet philosophy and theology arrive at these divine attributes from two different directions and on two different authorities. On the one hand, these attributes of God are deduced from the Bible through its teaching of the absolute autonomy of God. Because God is fully God in and of himself, he must be simple, immutable, and without passions. All that is in God must be God. This is what the Bible teaches. For Aristotle, on the other hand, these divine attributes are induced from the physical principle of causality. From the assumption that nothing can move itself, Aristotle concluded that God is immobile, and from divine immovability, he deduced that God is simple, immutable, and impassible.

Though philosophy and theology appear to arrive at the same destination from opposite directions, this is not the case. The Bible does not teach divine immovability. Of course, the Bible affirms that God didn't create himself. He didn't come into existence or need any external power to actualize any passive potency within him. God is God. He is self-existent and needs nothing outside himself to be who he is and to do what he wills to do. Yet God's aseity, independence, and absoluteness do not mean that God can't choose to exercise power or refrain from exercising power.

The biblical doctrine of divine simplicity and immutability does not mean, as Aquinas believed, divine immobility. As Herman Bavinck rightly claimed, "Immutability . . . should not be confused with monotonous sameness or rigid immobility."[4] For Aquinas, movement is linked with mutability because everything in the universe is both in motion and mutable. Because of this, Aquinas could not conceive of how movement is not an attribute of imperfection. Yet, though this may be true with created and dependent things in motion, it does not

---

4 Bavinck, *Reformed Dogmatics*, 2:158.

mean we can be certain that it is true in regard to how motion works in a Trinitarian God.

More importantly, the Bible does not teach that movement is an attribute of imperfection. Louis Berkhof echoed Bavinck's concern when he stated, "The divine immutability should not be understood as implying *immobility*, as if there was no movement in God."[5] And Puritan William Perkins identified the life of God as that "by which the Divine nature is in perpetual action, living, and *moving in itself*."[6]

There remains an irreconcilable difference between the god of Aristotle and the Trinitarian God of the Bible: the unmoved mover is undifferentiated, while the Trinity is differentiated. Besides the fact that the unmoved mover cannot be the moving cause of the universe, the unmoved mover cannot have any *ad intra* differentiations; otherwise, God's thought(s), will(s), and act(ions) are not all numerically the same. And without differentiation within God, there is no real possibility for God to subsist in three differentiated and distinct persons. In other words, if there is no *ad intra* differentiation in God, there is no Trinity.

DIVINE IMMOBILITY AND THE TRINITY

Thomas wanted to have it both ways—a God without differentiation and a God with differentiation. He explains the nature of God's undifferentiated oneness before he explains the nature of God's differentiated threeness. In Book 1 of *Summa Contra Gentiles*, God's nature is built on the foundation of sense experience, while in Book 4, the Trinity is derived from divine revelation. There is a reason Aquinas separated his explanation of God's nature from his explanation of the Trinity. Aquinas's natural theology, a "physical science built up by human reason," led to an undifferentiated monadistic God, whereas re-

---

5 Louis Berkhof, *Systematic Theology* (Grand Rapids: Eerdmans, 1996), 59.
6 William Perkins, "A Golden Chain," in *The Works of William Perkins,* ed. Joel Beeke (Grand Rapid: Reformation Heritage Books, 2019), 6:15. Italics mine.

vealed theology, through the gift of faith, teaches that God is both one and at the same time a differentiated trinity of persons.

Thomas admitted that natural reason does not lead to the doctrine of the Trinity. Through "natural reason," Aquinas stated, "we can know what belongs to the unity of the essence, but not what belongs to the distinction of the persons" (ST, 1.32.a.1). As an article of faith, the Trinity must be divinely revealed and accepted by faith. As Brian Davies stated, "Aquinas recognizes that philosophy can take us so far and no further."[7]

But just as it is impossible to reconcile the first and second proofs, reconciling Aquinas's doctrine of God's undifferentiated nature, which is a conjecture drawn from sense experience, with the biblical doctrine of the Trinity, which is an ontological reality revealed in Scripture, is likewise unattainable. For instance, Aquinas claimed in Part 1 of the *Summa Contra Gentiles* that God's mind, will, and actions are identical, and because they are identical, they are undifferentiated and indistinguishable within the mind of God. Yet in Book 4 of the *Summa Contra Gentiles*, Aquinas sought to explain the Trinity by inserting differentiations between the mind, will, and actions of God.

NATURAL THEOLOGY AND NO DIFFERENTIATION IN GOD

Because God is pure act, there can be no differentiation within God. Aquinas claimed that "in every compound, there must be actuality and potentiality. For a plurality of things cannot become one thing, unless there be actuality and potentiality" (SCG, 1.1.18). Because there is no potentiality in God, there is no differentiation within God.

No Differentiation between God's Essence and God's Knowledge

First, this means there is no differentiation between God's essence and that which God knows: "For his being is not only in conformity with his intellect, but is his very act of knowing; and his act of knowing is

---

7   Brian Davies, *The Thought of Thomas Aquinas* (Oxford: Clarendon, 1992), 190.

the measure and cause of all other being and all other intellect; and he himself is his own being and his own act of knowing" (ST. 1.16.5). In another place, Aquinas said, "If many things are known by God as known principally and essentially, it follows that God's knowledge is composed of many; and thus either God's essence will be composite, or knowledge will be accidental to God. But either of these is clearly impossible from what has been said. It remains, therefore, that that which is understood by God first and essentially is nothing else than his substance" (SCG, 1.48).

No Differentiation between God's Essence and God's Will

Second, and in the same way, God's knowledge is not distinct from his essence. Aquinas stated that God's "will is not distinct from his essence"—that is, "God's will is his very essence" (SCG, 1.73).

No Differentiation between God's Essence and God's Act(ions)

Third, God's act(ions) are identical to his essence. "Now God's power is his substance," Thomas claimed, "and his action is also his substance. . . . Therefore, God's power is not distinct from action" (SCG, 2.9).

No Differentiation between God's Knowledge and Will

As there is no difference between God's essence and God's knowledge, according to the "Doctor Angelicus," there is no difference between God's essence and God's will: "Since God is an intelligent being, as we have shown, it follows that there is a will in him: not that his will is something over and above his essence (as neither is his intellect, as we have proved above), but that his will is his very substance, it follows that in God intellect and will are one and the same" (SCG, 4.19).

REVEALED THEOLOGY AND DIFFERENTIATION IN GOD

If natural theology, without the aid of divine revelation, teaches us that God is the opposite of physical objects in motion, then Aquinas concluded with Aristotle that God is without differentiation. But as mentioned in the last chapter, the problem is how to reconcile the concept of an undifferentiated unmoved mover with the Trinitarian God of the Bible. Though Aristotle didn't have to worry about reconciling his beliefs with the Bible, Aquinas did. But no matter how hard Aquinas tried, he could not explain how the unmoved mover is a trinity of differentiated persons. For instance, Aquinas stated, "Those who follow the teaching of the catholic faith must hold that the relations in God are real. . . . Wherefore in God there must be some distinction not only in respect of creatures who differ from him in nature, but also in respect of someone subsisting in the divine nature" (QDP, 8.1).

Moreover, according to Aquinas, these distinctions within the persons of the Trinity must be real (*ad intra*) distinctions: "Now this distinction cannot be merely logical, because things that are only logically distinct can be predicated of one another. . . . Hence it would follow that the Father is the Son and the Son the Father: because seeing that names are given in order to distinguish things, it would follow that the divine Persons differ only in name, which is the heresy of Sabellius. It remains thus to be said that the relations in God are something real" (QDP, 8:1).

How could this be possible? According to Thomas, reason alone is not sufficient to answer (QDP, 8.1). For this reason, Gilles Emery states, "This project is not an attempt to 'comprehend' the Trinity, because our reason cannot fully grasp the mystery of relations in God."[8]

The Generation of the Son Is a Differentiation within the Mind of God

Nevertheless, Aquinas went on to define the procession of the Son as an internal movement that happens within the mind of God: "Procession exists in God only according to an action which does not tend to anything external, but remains in the agent himself" (ST, 1.27.a.3). Like a thought that originates and remains within the mind, the Son

---

8 Gilles Emery, *The Trinitarian Theology of St. Thomas Aquinas*, trans. Francesca Aran Murphy (Oxford: Oxford University Press, 2010), 79.

generates from within and remains within God. Aquinas explained it this way: "Whenever anyone understands because of his very act of understanding, something comes forth within him, which is the concept of the known thing proceeding from his awareness of it" (CJ, 1a.27.1).

And, according to Aquinas, this internal procession that takes place within the mind of God is God's knowledge of himself. This divine self-awareness, moreover, creates an internal *ad intra* differentiation within God. On the one hand, you have God as he is objectively. On the other hand, you have God's subjective awareness of himself. Though there is only one God, there exists a real distinction or relation within God. This internal procession is how Aquinas explained the eternal generation of the Son. As Ceslaus Velecky explains, "St. Thomas likens the procession of the Word in God to our act of self-awareness when the mind is both naturally and objectively identified with itself. So it is as if in thinking of himself that God begets God. He is pure intelligibility, and his act of understanding issuing in his Word is identical with his very being."[9] "The Son of God," according to Aquinas, "is the Word and concept of God understanding himself. Therefore, the Word of God is rightly called conceived or begotten wisdom, as being the wise conception of the divine mind" (SCG, 4.13).

The Procession of the Spirit Is a Differentiation in the Will of God

If the Son is generated by the Father's self-awareness, how does the Spirit proceed from the Father and the Son? According to Aquinas, the Spirit proceeds not from the mind of God but from the will of God. God cannot help but love himself by being fully aware of himself. "Moreover," Aquinas said, "the Word of God is born of God by the knowledge of Himself; and Love proceeds from God according as He loves Himself" (ST, 1.93.8). "The object loved is present in the lover," he claimed, "even as the object known is present in the knower" (ST, 1a.27.3). Therefore, because the Son generates from the Father's own awareness of himself, the Spirit proceeds from the Father and Son's

---

9 Quoted in Davies, *The Thought of Thomas Aquinas*, 196.

love of self: "For a thing would not be loved if it were not known in some way; nor is it the mere idea of the beloved object that is loved, but the object inasmuch as it is a good in itself. Hence the love whereby God is in his own will as the beloved in the lover must proceed both from the Word of God, and from God who utters the Word" (SCG, 4.19).

So, like Dionysius, Aquinas's origins (*generation* and *spiration*) of the Son and the Spirit are similar to God being the moving cause of creation. As God knows the particulars of the universe by knowing himself, God's knowledge of himself is the eternal origins (generation) of the Son. And as God's wills creation in willing himself, the eternal origin of the Spirit (spiration) is his eternal love for what he knows of himself. Yet for Aquinas, somehow the Trinity is necessary to God and the universe is not.

The Trinity Consists of Three Differentiations within God

Nevertheless, this means, in Aquinas's theology, that within God three separate relations and differentiations exist:

> And, in an intellectual nature, such action is that of the intellect, and of the will. The procession of the Word belongs to an act of the intelligence. As to the operation of the will, for us it gives rise to a different procession which is that of love, whereby the object loved is in the lover (in the same way that, by the procession of the Word, the thing spoken or known is in the knower). Hence, in addition to the procession of the Word, there exists in God another procession which is the procession of Love. (ST, 1.27.a.3)

In another place, Aquinas explained it thusly:

> There is in God, as there is in us, a sort of "circulation" (*circulatio*) in the operations of mind and will: for the will returns to that which understanding initiated. But with us the "circle" (*circulus*) closes in that which is outside of us: the external good moving

our intellect, our intellect moving the will, and the will returning through its appetite and love to the external good. But in God, the "circle" is completed within himself: for when God understands himself, he conceives his Word which is the "rationale" of everything known by him, since he understands all things by understanding himself; and through this Word, he "proceeds" to the love of all things and of himself. . . . And the circle being completed, nothing more can be added to it: so that a third procession within the divine nature is impossible, although there follows a procession toward external nature. (QDP, q. 9, a. 9)

THE TENSION

So according to natural theology, God is without differentiation, but according to revealed theology, God is not without differentiations. Gilles Emery defined the tension this way: "The intellect and will of God are really identical to the one single being and substance of God. So in God, intellect and will are a single, identical reality. But then how can one think the procession of two *really distinct* persons, when one uses the mode of two attributes (intellect and will or love) which are, in God, *really identical*? Would such an enterprise not be doomed to failure from the start?"[10]

In other words, if God's knowledge of himself proceeds perfectly from God's essence, and if God's knowledge of himself is identical with God's essence, how can there be any differentiation? If, as Aquinas said, "His intellect and its object are altogether the same" (ST. 1.14.2), then how can there be a real distinction between the Father and the Son? Karen Kilby remarked that the "more perfectly [something] proceeds, the more closely it is one with the source whence it proceeds." As explained by Aquinas concerning the Son proceeding from the Father, "the divine Word is of necessity perfectly one with the source whence he proceeds, without any kind of diversity (ST 1.27, 1 ad 2)." Kilby went on to explain the problem with this formation:

---

10   Gilles Emery, *The Trinitarian Theology of St. Thomas Aquinas*, trans. Francesca Aran Murphy (Oxford: Oxford University Press, 2010), 69. Italics original.

The Problems of Divine Immobility

"In God we precisely cannot think of difference between that which proceeds and that from which it proceeds: [undifferentiated] divine simplicity requires the denial of this. Thomas is presenting us with a procession that is so perfect that we in fact have no idea why it could not also be called 'not a procession.'"[11]

According to Thomas, the only difference is "mode of intelligibility," Kilby stated. "But, the difference we must affirm to be only in our way of understanding, not in God himself." Kilby continues: "Thomas went to great pains to insist that relations in God are real relations." Yet,

> he does also have a conception of merely notional relations, but to speak this way of relations in God would be to fall into Sabellianism. And if relations in God are real, they are also really distinct. Thomas insists on this point in article 3 of question 28: relations in God are distinguished not only in our understanding, but really in God. So to recap, we have one kind of distinction—between a subsisting relation and the essence—which exists only in 'the mode of intelligibility', not really in God—and another kind of distinction—between one subsisting relation and another—which Thomas insists exists not only in our understanding but in reality, in God. The subsisting relations are each really identical to the essence, and only different in our understanding, but they *really*, and not only in our understanding, differ from each other. The interesting thing here is the serenity with which Thomas seems to pass the question this raises by. He has laid things out in such a way as to make a problem more or less leap off the page at us—how can two things be absolutely identical with a third, and yet not identical with each other?—but he seems hardly to think it worth commenting on.[12]

Besides this difficulty, Robert Dabney rejected Aquinas's doctrine of the Trinity for four other reasons:

---

11 Karen Kilby, "Aquinas, the Trinity and the Limits of Understanding," in *International Journal of Systematic Theology,* Volume 7, Number 4, October 2005, 419, 420.
12 Kilby, 422.

First: The Scriptures inform us in advance, that God is inscrutable; and that we need not expect to explain his subsistence. *Second*: According to this explanation, both the *Νοῦς* and the *Ψυχὴ* would be compounded, the former of the two species of God's being and of His decree; the latter of two feelings, His moral self-complacency and His volition to effectuate His decree. *Third*: Neither the 2d nor 3d persons would be substance at all, but mere idea and feeling, which have no entity whatever, except as affections of the substance of the Father. This seems to our minds an objection so obvious and conclusive, that no doubt the student is almost incredulous that acute men should have seriously advanced a theory obnoxious to it. . . . *Fourth*: On this scheme of a trinity, I see not how the conclusion could be avoided, that every intelligent free agent is as much as finite trinity in unity as God is an infinite one. Let us then attempt no explanation where explanation is impossible.[13]

Nevertheless, by attempting to merge opposing worldviews together, Aquinas was forced to speak out of both sides of his mouth. According to Robert Letham, "Aquinas holds God to be without composition [internal distinction]." This is a result of Aquinas's commitment to Aristotle's natural theology. Nonetheless, Letham argues, "It becomes very difficult for him to conceive of three distinct persons while maintaining such a powerful idea of simplicity." The reason being, according to revealed theology, is that "three persons imply complexity and counteract absolute simplicity."[14] Vern Poythress summarized the inconsistency this way: "An Aristotelian-formed view of simplicity identifies God's intellect with his essence. Within God's essence there can be no differentiation. In particular, there can be no procession, because procession involves a source and a product that can be differentiated from the source. Moreover, God's essence is immutable, as his knowledge is immutable. Hence, if we accept Aristotle, there can be no procession in God or in his knowledge."[15]

---

13   Robert L. Dabney, *Systematic Theology* (Edinburgh: Banner of Truth, 1985), 180–181.
14   Robert Letham, *The Holy Trinity*, (Phillipsburg, NJ: P&R, 2004), 236.
15   Vern S. Poythress, *The Mystery of the Trinity: A Trinitarian Approach to the Attributes of God* (Phillipsburg, NJ: Presbyterian & Reformed, 2020), 316.

Thus, in the end, Letham rightly identified the problem: "This is as much a conflict between an Aristotelian doctrine of God and a biblical one."[16]

DIVINE IMMOBILITY AND BIBLIOLOGY

For Aquinas, it is not until death separates the soul from the body or until the beatific vision that we will escape the limitation that hinders us from truly knowing the unknowable God. As long as we remain bound to the physical realm of our empirical senses, we "cannot perfectly know God as He is in His essence" (ST, 1.2.3).

Even the Scriptures, according to Aquinas, are unable to reveal God's ineffable essence. The best the Scriptures can do is paint a symbolic and metaphorical picture of the transcendent God by using earthly names and terms that find their meaning in the world of sense experience. As Aquinas stated, "It is befitting Holy Writ to put forward divine and spiritual truths by means of comparisons with material things. For God provides for everything according to the capacity of its nature. Now it is natural to man to attain to intellectual truths through sensible objects, because all our knowledge originates from sense" (ST, 1.1.9). Hence, as Gilles Emery explains, "This question about properties as signified by abstract names is less a matter of the divine reality in itself than of *our human knowledge of the mystery*."[17]

This means that neither man, by the use of philosophy, nor God, by means of revelation, can penetrate the transcendental wall that separates God from man. All that man can say about God and all that God can say to man about himself is that which is metaphorical or symbolic. The symbolism of Scripture is not false information about God; it's simply not a real depiction of the hidden essence of God. There is simply no real point of connection between God and man.

---

16 Robert Letham, *The Holy Trinity* , 236.
17 Emery, *The Trinitarian Theology*, 34. Italics original.

It was Aquinas's pre-commitment to the metaphysics of Aristotle that led him to interpret Scriptures in such a fashion. For we must keep in mind that for Aristotle the unmoved mover cannot communicate to man. All that God can do is think of his undifferentiated and simple essence in an eternal state of self-contemplation. Man, therefore, is left to himself to learn what he can about God by the means of the physical world in which he is confined. And this philosophical framework was accepted by Aquinas. Though the unmoved mover is somehow able to know and to communicate to man by knowing himself, man's knowledge of God remains nevertheless bound to the physical realm of sense experience. God may be able to communicate, but his communication is restricted to the use of earthly symbols and physical metaphors.

Consequently, if this is the case, man is only able to have a symbolic and abstract knowledge of God. Man's relationship with God cannot be with the real God that remains locked behind the transcendental wall. Man can only have a relationship with a symbolic representation of God, and this symbolic representation of God can only exist in the mind of the knower. The Scriptural language that speaks of God's love, mercy, and compassion, according to Aquinas, is merely anthropomorphic.

But as mentioned in chapter 1, Aquinas placed natural theology as the framework to understand revealed theology. Rather than Scripture being sufficient in providing us with its own rules of interpretation (i.e., the analogy of the faith), Aquinas subjugated the language of Scripture to the metaphysics of Aristotle. Everything the Bible says about God, according to Thomas, must be understood through the extrabiblical lens of philosophy. Brian Davies, sympathetic to Aquinas, makes this very point:

> [On the one hand,] God is frequently depicted in the Bible (though chiefly in the Old Testament) in anthropomorphic terms, as being very like a human being. . . . On the other hand, however, biblical authors often insist on the difference between

God and everything else, on his otherness, on his majesty, on the mystery and hiddenness of divinity, and on God being the maker of heaven and earth. Talk emphasizing what we might call God's transcendence is as much in evidence in the Bible as is talk that strongly compares God to people. And Aquinas certainly takes it very seriously. Is he right to do so on biblical grounds? There seems to be no way of answering this question since the Bible does not interpret itself. Instead, it offers us, without comment, different ways of speaking of God, some criterion to which we might appeal when trying to decide which of these ways to favor. None is offered by biblical authors. There is, for example, no biblical text that tells us that biblical passages speaking of God anthropomorphically should be privileged over ones that do not, or vice versa. *So we clearly need some non-biblical grounds for determining how to read what the Bible says about God.* Aquinas thinks that we have such grounds. These lie in his reasons for saying that rational reflection can inform us about God to some extent (at least to the extent of being able to say that God exists and that certain things cannot be literally affirmed of him). In this sense, what we might call his philosophy of religion influences the way in which he reads the Bible.[18]

As we shall see, only when we start with the knowledge of God, which includes a knowledge of both God's transcendence and immanence, can we have a foundation for knowledge at all.

Conclusion

Reading Aquinas is frustrating. At least, it's frustrating to me because I reject Aquinas's epistemology, which is rooted in the epistemological commitments of Aristotle and Dionysius. Aristotle was an empiricist, and thus, his epistemology was based on the notion that all knowledge begins from and is confined to sense experience. Dionysius was a mystic, and so his epistemology is based on the notion that God is entirely unknowable and language about God—even biblical language—is

---

18 Brian Davies, *Thomas Aquinas on God and Evil* (Oxford: Oxford University Press, 2011), 120–121. Emphasis added.

at best merely symbolical or metaphorical. Hence, reading Aquinas is frustrating because rather than remaining consistent with his epistemological commitments and following his argument to its logical and unbiblical conclusion, he turns around and affirms the orthodoxy of his Catholic faith. In other words, though Aquinas rejected Aristotle's deism and Dionysius's pantheism, he upheld the empirical and mystical epistemological foundations behind their beliefs. And right when you think Aquinas is about to say something the Bible denies, he affirms the very biblical truths that are incongruent with his epistemology.

Aquinas wanted both the Bible and the philosophy of Aristotle to be true. He wanted the unmoved mover to be without differentiation while upholding the differentiations within the Trinitarian God of the Bible. He wanted God to be immobile and the moving cause of the universe. He wanted God to be unknowable and knowable at the same time. He simply wanted the impossible.

Though Aquinas desperately wanted to baptize Aristotle with the help of Dionysius, I am convinced he was unable to reconcile the conflict between these antithetical systems of thought. In the end, it is frustrating reading Aquinas because he leads his readers into a maze of irresolvable contradictions.

8

THE NECESSITY OF THE TRINITY

THOMAS OF AQUINO was a mystic. Though he gave his life to thinking about God, he believed God ultimately couldn't be reached by thinking. Because his philosophical theology placed God beyond the reach of all cognitive thought, Aquinas believed the best way to God is not through the mind but through an ineffable experience.[1]

Supposedly, it was an ineffable experience that caused Thomas Aquinas to abruptly abandon his life's work. From his youth, Thomas was unyielding in his determination to reconcile Aristotle with Christianity. He gave himself entirely to this endeavor. And when he was about to cross the finish line of his crowning achievement, his magnum opus, he suddenly came to a halt. He had nearly completed a multivolume set of books that summarized all his philosophical theology, *Summa Theologica*, when he gave up writing.

Thomas's decision was like an adventurer abandoning their life's objective of traveling around the world just a few miles short of reaching their goal. Who decides not to finish a book of over a million and a

---

1   See Bernhard Blankenhorn, *The Mystery of Union with God: Dionysian Mysticism in Albert the Great and Thomas Aquinas* (Washington DC: The Catholic University Press, 2015); and Jean-Pierre Torell, *Christ and Spiritualty in Thomas Aquinas*, trans. Bernhard Blankenhorn (Washington DC: The Catholic University Press, 2011).

half words? Of all his books, why didn't Aquinas complete this one? The *Summa Theologica* would be considered one of the most influential books of all time, but it has no ending. When he was working on the section regarding penance, he abruptly stopped. But why?

Why would Thomas, who accomplished so much through his unparalleled fortitude, suddenly opt to walk away from it all? When young Thomas resolved to become a Dominican, not even a lengthy imprisonment or the seductive lure of a prostitute could deter him. Obstacles only seemed to fuel his determination. It appeared that nothing could discourage him from his work. For years he was relentlessly driven to spend hours burning the midnight oil. He was so consumed with his studies, it is reported, he only spent a minimal amount of time eating and sleeping.[2] Like Alexander the Great who was determined not to lay down his sword until he had conquered the world, Aquinas appears to have been equally resolved not to lay down his pen until he had conquered every intellectual battle set before him. He was simply unwavering in his goal to subjugate "the Philosopher" under the Christian banner. Yet when he seemed to be making the most progress, at the prime of his intellectual power and at the height of his career, he purposefully decided to lay down his pen and write no more.

What had the power to demotivate the one who demonstrated unparalleled motivation? It appears to have been an unforeseen event that took place on December 6, 1273. While meditating and praying in isolation after attending Mass at the Chapel of St. Nicholas in Naples, Thomas entered into some type of a trance. He supposedly had an encounter with God that left him speechless—and some say, suspended in the air.[3]

Afterward, everything Thomas had ever written had suddenly appeared to him as rubbish. When his Dominican friend and secretary, Reginald of Piperno (c. 1230–c. 1290), urged him to continue his

2   See Grabmann, *Thomas Aquinas: His Personality and Thought*, 31.
3   See G. K. Chesterton, "St. Thomas Aquinas," The Society of Gilbert Keith Chesterton, accessed March 30, 2020, at https://www.chesterton.org/st-thomas-aquinas.

writing, Thomas responded by saying, "I can write no more." Thinking something was severely wrong and after a long delay, Reginald asked him why. "Reginald," Thomas answered, "Everything that I have written seems straw in comparison with what I have seen."[4] What had meant the world to him before he entered the Chapel of St. Nicholas seemed like stubble after he exited the chapel. He viewed his life works as nothing more than dry, uprooted grass fit only to be burned or driven by the north wind into the Tyrrhenian Sea.

Believing this mystical experience was a true divine encounter, Josef Pieper explains, "He is silent, not because he has nothing further to say; he is silent because he has been allowed a glimpse into the inexpressible depths of that mystery which is not reached by any human thought or speech."[5] Because mystical experiences are ineffable by their very nature, they are incommunicable; and because they are incommunicable, Thomas didn't even attempt to explain his life-changing experience. Though there is no way of knowing anything about what Thomas claimed he had encountered, I tend to think it was not a mystical experience at all. The accounts of Thomas levitating while having this mystical encounter seem fantastical and altogether unbelievable.[6]

I would like to believe that what caused Aquinas to suddenly stop writing was not a mystical experience but the sudden realization he was wrong. Perhaps he realized his philosophical theology was riddled with irresolvable tension and it finally dawned on him, in a moment of intense meditation, that the Trinity (and not the undifferentiated oneness of the unmoved mover) was the answer to all his conundrums. He might have concluded that—rather than the oneness of the unmoved mover being the foundation of his theology—unity and diversity are both equally ultimate. And maybe he determined that only the Trinity can explain the relationship between God's transcendence and

---

4 Torell, *Christ and Spiritualty in Thomas Aquinas*, 20.
5 Josef Pieper, *The Silence of St. Thomas*, trans. by John Murray, S. J. and Daniel O'Connor (South Bend, IN: St. Augustine's Press, 1963), 38.
6 See Chesterton, "St. Thomas Aquinas."

immanence. Sadly, this is only wishful thinking on my part, and I am certain it was not the case.

SIMPLICITY IS NOT ULTIMATE

Throughout his life, however, Thomas erred in making simplicity/oneness ultimate. This simple mistake was made at the beginning of his philosophical theology. By embracing Aristotelianism, he viewed the oneness of God as the ultimate reality. Using Aristotle's epistemology (that all knowledge comes from and is confined to sensory experiences), Thomas deduced that ultimate reality is the opposite of all that is in motion. And by stripping away all the attributes of motion, Aquinas concluded that God is undifferentiated in his simplicity.

Though Thomas sought to use the Bible to guide and perfect his natural theology (making room for the trinity of persons), he remained committed to the epistemology behind it. That is, though he made room for the Trinity, he remained committed to the notion that the simplicity of God's oneness is ultimate over the complexity of God's threeness. And though it was the Bible that prevented Aquinas from embracing the deism of Aristotle and the pantheism of Dionysius, it was the philosophy of Aristotle and Dionysius that shaped Aquinas's interpretation of the Bible.

By looking to natural theology before looking to revealed theology, Aquinas placed the simplicity of the unmoved mover as the foundation of his understanding of the complexity of the Trinity. According to Philip Butin, "In contrast to Lombard's intrinsically trinitarian way of treating the doctrine of God, medieval theology from Aquinas on typically placed the treatise 'On the Triune God' after a prior treatise 'On the One God.'" And the motivation behind this shift, according to Butin, was Aquinas's desire to reconcile philosophy with Christianity: "A prominent concern reinforcing this way of treating the Trinity was the desire to reconcile logically the Christian concept of the triune

God with the (also influential) Greek philosophical understanding of God as utterly transcendent, ineffable being."[7]

Because of this, Thomas had difficulty in making sense of differentiations within the Trinity, as Robert Letham points out:

> Thomas Aquinas (1225–1274), in his *Summa contra Gentiles*, and also in his *Summa Theologiae*, separated his discussion of the one God from that of the trinity. In *SCG* the whole of Book One considers the existence, nature, and attributes of God, while the trinity is relegated to Book Four. The same pattern follows in *ST*, although the two are consecutive rather than separated. Of particular note is that *ST* begins with an emphatic discussion of the simplicity of God. . . . But with Aquinas, so dominant is the theme it becomes difficult to account for the three persons. With the strong priority of the essence—the essence is before the persons—a fundamentally *impersonal* doctrine of God results. . . . However, what is striking in Aquinas is the place he gives it and the emphasis he places on it. He goes as far as to equate the being of God and his attributes—due to his doctrine of simplicity, the will of God is identical to and indistinguishable from his being. This would lead logically to a doctrine of the necessity of creation, or to the coeternity of matter (both of which Aquinas denies).[8]

Likewise, Kilby concludes that "the impression this leaves, according to Rahner and many who have taken up his complaint, is that one can first say a great deal about God—about God's simplicity, perfection and eternity— . . . before one ever comes to reflect on God as Trinity. The Trinity becomes a kind of afterthought, which one

---

7 Philip Walker Butin, *Revelation, Redemption, and Response: Calvin's Trinitarian Understanding of the Divine-Human Relationship* (New York: Oxford University Press, 1995), 12.

8 Robert Letham, "John Owen's Doctrine of the Trinity in Its Catholic Context and Its Significance for Today," in *John Owen: The Life, Thought, and Writings of John Owen (1616–83)*, accessed March 30, 2020, http://johnowen.org/media/letham_owen.pdf.

struggles valiantly but not very successfully to make sense of in the context of an already drawn picture of God."[9]

And this is the basic problem behind Thomas's ontology. By making the oneness of God primary, the diversity of God becomes hard to explain. This has led Craig Cater to comment:

> We can say nothing about the difference between the three persons except what is revealed in Scripture, namely, the relations of origin. We cannot say what is the exact ontological difference between hypostasis and ousia. Originally these two Greek words were synonyms; the decision to apply one to the Father, Son and Spirit and the other to God in general was made in order for us to be able to say different things about God's being and the three and not be confused. But we do not know what the difference is beyond the fact of the relations of origin. This is the border of mystery.[10]

Making the oneness of God ultimate and the prism in which the three persons of the Godhead are understood leads to a host of other problems. It rules out not only any knowable distinctions within the three persons of the Godhead but also a temporal universe. More than that, it rules out a knowable and relatable God. Though placing God's simplicity over God's diversity may highlight God's absoluteness and transcendence, it does so at the expense of God's relatability and immanence. A God who is wholly other is a God who is wholly unknowable. A God who is immobile is a God who is without differentiation. And a God without differentiation is a non-Trinitarian God who cannot create, communicate, or relate. Craig Carter, for instance, denied God's relatability. He goes so far as to say, "The false gods are relational because they are creatures; Yahweh is not relational because he is not a creature. Therefore, to worship a relational god is to worship

---

9   Karen Kilby, "Aquinas, the Trinity and the Limits of Understanding," in *International Journal of Systematic Theology*, Volume 7, Number 4, October 2005, 414–427, 415.
10   Craig A. Carter, "Contemplating God with the Great Tradition: An Interview with Craig Carter," *Credo Magazine*, Vol. 10, Issue 2. June 22, 2020. https://credomag.com/article/contemplating-god-with-the-great-tradition.

the creature rather than the Creator, which is Paul's definition of idolatry in Romans 1:22."[11]

DIVERSITY IS NOT ULTIMATE

To combat such difficulties, open theists have gone too far in the opposite direction and have made God's *diversity* ultimate rather than God's *complexity*. Instead of God being the unmoved mover, he is, according to Clark Pinnock, the most moved mover. "Do we really want to assume," Pinnock asks, "that God is an unmoved mover or something approximating it?"[12]

According to Pinnock, there is no mediating position between an absolute God and a relatable God. He is either one or the other. He is either unmoved or "the most moved mover." If God is independent, he can't be personal. Or if God is personal, he is no longer independent. In other words, God cannot be transcendent and immanent at the same time for, as Pinnock claims, "the conventional attributes rise and fall together. If God is personal and enters into relationships, God cannot be immutable in every respect, timelessly eternal, impassible, or meticulously sovereign. Piecemeal reform will not do the job; we need some thorough rethinking."[13]

Therefore, Pinnock placed God's immanence and relatability over God's transcendence and absoluteness: "We ought to view God in personal not absolutist terms. The primary category in Christian theism is person not substance."[14] According to Pinnock, God can relate because he is not absolute. And God is open to change because he is not immutable.

---

11   Carter, "Contemplating God."
12   Clark Pinnock, *Most Moved Mover: A Theology of God's Openness* (Grand Rapids: Baker Academic, 2001), 70.
13   Pinnock, 72.
14   Pinnock, 79.

In the end, though open theists emphasize God's immanence and reliability, they do so at the expense of God's transcendence and independence. God is so much like us that he ceases to be independent of us. Like Aristotle, open theists destroy God's independence but do so by traveling from the other direction. In such a fashion, open theists place God's diversity over God's simplicity. Ultimately, God is the most moved mover because he is moved by everything outside himself.

SIMPLICITY AND DIVERSITY ARE EQUALLY ULTIMATE

Yet the Bible does not place God's simplicity over his diversity or his diversity over his simplicity. Rather, *the one* and *the many* are equally ultimate in God. God is both simple and diverse. Because God is both one (in his essence) and many (in the diversity of his persons), both the simplicity and differentiation in God are coeternal and co-necessary. The one and the many, by logical necessity, must be co-essential, or otherwise, if the one was ultimate, there is no logical explanation for the existence of the many. And, conversely, if the many were ultimate, there is no logical explanation for the existence of the one. [15]

God's simplicity, therefore, must be understood in light of God's diversity, and God's diversity must be understood in light of God's simplicity. Augustine claimed God was both simple and multiple: "For God it is the same thing to be as to be powerful or just or wise or anything else that can be said about his simple multiplicity or multiple simplicity to signify his substance."[16] Likewise, following Augustine,

---

15 Cornelius Van Til claimed, "Using the language of the One-and-Many question, we contend that in God the one and many are equally ultimate. Unity in God is no more fundamental than diversity, and diversity in God is no more fundamental than unity. The persons of the Trinity are mutually exhaustive of one another. The Son and the Spirit are ontologically on a par with the Father" (*Defense of the Faith*, 25). And Vern Poythress says, "The unity does not arise subsequent to the diversity, as if God started off as three independent persons who agreed at some point to combine their efforts and become one. Or does the diversity arise subsequent to the unity, as if God started off as a purely undifferentiated unity and then split into three, or manifested himself in three ways" (*Redeeming Philosophy*, 57).

16 Augustine, *The Trinity*, trans. Edmund Hill, ed. John E. Rotelle (Hyde Park, NY: New City, 1991), 209.

Bavinck said, "God is therefore simple in his multiplicity and manifold in his simplicity."[17] Calvin said, "That passage in Gregory of Nazianzus vastly delights me: 'I cannot think on the one without quickly being encircled by the splendor of the three; nor can I discern the three without being straightway carried back to the one.'"[18]

We can't properly understand God's simple essence without understanding the trinity of persons within the Godhead.[19] Though God is simple and absolute in his essence, he is also inherently personal within the interrelationships of the three divine persons. Francis Turretin said there is a clear distinction between the one essence of God and the three persons of God. "The former," he claimed, "is absolute, the latter are relative."[20] God, in himself, is both absolute and personal. According to Robert Letham, "The doctrine of the Trinity affirms that God is personal, his actions being those of a personal agent, which other religious conceptions cannot allow."[21]

Because God is triune, there are eternal and intrinsic distinctions between the three persons of the Godhead. The Father knows, for instance, that he is neither the Son nor the Spirit; the Son knows he is neither the Father nor the Spirit; and the Spirit knows he is neither the Father nor the Son.[22] The interaction and fellowship between the

17 Bavinck, *Reformed Dogmatics*, 2:177.
18 Calvin, *Institutes*, 1.13.17. The passage Calvin was referring from Gregory of Nazianzus reads, "No sooner do I conceive of the one than I am illuminated by the splendor of the three; no sooner do I distinguish them than I am carried back to the one. When I think of any one of the three, I think of him as the whole, and my eyes are filled, and the greater part of what I am thinking escapes me. I cannot grasp the greatness of that one so as to attribute a greater greatness to the rest. When I contemplate the three together, I see but one torch, and cannot divide or measure out the undivided light" (*Orations*, 40.41).
19 For an excellent article on the relationship between divine simplicity and the Trinity, see Thomas H. McCall, "Trinity Doctrine, Plain and Simple," in *Advancing Trinitarian Theology* (Grand Rapids: Zondervan, 2014).
20 Frances Turretin, *Institutes of Elenctic Theology*, trans. George Musgrave Giger, ed. James T. Dennison, Jr., (Phillipsburg, NJ: Presbyterian and Reformed, 1992), 1:278.
21 Letham, *Systematic Theology*, 46.
22 The Eunomians (i.e., neo-Arians) denied the orthodox doctrine of the Trinity by applying Aristotelian logic to the doctrine of divine simplicity. They argued that if there are no distinctions within God, then only the Father exists *a se* (dependent on nothing outside himself).

three persons of the Godhead can be seen in the biblical doctrine of the covenant of redemption, where the Father gave the Son a chosen people (John 6:37–39).

Regardless, God's simplicity and diversity are as equally ultimate as they are equally necessary and coeternal. When doctrine of simplicity is understood in light of the diversity of God, it prevents us from falling into an undifferentiated, impersonal, and ineffable understanding of the doctrine of simplicity. Robert Dabney explained the doctrine of divine simplicity this way:

> Divines are accustomed to assert of the divine substance an absolute simplicity. If by this it is meant that He is uncompounded, that His substance is ineffably homogeneous, that it does not exist by assemblage of atoms, and is not discerptible, it is true. . . . But that God is more simple than finite spirits in this, that in Him substance and attribute are one and the same, as they are not in them, I know nothing. The argument is, that as God is immutably what He is, without succession, His essence does not like ours pass from mode to mode of being, and from act to act, but is always all modes, and exerting all acts; hence His modes and acts are Himself. God's thought is God. He is not active, but activity. I reply, that if this means more than is true of a man's soul, viz: that its thought is no entity, save the soul thinking; that its thought, as abstracted from the soul that thinks it, is only an abstraction and not a thing; it is undoubtedly false. For then we should have reached the pantheistic notion, that God has no other being than the infinite series of His own consciousnesses and acts. Nor would we be far off from the other result of this fell theory; that all that is, is God. For he who has identified God's acts thus with His being, will next identify the effects thereof, the existence of the creatures therewith.[23]

Ultimate *oneness* is reducible to the Father—he alone possesses the simple essence of divinity. The essence of the Son is generated from the Father, and the essence of the Spirit proceeds from the Father and Son as they are ontologically and eternally subordinate to the Father, who alone is Almighty God. See McCall "Trinity Doctrine, Plain and Simple," 46.

23　Robert L. Dabney, *Systematic Theology* (Edinburgh: Banner of Truth, 1996), 4344.

And for this reason, Vern Poythress places his finger on the heart of the problem:

> The difficulty is that unless we understand that the Trinitarian character of God is ontologically basic, we will do as Aristotle did. We will use autonomous reason to produce an ultimate system of categories. And then we end up using a framework of categories that prioritizes unity or else prioritizes diversity. That is, we accept some kind of prioritizing, instead of starting with the Trinity. If we do that, we do not accept the ultimacy of both unity and diversity in the Trinity. And we do not move from the Trinity in order to consider how God may have created the world with a structure of unity and diversity in harmony with who he is as the Trinitarian God.[24]

A system that prioritizes unity tends to end up with a supreme principle of unity that contains no diversity. Diversity comes only later. Then we have some form of Unitarianism or modalism or Plotinus's "One" or an Aristotelian view of simplicity and of the unity of Aristotelian form.

The Trinity Allows for a Self-Moving God

The Trinity, therefore, is the solution to one of the most complexing problems in philosophy and theology—the problem of "the one and the many." Consequently, God is neither the unmoved mover nor the most moved mover. The unmoved mover can't move himself, and the most moved mover is moved by things outside himself. The unmoved mover is not personal, whereas the most moved mover is not absolute.

The Trinity is the only being (because he is both one and many) who can move himself *ad intra*. Aristotle observed that nothing in the universe can move itself. For something to be self-mobile, it has to be unmovable and movable at the same time. And this, according to Aristotle, seemed impossible. Yet Aristotle had no concept of a triune being.

---

24 Poythress, *The Mystery of the Trinity*, 320.

But a self-moving God is what we find in the Trinitarian God of the Bible. God is both immutable in his essence without being restricted to a static and motionless state within the relations of the three persons. The Father, as a distinct person, is intrinsically moved to love and glorify the Son, and likewise, the Son and the Spirit are moved to love and glorify the Father. The Son eternally proceeds from the Father, and the Spirit eternally proceeds from the Father and the Son. Each of the three distinct persons are moved *ad intra* to share, communicate, give, love, and glorify the other by the infinite worth they consistently see in the other. They are in an eternal state of relating, communicating, interacting, and sharing their glory with each other. That is, within the Godhead, there is a necessary and eternal state of movement (i.e., procession and interaction) between the three persons without any change taking place in the unity of their simple essence.[25]

The word *automobile* originated from the compound of two French words *auto*, which means "self," and *mobile*, which means "movable." Thus, an automobile is something that moves itself. But truly this cannot be said of man-made vehicles that require a driver and fuel. Vehicles don't move themselves. Strictly speaking, the word *automobile* applies only to God. Only the triune God is autonomously self-moving. Unlike Aristotle's unmoved mover, the God of the Bible does not need the universe as a vehicle of movement. God is not dependent on anything

---

25 The Trinity can interact with creation in a personal and immanent way because he is inherently able to differentiate between things within himself and things outside himself. Because diversity is essential to the Godhead, God can distinguish between his thoughts, emotions, acts, and time-related events. Yet he remains transcendent and separate from creation because his unity is also equally essential to his nature. Because he can differentiate between his will of decree and his will of command, he is able to providently and emotionally interact with creation in a personal way. But God also knows and sees all things at once. And ultimately nothing can cause God to suffer because he knows and controls all things without there being any change within himself. In sum, without the diversity of the three persons, God's simplicity would lead to pantheism. Conversely, without the oneness of God's essence, the relational properties inherent within the Trinity would lead to open theism. Though from different directions, both pantheism and open theism make God dependent on creation. The equal ultimacy of the oneness and diversity of the Trinity is the only safeguard to keep us from falling on either side of the ditch.

outside himself. God is not cemented in an immovable state, for he can act, move, create, destroy, and do as he pleases.

Moreover, this eternal state of movement within the Trinity is not a change in the immutability of God. Self-movement is not an attribute of imperfection. It is the exact opposite. If God could not move himself, he would not be perfect—as he could not love, create, or relate. If he could not move himself, he would be dependent on something outside himself to love, create, and relate. For this reason, the English Puritan Thomas Goodwin observes, "If the divine nature had not afforded in having in it three persons really distinct, knowing, rejoicing in, glorying of, and speaking unto each other, there had not been a perfection of blessedness."[26]

The Trinity Allows for a Temporal Universe

Because a monistic and undifferentiated deity cannot display intentional and temporal acts of power, a temporal universe could not have come into existence out of nothing. Aquinas admitted that philosophy, through reason alone, does not lead to a temporal universe but, rather, a temporal universe had to be an article of faith. In all this, he was unable to reconcile how God could be both immobile and the efficient cause of a temporal universe.

But the answer is simple if we throw out Aristotle's unmoved mover and put the Trinity in its place. Because God is triune, he is not immobile. Because he is able to move himself, he is the moving cause of the universe. Because he is not stuck in a motionless state, creation does not have to be necessary or eternal. The self-moving God is free to create, govern, and relate without altering his simple essence in the process. God does not have to take on new properties to create; he simply had everything he needed within his immutable, eternal, and triune nature to freely act in time and space.

---

26 Thomas Goodwin, *The Works of Thomas Goodwin* (Edinburgh: James Nichol, 1864), 9:145.

The Trinity Allows for a Knowable God

The Trinity also allows for real differentiation within the knowledge of God. The Father knows he is not the Son, and the Son knows he is not the Father. Such cognitive distinction within God gives us reason to believe that God is able to make other distinctions within himself. Without such distinctions, Aristotle was right when he stated, "If they are one in number, all things will be the same" (*Metaph.*, 11.2). And if God can't distinguish between his mind, will, and acts, then God couldn't communicate these distinctions to us.

Calvin says that without differentiation within God, "only the bare and empty name of God flits about in our brains, to the exclusion of the true God."[27] Commenting on this, B. B. Warfield remarks, "According to Calvin, then, it would seem, there can be no such thing as a monadistic God; the idea of multiformity enters into the very notion of God."[28] And Bavinck claims, "On the basis of God's revelation it is our obligation . . . to hold onto the belief that, though every attribute is identical with the divine being, the attributes are nevertheless distinct." He continues: "This diversity of attributes, moreover, does not clash with God's simplicity."[29] In way of explanation, Geerhardus Vos states,

> May we also say that God's attributes are not distinguished from one another? This is extremely risky. We may be content to say that all God's attributes are related most closely to each other and penetrate each other in the most intimate unity. However, this is in no way to say that they are to be identified with each other. Also in God, for example, love and righteousness are not the same, although they function together perfectly in complete harmony. We may not let everything intermingle in a

27 Calvin, *Institutes*, 1.13.2.

28 B. B. Warfield, *Calvin's Doctrine of the Trinity*, in *Works of Benjamin B. Warfield* (Grand Rapids: Baker Books, 2003), 5.191. "To avoid the blank identity of pantheism," Van Til claims, "we must insist on an identity that is exhaustively correlative to the differentiations within the Godhead." *An Introduction to Systematic Theology* (Phillipsburg, NJ: P&R, 2007), 273.

29 Bavinck, *Reformed Dogmatics*, 2:125, 2:127.

pantheistic way because that would be the end of our objective knowledge of God.[30]

The Trinity Allows for an Absolute and Relatable God

A monadistic or pantheistic deity is utterly unknowable. Because such a god cannot be understood by any human terms or concepts, such a god is entirely transcendent and unreachable. Yet it is apparent that the triune God of the Bible can reveal himself. More than that, the triune God of the Bible can enter into a real relationship with us. The properties needed for the triune God to enter into new relationships were already present in him from all eternity. If the Father, Son, and Holy Spirit were not in an eternal state of communicating and relating with themselves, then communication and relating would not be an essential part of God's nature. Communicating and relating are nothing new to God.

Thomas Goodwin spoke of the eternal relationship between the three persons of the Godhead, which he said consisted of the mutual sharing of "life," "interest," "communication," "knowledge," "discovery of each other's mind," "love," and "glory," as the bases for the relationship that God enters into with his people.[31] "This motive, drawn from the Trinity," Goodwin argues, "divides itself into two branches, which in themselves are distinct, and apart to be considered."[32] Goodwin elucidates:

1. Their oneness in essence; or that the Father, and Son, and Spirit, have, in their common and blessed enjoyment, one and the same Godhead, and all the perfections thereof; and how this did move them to make creatures partakers of the same enjoyment, as far as creatures possibly are capable of.

---

30 Geerhardus Vos, "Theology Proper," in *Reformed Dogmatics*, trans. and ed. Richard B. Gaffin (Bellingham, WA: Lexham, 2012–2014), 1:5.

31 See Thomas Goodwin, "The Knowledge of God the Father and His Son Jesus Christ," in *The Works of Thomas Goodwin* (Grand Rapids: Reformation Heritage Books, 2006), 4:365.

32 Thomas Goodwin, "A Discourse of Election," in *The Works of Thomas Goodwin* (Edinburgh: James Nichol, 1864), 9:133.

> 2. The second is, their mutual intercourse and society, as persons, one with another, and the sweetness of that converse those three persons had among themselves; that also was an inducement to take up creature-fellowship and communion into a participation of that sweet society.

> These are different notions and considerations; the first being founded upon the oneness of the three persons in an one enjoyment of that one Godhead; the other upon their converses had between themselves, as persons subsisting in that Godhead, glorifying, loving, and speaking to each other from everlasting.[33]

In other words, the triune God didn't have to take on new properties to communicate or relate. Loving, sharing, and communicating are all intrinsic abilities within the triune God. And, according to Michael Reeves, love was "the motive behind creation." As he explains, "The Father loved him [the Son] before the creation of the world, and the reason the Father sends him is so that the Father's love for him might be in others also. That is why the Son goes out from the Father, in both creation and salvation: that the love of the Father for the Son might be shared."[34]

And this same love that moved God to create is the same love that moved God to enter into individual relationships with his elect people. The Father, out of love for his Son, gave his Son a people. And the Son, out of love for his Father, agreed to redeem his people for the Father. The Spirit's love for the Father and the Son motivated him to reveal the Father and the Son to God's people in salvation. God did not have to create, but out of love for his own glory, he freely chose to do so (Eph 1:3–14). And for his own glory, God chose to share his love with us. According to B. B. Warfield,

---

33 Goodwin, 9:133.
34 Reeves, *Delighting in the Trinity*, 47, 44.

Difficult, therefore, as the idea of the Trinity in itself is, it does not come to us as an added burden upon our intelligence; it brings us rather the solution of the deepest and most persistent difficulties in our conception of God as infinite moral Being, and illuminates, enriches and elevates all our thought of God. . . . It has accordingly only stable theism. That is as much as to say that theism requires the enriching conception of the Trinity to give it a permanent hold upon the human mind—the mind finds it difficult to rest in the idea of an abstract unity for its God; and that the human heart cries out for the living God in whose Being there is that fullness of life for which the conception of the Trinity alone provides.[35]

The Trinity Allows for God to Be Both Transcendent and Immanent

With the Trinity, there is a clear Creator/creature distinction since God created the universe out of nothing in a particular point in time. The triune God alone existed before the foundation of the world. There was nothing else but God until God intentionally spoke the universe into existence out of nothing. And because God and the universe do not consist of the same ontological substance, God remains transcendent. But God is also immanent because he is not barred from time and space as he personally interacts with those whom he has made after his own *ethical* likeness. "While immutable in himself," Bavinck states, "he nevertheless, as it were, lives the life of his creatures and participates in all their changing states." For, as Bavinck goes on to say, "though eternal in himself, God can nevertheless enter into time and, though immeasurable in himself, he can fill every cubic inch of space with his presence. In other words, though he himself is absolute being, God can give to transient beings a distinct existence of their own."[36] In this, we see how God both remains above us and lives among us.

This, according to Bavinck, is what makes God so glorious. It is one thing for the perfect being to dwell in the high and lofty place, but all the more glorious that this transcendent being chooses to dwell with

---

35 Benjamin B. Warfield, *Biblical Doctrine* (Edinburgh: Banner of Truth, 1988), 139.
36 Bavinck, *Reformed Dogmatics*, 2:158.

those of a low and contrite spirit (Isa 57:15). "It is a mark of God's greatness," Bavinck remarks, "that he can condescend to the level of his creatures and that, though transcendent, he can dwell immanently in all created beings. Without losing himself, God can give himself, and, while absolutely maintaining his immutability, he can enter into an infinite number of relations to his creatures."[37]

The Absurdity of Natural Theology

Without the Trinity, everything falls apart. Douglas Kelly was right when he stated, "Systems of thought that reject the Holy Trinity need some other ultimate reference point to make their system work; some necessary thing."[38] Therefore, Thomas Aquinas correctly said that philosophy has its limits. Yet the limits of philosophy are more limited than Aquinas realized. Philosophy is unable to explain not only a temporal universe and the Trinitarian diversity within the Godhead but also the true nature of God's oneness. Philosophy is good at raising questions but not so good at answering them, because it does not have access to the necessary data (i.e., the Trinity) needed to construct a consistent worldview.

As already mentioned, it was in the wisdom of God that God determined that man in his wisdom is unable to come to the knowledge of God (1 Cor 1:21). Without submitting to divine revelation, humanity is left to themselves to grope around aimlessly in the darkness. This is because natural theology, no matter what direction it takes, leads to inherent contradictions. Principally, philosophy, by the use of reason alone, can't explain the relationship between the absolute God and a contingent universe. "Why is there something rather than nothing" is one of the fundamental questions of philosophy.[39] But it is a question that philosophy can't answer.

---

37 Bavinck, 2:159.

38 Kelly, *Systematic Theology: Grounded in Holy Scripture and Understood in Light of the Church* (Fearn, Ross-shire: Christian Focus, 2008-2014), 1:74–75.

39 See Gottfried Leibniz, *The Monadology*, trans. Nicholas Rescher (Pittsburgh: University of Pittsburgh Press, 1991), 135.

On the one hand, the universe can't explain itself. A contingent universe does not make sense without an absolute creator. Without something fixed, unmovable, and absolute, everything is in process. And those who accept this conclusion can't help but fall into some type of relativistic absurdity. For instance, a committed materialist, William Provine, understood the logical consequence of a closed universe when he concluded, "No inherent moral or ethical laws exist, nor are there absolute guiding principles for human society. The universe cares nothing for us and we have no ultimate meaning in life."[40] Without an absolute God, there is no unifying standard for truth. For those who even care to try to pick up the irregular and broken fragments, all that remains are various incoherent and self-referentially absurd systems of thought, such as various forms of existentialism, relativism, and nihilism.

On the other hand, it is hard to make sense of how an absolute God, such as Aristotle's unmoved mover, can create a contingent universe without losing his absoluteness in the process. Of course, Aristotle didn't think it was possible. For once God creates and relates, he then ceases to be the unmoved mover. It appears that an absolute God can't relate, and a relating God can't be absolute. No matter what direction philosophers take, either God's transcendence will override God's immanence or God's immanence will override God's transcendence; and in both cases (seeing that there is the universe), God's independence is destroyed in the process. Thus, without divine revelation of the triune nature of God, the mystery of why there is something rather than nothing remains.

THE FATAL FLAW OF THE COSMOLOGICAL ARGUMENT

The fatal flaw of the philosophical theology of Thomas of Aquinas is his insistence on divine immobility. The foundation of Aquinas's philosophy and theology is the cosmological argument. Yet divine im-

---

40 William Provine, "Scientists, Face It! Science and Religion Are Incompatible," *The Scientist* 2[16]:10, September 5, 1988.

mobility—the conclusion of the cosmological argument—is neither rooted in special revelation (i.e., the Bible) nor in natural revelation. In fact, divine immobility is not even a necessary consequence of natural science. Even some of the most notable Thomistic scholars, such as Gilson and Feser, have admitted that sense experience does not establish "a divine unmoved mover" as a scientific fact.[41]

If the concept of a divine unmoved mover is not derived from revelation or science, then where does it come from? It comes from a philosophical postulation. This would not be a bad thing if such a postulation makes sense of all the known data. Some type of transcendental conception of God is necessary to make sense of the universe. Our universe, with all its moving parts, cannot explain itself. Because science cannot explain itself, naturalism cannot explain itself, in that our empirical senses can't discern and explain the existence of logic, mathematics, and ethics. And science is impossible to carry out without presupposing the existence of logic, mathematics, and ethics. Thus, without the right transcendental conception of God, knowledge (all knowledge) is impossible. Without the right transcendental postulation (or presuppositions), it does not make sense why there is something rather than nothing.

The question is what type of transcendental conception of God makes sense of the universe. Atheism and deism provide us with no assistance as they each leave us with the same incoherency of naturalism. Without a God who communicates, we are left in the darkness with no absolute, meaning, or purpose. Neither a pantheistic nor a panentheistic conception of God can make sense of the unity and diversity in the universe either. As we have already pointed out, to make sense of the universe, we need a God that is both transcendent and immanent. Yet both pantheism and panentheism destroy God's transcendence because they both destroy God's absoluteness. They both destroy God's absoluteness because they both make the universe necessary to God's existence. Neither pantheism nor panentheism allow for God to

---

41   See Gilson, *The Philosophy of St. Thomas Aquinas*, 75, and Feser, *Essays*, 60–62.

communicate, which leaves man in the same darkness of atheism and naturalism.

Moreover, according to Feser, William Paley's argument for a divine designer fails to be a fitting explanation for the universe. Feser contends that the argument from design does not necessarily lead to an all-powerful and self-existing God. "Now it is often acknowledged," Feser states, "that Paley's argument gets us at best to a designer who is extremely powerful and intelligent, but who for all we know may yet be finite and thus non-divine."[42] Proving that the world had to have a designer does not prove that the designer is God. And this only pushes the problem back to the question: Who designed the designer?

Supposedly, for Feser, the cosmological argument is superior to the argument from design because it points to a more divine-like God. The cosmological argument claims that God is the unmoved mover—and this prevents us from having to ask who moved/created God. Yet such a postulation of God, as we have seen, is also an inadequate explanation of why there is something rather than nothing. The idea of unmoved mover may do a good job of explaining the transcendence and unity of God, but it fails in explaining how the unmoved mover can freely create, know, communicate, and relate with the universe.

Feser ruled out Paley's designer as a suitable solution for a second reason: "The problem is not just that Paley's designer may *be* something other than God as classical theism understands Him. There is reason to think that Paley's designer could not be God as classical theism understands Him."[43] But what Feser fails to realize is that this criticism can also be levied at Aquinas's unmoved mover. The unmoved mover, with its undifferentiated oneness, may agree with divine simplicity and immutability, but it does not allow for such a being to subsist in three relationally distinct persons that interact and communicate with one another.

---

42 Feser, *Essays*, 74.
43 Feser, 75.

As we have seen, only the Trinitarian God of the Bible can make sense of the universe and the laws of nature. That is, we must presuppose the Trinitarian God of the Bible to be able to construct a consistent worldview that does not fall into absurdity under its own weight. For all worldviews (besides the Trinitarian worldview) are self-referentially absurd.[44]

CONCLUSION

For this reason, I would like to suppose that what caused Thomas to cease writing, viewing his life's work as straw, was not a mystical experience but the realization that the Trinity was the solution of all the inherent tension riddled throughout his philosophical theology. It appears that Aquinas did come close to seeing this, as he stated, "The knowledge of the divine persons [is] necessary . . . for the right idea of creation. The fact of saying that God made all things by His Word excludes the error of those who say that God produced things by necessity. When we say that in Him there is a procession of love, we show that God produced things not because He needed them, but on account of the of His own goodness" (ST, 1.32., a.1. ad 3).

Gilles Emery stated that, according to Aquinas, "Trinitarian faith is required for a firm grasp on God's creative activity in the world," in that it is the doctrine of the Trinity that prevents us from drawing the same conclusions of Aristotle—that the world is eternal and necessary, and God is unconcerned and uninvolved in its affairs.[45]

At this point, I am not sure why Aquinas didn't decide to throw the pagan philosopher out of the baptistery. For if the Trinity, which is only understood by divine revelation, is needed to prevent natural theology from drawing the wrong conclusions, then why trust natural theology in the first place?

---

44 See Jeffrey Johnson, *The Absurdity of Unbelief* (Conway, AR: Free Grace Press, 2016).
45 Emery, *The Trinitarian Theology of St Thomas Aquinas*, 8.

But sadly, it does not appear the Angelic Doctor came to this conclusion. Though he came close to realizing that the unmoved mover is incompatible with the Trinitarian God of the Bible, he never made any retractions. He may have had an experience that caused him to stop writing, but it seems he held on to the false belief that the philosophy of Aristotle could be used as a handmaiden to theology.

9

Analogical Language

Thomas of Aquino was ambitious. However his ambition was not for power or wealth. The lure of earthly rank never appealed to him. He had no aspiration for such things. He had no desire to become a bishop or archbishop or even the pope. Such positions of authority would have only taken him off task; they would have been a distraction. For instance, Torrell claims, "He always stubbornly refused ecclesial honors that would inevitably have involved him in temporal affairs, whether it was a matter of the abbacy of Monte Cassino, the archbishopric of Naples, or a cardinal's hat. William Tocco confirms that he even prayed that he would be spared such involvements."[1]

He was content to be a lowly friar because his ambition laid elsewhere. All he wanted was to be a scholar. He was a shy person who would rather contemplate in isolation than be burdened with the task of administration. He would rather be poor and left alone with his books than be rich and constantly burdened with the affairs of this world.

---

1 Jean-Pierre Torrell, "The Person and His Works," in *St. Thomas Aquinas*, trans. Robert Royal (Washington, DC: The Catholic University of America Press, 2005), 1:14.

He indeed chose books over wealth and a study desk over an ecclesiastical chair. When he defied the wishes of his family by joining a mendicant order, he turned his back on becoming the abbot of the famed Monte Cassino. Sometime later, the pope offered him this same position, but again, this was not what he wanted. Once more, at the end of his life, it appears he had an opportunity to become a bishop like his friend Bonaventure, but even until death he remained uninterested.

As the story goes, after the life-altering mystical experience in the Chapel of St. Nicholas, Aquinas was called to the critical Second Council of Lyon in 1274. The Roman Catholic Church and the Eastern Orthodox Church had been divided for over 250 years, and the two branches were convening in Lyon to discuss the possibility of reuniting. Pope Gregory X desired the best Catholic minds to be present, so the Roman pontiff summoned Thomas as well as Bonaventure to attend the discussions.[2] On Thomas's long journey north to Lyon, his trusted friend and traveling companion, Reginal, commented to Thomas, "Now you are on your way to the Council, and there are many good things that will happen; for the whole Church, for our order, and for the Kingdom of Sicily." Optimistically, Thomas replied, "Yes, God grant that good things may happen there."[3] One of those good things Reginal believed would transpire was an ecclesiastical promotion for Thomas. Reginal went on to say, "You and Friar Bonaventure will be created cardinals, to the great glory of your Orders,"[4] to which Thomas responded, "I shall never be anything in our Order or in the Church, . . . [for] I cannot serve our Order better in any other state than my present one."[5] Apparently, teaching future bishops and cardinals his philosophical theology was deemed weightier by Thomas than becoming a bishop or a cardinal.

---

2 See Grabmann, *Thomas Aquinas*, 15.
3 See Pieper, *The Silence of St. Thomas*, 40.
4 Maritain, *St. Thomas Aquinas*, 26.
5 Maritain, 26.

ANALOGICAL SYMBOLIC LANGUAGE

By joining philosophy and theology together, Aquinas taught that all knowledge of God is analogical. "For in analogies the idea is not, as it is in univocals, one and the same, yet it is not totally diverse as in equivocals; but a term which is thus used in a multiple sense signifies various proportions to some one thing" (ST, 1.13.4). For Aquinas, then, "no name belongs to God in the same sense that it belongs to creatures. . . . Therefore whatever is said of God and of creatures is predicated equivocally" (ST, 1.13.5).

Yet when Aquinas said all knowledge of God is analogical, he meant that all knowledge of God is *metaphorical*, and this for two reasons. The first reason why all knowledge of God is metaphorical, according to Thomas, is because *we have no direct access to God*. God stands on the other side of a transcendental wall, and there is no way for us to know anything about what lies on his side of the wall. God surpasses every word or conception or idea that we can possibly have about him. Every word or concept or idea we use to define God has been derived from the realm of sensible things in which we are confined. Even our philosophical speculation and words we coin to refer to metaphysical things that transcend the realm in which we live are still derived from our side of the wall. Words such as *being, unity, simplicity, pure actuality*, and *transcendent* do not communicate what God is from God's own point of view. Thomas believed an infinite chasm separates us from God. Because there is no probation or gradation between the finite and the infinite, our communication of God, from Aquinas's perspective, is at best metaphorical, if not altogether mystical.

The second reason why all knowledge of God is metaphorical, Aquinas presumed, is because *God has no direct access to us*. God can't reveal his own knowledge of himself to us because he is bound to his timeless realm of immobility. As we are bound to the realm of movement and diversification, God is bound to the realm undifferenced simplicity. God's knowledge of his own undifferentiated self will always remain locked within his own mind. God cannot reveal his un-differentiated knowledge of himself even if he wanted.

How, then, has God revealed himself to us? According to Aquinas, not by entering time and directly speaking to us after he created us but by indirectly speaking to us in the act of creating all things. In other words, when God created all things after the representation of himself, he revealed himself symbolically through the things he created. All things are created in God's likeness because, as Thomas said, "every effect in some degree represents its cause, but diversely" (ST, 1.45.7). "All created things, so far as they are beings, are like God as the first and universal principle of all being" (ST, 1.4.3). Concerning this, Tommaso Cajetan explains, "Every concept of a creature is a concept of God, just as every creature is a kind of likeness of God."[6] In this way, all creation, especially man, functions as a symbolic picture or metaphorical image of God.[7]

This means, for Aquinas, that we only know God by knowing the universe. By knowing the universe, we know at least something (metaphorically) about God. Though we cannot know God in his essence, we can at least know something of his goodness by knowing the goodness is in all things. We can know a bit about the cause by knowing something about the effects. "Now because we do not know the essence of God, the proposition is not self-evident to us; but needs to be demonstrated by things that are more known to us, though less known in their nature—namely, by effects" (ST, 1.2.1).

---

6 Tommaso de Vio Cajetan, *The Analogy of Names and the Concept of Being*, trans. Edward A. Bushinski (Eugene, OR: Wipf & Stock, 2009), 80.

7 "Effects disproportionate to their causes do not agree with them in name and essence. And yet some likeness must be found between such effects and their causes: for it is of the nature of an agent to do something like itself. Thus also God gives to creatures all their perfections; and thereby he has with all creatures a likeness, and an unlikeness at the same time. For this point of likeness, however, it is more proper to say that the creature is like God than that God is like the creature" (SCG, 1.1.29).

Like learning about the sun in the sky by observing shadows reflected on the ground, we can learn about God in heaven by looking at his likeness represented in created things here below. Though we are not to make graven images of God, this did not prevent God from creating diverse images of himself. It is only by knowing something about the various differentiated images of God that we can know anything at all about the undifferentiated God.

Yet, we must bear in mind that knowing something about these differentiated images of God is not the same thing as knowing the ineffable God behind these created images. For, as Thomas said, "the knowledge of God by means of any created similitude is not the vision of His essence" (ST, 1.12.11). Even by reading the Scriptures, according to Thomas, we don't know God; we only know a metaphorical reflection of God. "Whatever names denote properties that are caused in things by their proper specific principles," claimed Thomas, "cannot be predicated of God otherwise than metaphorically" (SCG, 1.1.30).

Thus, for these two reasons, what Aquinas means by *analogical* language is really *metaphorical* or symbolical language. But this has its consequence—it not only destroys any real knowledge of God but it also destroys any real covenantal relationship with God.

Divine and Human Relations

For Aquinas, in the same way that we can only know God by knowing the universe, God can only know us by knowing himself. God does not know us by gazing his mind's eye on us; he only knows us by keeping his mind's eye on his undifferentiated self. God and man are each stuck on their respective side of the transcendental wall. According to Aquinas, we can only know what's on God's undifferentiated side by studying the differentiated contents on our side of the wall. Likewise, God can only know what's on our side by looking at himself. He knows the effects by knowing himself as the first cause, and we can know the first cause by knowing something of the effects.

Subsequently, for Aquinas, God can't enter into any new relationships, and we can only have a relationship with a created and metaphorical representation of God. And this has its consequences.

Our Relationship with God

First, since we can only know God by knowing him indirectly through his creation, our personal relationship with God is limited to a relationship with the universe—a created and symbolic representation of God. Though we participate in his likeness and are dependent on him for our own existence, there can be no personal relationship or direct connection with the God who is locked behind the creative symbols. We can only know and relate to the creation and not the Creator. Our "personal" relationship with the symbolic manifestation of God, moreover, is only a relationship that exists in our minds.

God's Relationship with Us

Second, if God can only know us by knowing himself, God can't enter into a personal relationship with us. For Aquinas, God is immanent and omnipresent because he is the first cause of all immanent effects. He is immanent only in the sense that his perfections (wisdom, power, etc.) are present in every effect around us. "God is in all things," Aquinas said, "not, indeed, as part of their essence, nor as an accident, but as an agent is present to that upon which it works" (ST, 1.8.1). God, as he is in his ontological essence, however, cannot enter the time and space we occupy. This would be a change within the immovable God. Consequently, God cannot relate to us in any real or personal way.

Though God knows about us by knowing himself, he cannot enter into any experiential relationship with us without change and movement happening within himself. Though he can logically know about us (as we share a bit of his likeness) by knowing his own likeness perfectly, he cannot relate to or connect with us. "In God," Aquinas claimed, "there is no real relation to creatures (ST, 1.13.7). Again, he said, "relations of God to creatures are not real in Him" (ST, 1.28.4).

Because God remains in an undifferentiated state of immobility, he can only have a logical rather than a personal relationship with us.

According to Aquinas, God is like an immobile column that remains in the same location and in the same state of mind whether we move to the left or the right of him (ST, 1.13.7). The same state he was before the world was created is the same state he remains after the world was created. In fact, God never changed from non-creator to creator—for he never was not creating a temporal universe.

God's affections and emotions are completely unaltered. The fall of man supposedly did not grieve God any more than the death of Christ appeased him. All change takes place on our side of the "relationship." God's wrath was neither kindled when we, in unbelief, sinned, nor was his wrath appeased when we, by faith, entered a state of grace. Remaining in an immovable and apathetic state, God cannot experience any personal communion with his people. Any biblical language that says or implies otherwise is merely metaphorical and anthropomorphic.

When the empiricism and unmoved mover of Aristotle become the hermeneutical framework in which the language of Scripture is understood, then this is the high cost that must be paid. God may be absolute and transcendent, but his transcendence consumes his immanence and relatability in the process. It is hard to see how a God of this nature actually loves and cares.

ANALOGICAL PREDICATION LANGUAGE

Though we may disagree with Aquinas, we must be careful of overcorrecting. It's not that language describing God is univocal. Because God is ontologically distinct and transcendent, language about God has to be analogical, and the language of Scripture is no exception. I wholeheartedly affirm this. It is impossible to know God exhaustively at any given point. He is not like us. To know God perfectly as God knows himself is impossible. Therefore, no word or name describing God is univocal. The creator-creature distinction must be maintained.

Yet this also does not mean that all words and names describing God are symbolical or anthropomorphic. Rather than God's self-revelation being analogically symbolic, it is what I call *analogically predicate*. By the word *predicate*, I mean something is not metaphorical or symbolic or anthropomorphic. For the language of God to be analogical, there has to be a real point of similarity between God and man. There must be a direct point of connection, or there is no connection at all. For example, oranges and apples are different but similar—they are analogous. They are analogous in that they are different types of fruit, but they are both round pieces of fruit. The real point of similarity is that the word *round* and the word *fruit* carry the same meaning for both oranges and apples.

In the same way, for language of God to be truly analogical, some words must have the same meaning for God as they do for us—such as the word *love*. Of course, we don't have an exhaustive understanding of the word *love*, nor do we even come close to knowing love as God knows love. But if the word *love* for God and the word *love* for us does not at least have a small point of identity, we can no longer speak of language as being analogical. If there is no point of similarity, then the statement "God is love" means nothing at all.

Therefore, there must be a real point of connection between God's knowledge of himself and the knowledge of himself he has chosen to reveal to us in Scripture. And this for two reasons: (1) God is immanent, and (2) man was made in God's likeness.

God Is Immanent

First, God is able to access us and reveal something of his own knowledge of himself to us because he is not only transcendent but also immanent. For there to be knowledge of God at all, God must be immanent, relatable, and personal. If God is wholly other, then God's knowledge of himself is entirely incommunicable. If there is not a point of connection between God and man, Scriptural language used to define God, such as "God is love," breaks down altogether.

Although the Bible teaches that God is transcendent, it also teaches God is immanent. God is absolute, but God is also personal and relatable. God's immanence, moreover, is not restricted to his likeness being symbolically represented in all created things. Rather, God is immanent because he has chosen to enter our realm and directly walk and speak with us. God is omnipresent.

And this leads us to the second reason why the analogical language of Scripture is not entirely symbolical.

Man Is Made in God's Moral Likeness

Second, God is able to enter into relationships with us because he made us in his own moral likeness. This means two things. First, it means that man is a moral agent. Second, it means that God is a moral agent.

Man Is a Moral Agent

According to Aquinas, however, man is not made in the moral likeness of God. He did claim that man was created after the likeness of God, but only in the sense that all created things are made in the likeness of God. Every effect, Thomas claimed, participates (in various degrees) in the likeness of God, the first cause.

Yet, according to Scripture, the *imago Dei* is not something that properly describes all created things. There is something uniquely true about man that is not true about any other created thing. Though man was not created in the ontological likeness of God (being made from divine essence), man was made in the *ethical* likeness of God in that the Bible says that man was originally created morally upright (Eccl 7:29). "The image of God in which man was created," claims Louis Berkhof, "certainly includes what is generally called 'original righteousness,' or more specifically, true knowledge, righteousness, and holiness."[8] Though God's image in man was defaced by the fall, it is renewed again "after the likeness of God in true righteousness and holiness" (Eph 4:24). In other words, the *imago Dei* does not mean sharing in the ontological goodness of God but reflecting the moral or ethical goodness of God.

And this moral likeness is important because it's what allows for God to have a covenant relationship (based on God's own moral law) with man. As God made Eve after the likeness of Adam (1 Cor 11:7) so that man and woman can enter into a covenant relationship with each other (Gen 2:18–24), God created man after his likeness so they can enter into a covenant relationship. "Adam," claimed John Owen, "was fully furnished with the wisdom and moral light required to enter this relationship. He was enabled to know God."[9] Unlike the various inanimate objects in the universe and even the beasts of the field, the birds of the air, and the fish of the sea, man (and only man) was designed to enjoy a personal and covenantal relationship with God.

God Is a Moral Agent

But this leads to the second point—this also means that God must be a moral agent. For God to relate to man, he must be a moral and ethical being. But this too was something Aquinas denied.

Aquinas believed that though God is good, he's not morally or ethically good. In explaining Aquinas's position, Brian Davies states, "God is good because he somehow contains in himself the perfections of his creatures, all of which reflect him somehow."[10] God is good because God is without motion. God is good because he is pure actuality without any potentialities and deficiencies. It is because God's goodness is

---

8   Berkhof, *Systematic Theology*, 204.

9   Owen, *Biblical Theology*, 25.

10   Brian Davies, *An Introduction to the Philosophy of Religion* (Oxford: Oxford University Press, 1993), 48.

without potentiality that Aquinas believed that God (*pure actuality*) is not *morally* good.

According to Aquinas, God cannot be morally good because moral goodness requires "certain duties or obligations" between two relating parties.[11] Only those who interact with others are obligated to comply with a standard of conduct, and only those who are obligated to a standard of conduct can be moral agents. Therefore, because God cannot enter into any real relations with his creatures, he can't be under any moral obligations to them. As Brian Davies sought to explain, "Christians will not find it amiss to speak of God as just. But they cannot mean by this that God gives others what he owes them (commutative justice), for the notion of him being indebted to them makes no sense. As source of everything creaturely, God cannot receive gain by what is creaturely and then return it."[12]

Thus, for Aquinas, God cannot enter into a relationship with man for two reasons: (1) God is entirely transcendent, and (2) man is not made in God's ethical likeness any more than God is an ethical being.

The Trinity Is the Reason God Is Immanent and Relational

But again, the heart of the problem is that Aquinas placed God's simplicity or his oneness above the complexity and diversity of God's threeness. In so doing, he failed to see how the personal relations between the Father, Son, and Spirit explain how God can be inherently personal and relational. Thomas's understanding of the Trinity does not allow for the Father, the Son, or the Holy Spirit to have their own distinct self-awareness. And without each of the three persons being self-aware, there can be no communication or interaction between them.

Thus, for Aquinas, the Father could not have given his Son a people before the foundation of the earth (John 6:37). Nor could the Son

---

11 Davies, 49.
12 Davies, 50.

have accepted this gift from the Father and then have decided to take on the form of a man to redeem these people (Phil 2:6–7). And the Spirit, as a distinct person, is unable to speak, according to his own mind, to the Father as when he does when he intercedes on our behalf in accordance with the will of the Father (Rom 8:27).

Yet the Scriptures teach there is real interaction between each of the three persons of the Trinity. What is more, their interaction is rooted in their love for one another. In this love, they glorify each other (John 17:1, 24). Though no law exists independent of or above God, God's inherent righteousness will always be on display in the manner in which the Father, Son, and Spirit interact and relate with each other. The Father will always love and glorify the Son and the Spirit perfectly, and the Son and the Spirit will likewise always love and glorify the Father and each other perfectly. Thus, each person of the Trinity is not just good, they are *morally* good in their interaction with each other.

This moral goodness in God is important because God made man in his likeness. All the felicities needed for man to be moral, rational, and ethical agents (i.e., the law written on his conscience) were given to man. Man is made in the moral likeness of God by having the law embedded in his conscience. This law, according to John Brown of Haddington, "must necessarily correspond with the nature of God, who imposes it, and of men, who are subject to it."[13]

And this is true. The law that governs our earthly relationship is the eternal law that finds its foundation in the nature of the triune God. Because God is triune, each of the three persons have all the *ad intra* qualities needed to be ethical and relational. The Father, Son, and Holy Spirit can love and communicate and relate to us because the Father and the Son and the Holy Spirit have been in an eternal state of loving and communicating and relating among themselves. This moral similarity between God and man (which could be identified by the

---

13 John Brown, *Systematic Theology: A Compendious View of Natural and Revealed Religion* (Grand Rapids: Reformation Heritage Books, 2015), 1.

word *love*) is what allows for God to be immanent and near in either judgment or peace with all those he created in his image.

This ontological and ethical framework brings us back to a right understanding of biblical epistemology. The reason God can effectively communicate and speak to us is because we are made in his ethical likeness. This common ground between God and man is what makes communication possible.[14] In short, because God is triune (and not just simple), he is able to come near to us and we are able to be drawn near to God.

Because of the Trinity, We Can Truly Know and Relate to God

Being made in God's moral likeness, we were created to live in a covenant relationship with God. Without a real point of connection between God and man, a personal relationship between God and man is impossible. Because this relationship is based on God's moral and covenantal goodness, man's separation from God is the result of sin, and believers' re-union with God is based on Christ's moral obedience.

Though God is not under any external law that stands above him, he swore by himself and entered into a covenant with mankind to remain faithful to his own moral goodness. The same moral goodness on eternal display within the internal relationship between the Father, Son, and Holy Spirit is the moral goodness on display toward his image-bearers.

God will always be true to himself. He will always be morally good. He will always be holy. He is immutable in his nature. But immutability does not mean immobility (as evidenced by the fact that Christ is mobile and immutable [Heb. 13:8]). God has promised to uphold justice both by rewarding those, such as Jesus Christ, who obey him and by punishing those, such as Adam and his fallen descendants, who disobey. Because God is ethically immutable, his interaction and

---

14 This is also why depravity—the depuration of divine love—prohibits the natural man from embracing the knowledge of God (1 Cor 2:14).

relationship with ethically mutable man changes. And though sinners have lost fellowship and communion with God in Adam, believers have regained fellowship and communion with God through the second Adam (Rom 5:12–17).

But it must be noted that it is man's nature that changes, not God. English Puritan Stephen Charnock understood this:

> God is not changed, when of loving to any creatures he becomes angry with them, or of angry he becomes appeased. . . . God always acts according to the immutable nature of his holiness, and can no more change in his affections to good and evil, than he can in his essence. . . . Though the same angels were not always loved, yet the same reason that moved him to love them, moved him to hate them. It had argued a change in God if he had loved them always, in whatsoever posture they were towards him.[15]

Because both God and man are moral beings, and because the moral standards of the covenant are fulfilled in Christ, believers have been brought into an experiential relationship with God. This knowledge of God, moreover, comes by faith in God's Word. With Christ dwelling in believers' hearts by faith, they are rooted and grounded in God's love and filled with all the fullness of the Godhead (Eph 3:17–19). Truly, by faith, believers—being filled with the Spirit of God, actually and personally and experientially know and relate to the real God of the Bible.

Because of the Trinity, God Can Truly Know and Relate to Us

In addition, because God is triune, he is both immutable and self-mobile at the same time. God's essence does not change, but this does not hinder him from entering into new relationships with ethical people who do change. God is not barred from time or space but is able to experientially interact with his creation. Though he dwells in the high and lofty space, this does not prevent him from dwelling with those and in those who have a contrite spirit (Isa 57:15).

---

15   Stephen Charnock, *The Existence and Attributes of God* (Grand Rapids: Baker, 1996), 1:345.

Because God can make internal differentiations within himself, he can make differentiations about things that change. Though God's eternal blissfulness does not alter, he does have particular opinions about everything that does.

Consequently, God was grieved by the first Adam eating fruit from the forbidden tree and appeased by the second Adam dying on a tree. In other words, he who controls time can differentiate between time-related events. Truly, God is both absolute and personal. He is transcendent and immanent because he is a Trinity consisting of a single essence and a plurality of persons. This allows God to be ontologically distant and morally similar to those created in his likeness.

Symbolical vs. Predication

We can know something about God because we are not entirely different from God. Though the biblical language of God is analogical and, at times, anthropopathic, it is not entirely metaphorical.

How God describes love in the Bible, for instance, is not completely different from how God understands love. Yet for Aquinas, the phrase "God is love" is altogether metaphorical. Because God transcends all categories of thought, we have no idea how the concept of love actually relates to God's hidden essence. Aquinas held that the human notion that God is love is merely a part of the created manifestation of God. But according to the Scriptures, by knowing that God is love we know something truly (though not exhaustively) about the ontological essence of God. And if we have the love of God poured out into our hearts by faith, we have some real experiential knowledge of God's essence in our hearts and minds (Eph 3:17). "For love is from God, and whoever loves has been born of God and knows God" (1 John 4:7).

When the Bible uses anthropomorphisms to describe God, we know they are metaphorical because of the analogy of Scripture. Since the Scriptures teach us that God is an infinite spirit, we know that God does not have eyes, arms, or legs. We know that God cannot repent because the Bible says that God cannot err. In this, we have Scripture (not philosophy) to determine when the Bible is using anthropomorphic language. Scripture alone is the source of our hermeneutical principles. Therefore, all Scriptural language is analogical, but not all is metaphorical.

THE NECESSITY OF REVELATION

The problem with Aquinas's epistemology is that it is rooted in a "philosophical science built up by human reason." The Bible does not teach that all knowledge arrives and is confined to sense experience. Aquinas assumed empiricism as his starting presupposition and then went on to use it to interpret Scripture. Such a maneuver subjugated all Scripture to an extrabiblical and faulty foundation.

Yet our hermeneutics must be derived from revelation alone. Special revelation, moreover, teaches us that knowledge of God begins and ends with divine revelation. Contrary to Aquinas's commitment to the empiricism of Aristotle, Calvin claimed that all knowledge begins with the knowledge of God. According to Calvin, "The human mind, by natural instinct, possesses some sense of a deity."[16] In summarizing Calvin's view of revelation, B. B. Warfield stated, "The knowledge of God is innate (I.iii.3), naturally engraved on the hearts of men (I.iv.4), and so a part of their very constitution as man (I.iii.1), that it is a matter of instinct (I.iii.3, I.iv.2), and every man is self-taught it from his birth (I.iii.3)."[17]

This means that, for Calvin, God made us to be proper recipients of divine communication. Likewise, Beeke and Smalley claim "that God created man [as image-bearers] with a capacity and inclination to

---

16   Calvin, *Institutes*, 1.3.1.
17   B. B. Warfield, "Calvin and Calvinism," in *The Works of B. B. Warfield* (Grand Rapids: Baker, 2003), 5:33.

receive divine revelation."[18] Because of this, man is not left to himself. Rather, he is equipped by God with the moral apparatus to know God through natural and special revelation. Because man has a sense of the divine within, man cannot help but immediately know God in natural revelation. Consequently, according to Calvin, as man cannot help but know himself, man cannot help but know God.

Likewise, having the sense of God and his moral law within, man is equipped with the natural ability, especially when his heart is renewed by the regenerating work of the Spirit, to cognitively understand natural and special revelation. In other words, divine revelation communicates effectively because man was made in the moral likeness of God.

Conclusion

Adding water to wine doesn't create more wine. Philosophy, as it turns out, is a detractor rather than a handmaiden to theology. This is because philosophy is neither built on the same foundation as revelation nor leads to the same conclusions of revelation.

Natural revelation reveals that God is both transcendent and immanent, but it does not explain how God can be both transcendent and immanent. But all men know these two realties about God, nevertheless. This revelation is consistent with special revelation, which helps us understand how God can be both transcendent and immanent in the fact that he is triune.

You see, natural revelation is consistent with special revelation, but natural revelation is not sufficient to construct a cohesive worldview without special revelation. As it was before the fall, natural and special revelation were not designed to be separated. Natural revelation was

---

18 Beeke and Smalley, *Reformed Systematic Theology*, 1:183. And John Murray stated, "It was of his sovereign will that God created the universe and made us men in his image. But since creation is the product of his will and power the imprint of his glory is necessarily impressed upon his handiwork, and since we are created in his image we cannot but be confronted with the display of that glory." *Collected Writings of John Murray*, 4:1.

never designed to be sufficient. It's merely enough to condemn man. It is enough to tell him that without God, he remains in the darkness.

So when natural man rejects what God has already communicated to him in natural revelation and seeks to philosophize his own way to God, he will either create an entirely transcendent god or one that is entirely immanent. When man rejects the light he has been given, he will only move further away from the light into more darkness.

Because philosophy can't lead its adherents to the doctrine of the Trinity, philosophy is a dead end. It is not that philosophers lack cognitive strength. It is that they don't have access—without submitting to divine revelation—to the needed information (i.e., the Trinity) to establish a coherent worldview that maintains the proper balance between God's transcendence and his immanence. And as we have seen, when God's transcendence and immanence are not equally maintained, one's worldview falls into absurdity.[19]

For God, in his wisdom, has determined that philosophers, in their wisdom, are incapable of arriving at a proper knowledge of God (1 Cor 1:21). Without bowing the knee to divine revelation, which comes from above, man has no access to the information needed to understand how God is both transcendent and immanent. Because worldly wisdom and heavenly wisdom are incongruent, philosophy only dilutes theology when combined with it. For this reason, we must root our apologetics in our theology; otherwise, our theology will be rooted in our apologetics.

Thomas Aquinas built his theology on Aristotle's cosmological argument. Yet he was unable to smooth out the tension created by uniting the god of Aristotle with the Trinitarian God of the Bible. He wanted desperately to baptize the pagan philosopher, but he failed to realize that baptism requires death. To become a Christian, the pagan philosopher would have to die to self, renounce all claims of intellectual autonomy, and fully submit to the truth-claims revealed by God.

19   See Jeffrey Johnson, *The Absurdity of Unbelief* (Conway, AR: Free Grace Press, 2017).

Nevertheless, Aquinas gave his life to carry out the impossible: unifying the Bible with the unorthodoxy of Aristotelianism. Rather than
throwing out the dry wineskin of Aristotelianism, as he should have
done, Aquinas sought to rescue Aristotle's worn-out container by fill-
ing it with the new wine of orthodoxy. It is no wonder that Aquinas
had difficulty maintaining orthodoxy when he failed to realize that
Aristotelianism can neither contain nor support the biblical worldview.

The foundation and container of the biblical worldview is not man's
intellectual autonomy or human achievement or rationalism or empiricism or philosophical speculation or "philosophical science built up by
human reason" or any other humanistic concept that comes from below. The foundation of the biblical worldview is divine revelation—and
such revelation is a gift that must be submitted to by faith as coming
from God. Without submitting to the God of natural and special revelation at the start, there is no arriving to the God of revelation at the
end of our inquiry. In other words, what does not begin with God does
not end with God.

Nevertheless, Thomas was relentless in rescuing his favorite pagan
philosopher and continued to dedicate himself to writing on this subject until a mystical experience moved him to stop writing altogether.
About three months after this life-changing experience and while en
route to the Second Council of Lyon, Thomas grew ill. Some accounts
report that he became unwell after hitting his head on a low-hanging
tree branch.[20] Others claim that his sickness was the result of burning
himself out with relentless study—with such sleeplessness and long
hours of dedicated study, his body broke down in sheer exhaustion.
According to Grabmann, "The last years of Thomas indicate clearly
that he was exhausted and overworked, that his bodily vigor had not
been able to keep up pace with his astounding mental energy."[21] And
regardless of if he suffered from a head injury, it appears that death had

20 Feser, *Aquinas*, 6.
21 Grabmann, *Thomas Aquinas: His Personality and Thought*, 15.

been chasing Thomas for a good while. His furious drive and relentless work ethic only increased death's pace.

On his way to Lyon, death began to overtake him. Even before reaching Rome, he was forced to delay his journey and take rest at Monte Cassino. Though he regained enough strength to continue his travels, he didn't make it too far before he had to stop again—this time at Campania. Maritain reports that "he had scarcely arrived when he fainted for weariness, and sickness took hold of him."[22]

After four days, and realizing that he was not likely to recover, Thomas asked to be transported to the neighboring monastery of Santa Maria at Fossanova. "As he made his way in, he leaned against the wall and said: 'This is my rest for ever and ever: here will I dwell, for I have chosen it.'"[23] There, about sixty miles southeast of Rome, just a few miles from where he was born, the great Schoolman spent the last few days of his life. Knowing his time was at hand, he confessed his sins to a priest and reaffirmed his commitment to the Catholic Church. Thomas claimed, "If I have said anything amiss, I leave it all to the correction of the Roman Church."[24] And, at the relatively young age of forty-nine, on March 7, 1274, the great Thomas of Aquino died.

---

22 Maritain, *St. Thomas Aquinas: Angel of the Schools*, 27.
23 Maritain, 27.
24 Kenelm Foster, ed., *The Life of Saint Thomas Aquinas: Biographical Documents* (Baltimore: Helicon, 1959), 110.

Not among the Protestants

Thomas of Aquino was a member of the heretic hunters: the Dominicans, a special order of priests sanctioned by the pope to deal with heretics, such as the Waldensians. The Roman pontiff viewed the Waldensians as a threat. They were not just a threat to Rome's authority; they were supposedly a threat to the eternal souls of men. Their unauthorized preaching was viewed as an act of treason. By disobeying the authority of Rome, the Waldensians were seen as schismatics. And such rebellion could not be tolerated. Because the Waldensians were a danger to themselves and to those with whom they came into contact, they had to be suppressed. These poor preachers had to be stopped no matter the cost. Though they didn't carry weapons of war, weapons of war were sanctioned by the Catholic Church to be used against them. If the Waldensians were to be stopped, they first had to be hunted down and tried. And this task was given to the Dominicans.

In a way, the Dominicans were the Catholic's counter version of the Waldensians. Like the Waldensians, the Dominicans were a group of poor preachers. Both the Waldensians and the Dominicans turned their backs on the world to give their lives to preaching. And unlike ordinary priests who remained within the walls of monasteries and chapels, the Waldensians and the Dominicans took their message to the public squares. They were evangelists who sought to mingle with the people.

The Waldensians came first, however. They were the followers of the pre-Reformer Peter Waldo (c. 1140–c. 1205), a wealthy merchant who lived in Lyon. Around 1173, Peter decided, after the death of a friend, to give his riches away and dedicate the rest of his life to preaching the gospel.[1] In so doing, he taught against the papal extravagances, transubstantiation, and purgatory. Both Peter's example and teaching began to spread.

The Reformation of the sixteenth century was based on the biblical principle that every believer was a priest before God—meaning that every believer had the freedom of conscience. This commitment of the Reformation was the same commitment of Peter Waldo. In opposition to the authority of the Catholic Church, Peter was convinced that one's conscience—as it is bound to God alone—can only be rightly ruled by the Scriptures.

Thus, Peter Waldo, like the Reformers who would follow, desired the Word of God to be understood by all. Peter wanted the Bible to be translated into the common language of the people. If truth would increase and the errors of the Catholic Church be exposed, people needed to judge the truth for themselves. So Peter had the Latin Vulgate translated, possibly for the first time, into the vernacular of his day.

In January 1179, Peter met with Pope Alexander III in Rome to debate his views on the vernacular translation of the Bible and his belief concerning the priesthood of every believer. Just a few months later, in March, at the Third Lateran Council, the teachings of Peter Waldo were condemned. Peter and his followers had to flee from Lyon into the mountains and valleys in southern France and northern Italy. In

---

1 See Jenifer Kolpacoff Deane, *A History of Medieval Heresy and Inquisition* (Plymouth, UK: Rowman & Littlefield, 2011).

1184, Pope Lucius III excommunicated Peter at a synod held at Verona. Finally, just a decade before the birth of Aquinas, the Waldensians were officially condemned as heretics at the Fourth Lateran Council of 1215.

Though condemned and exiled, the Waldensians continued to grow in number. Their movement only spread the more they were persecuted. The more the Waldensians grew, the more they became committed to the teachings of Scripture. And the more they were committed to the Scriptures, the more the Catholic Church was bent on rooting them out.

Because it did not appear that the movement would die out on its own, something had to be done. The poor lay preachers had to be suppressed and stomped out. Seeing that excommunication was not working, a new tactic was needed, and this is where the Dominicans came into the picture.

The Dominicans sought to imitate the Waldensians. The Waldensians were not interested in money or power. They were lay evangelists, honest and humble Christians, who shunned personal and economic gain to take their teaching to the people in the streets. This is one of the reasons the Waldensians were so influential, or dangerous. Hence, the Catholic Church decided that if they couldn't eliminate the self-impoverished preachers by intimidation and persecution alone, they would replicate them. The Catholics decided to counter the Waldensians by becoming like them. So, they established a new order of preachers who took oaths of poverty. Most importantly, the Dominicans followed the example of the Waldensians and took their Catholic doctrine to the people.

The Dominicans began with the efforts of the Spaniard Dominic of Caleruega (1170–1221). In 1215, the same year the Waldensians were condemned by the pope, Dominic went to Rome to gain the approval of Pope Innocent III to start a new order of mendicant preachers.

One year later, with the sanction of the new pope, Honorius III, Dominican order was officially established.

Consequently, in his fight against the Waldensians, the pope called the Dominicans to carry out (along with another newly established order, the Franciscans) the Inquisition. Because these mendicant orders were directly commissioned by the pope, they were not under the normal hierarchical jurisdiction of the Catholic Church. This gave them the freedom and authority to move about Europe without being restricted by various diocesan bishops. In other words, they could chase down fleeing heretics. And this is what happened when the Dominicans were appointed by Pope Gregory IX in 1231 to hunt down the Waldensians in the Inquisition.

The Dominican Robert le Bougre was especially eager to root out and exterminate the heretics. Robert was known as the "Hammer of Heretics" because of his extreme cruelty against them. In 1248 and 1249, a manual of operations was drawn up for inquisitors in Carcassonne. According to Edward Peters, "The manual begins with a letter of commission to inquisitors, sent by the Dominican provincial to two members of the order, charging them that, 'for the remission of your sins, you are to make inquisition of heretics and their believers, factors, receivers, and defenders, and also of persons who are defamed.'"[2]

The Inquisition was in full force in 1243 when Aquinas joined the Dominican order, and it would continue to rage across Europe with all its medieval cruelty throughout the life of Thomas Aquinas. Author Michael Novak reveals, "In southern France, men and women alike were accused of being heretics, given no way to defend themselves except by enduring torture, and if found guilty covered with pitch and set aflame. Swords aloft, soldiers were set free upon entire settlements of heretics, which they torched. During the lifetime of Aquinas, all of

---

2 Edward Peters, *Inquisition* (Berkeley: University of California Press, 1989), 58.

Provence was swept by violence against heretics—some of whom were living, according to their own lights, admirable evangelical lives."[3]

Though Aquinas didn't directly take part in the Inquisition, he supplied its barbaric tactics with his intellectual support. Following the spirit of the age, Aquinas believed heretics needed to be killed:

> With regard to heretics there are two points to be observed, one on their side, the other on the side of the Church. As for heretics their sin deserves banishment, not only from the Church by excommunication, but also from this world by death. To corrupt the faith, whereby the soul lives, is much graver than to counterfeit money, which supports temporal life. Since forgers and other malefactors are summarily condemned to death by the civil authorities, with much more reason may heretics as soon as they are convicted of heresy be not only excommunicated, but also justly be put to death. (ST, 2–2.11.3)

And even though he did not personally involve himself in hunting down the Waldensians, as he was too busy to leave his studies, he joined the Dominican order, knowing all the while what the Dominicans were commissioned to carry out.

NOT A PRE-REFORMER

The irony is that the Waldensians were the ones moving away from heresies, while Aquinas, the Dominican, was rooting the Catholic Church deeper into its heresies. When the sixteenth-century Reformation occurred, the Waldensians joined forces with the Reformers by integrating into their churches, whereas Thomas's *Summa Theologica* was the main text used in the Counter-Reformation of the Catholic Church.

For instance, it was a Dominican and committed Thomistic scholar, Sylvester Mazzolini (1460–1523), who was the first to draft heresy

---

3 Michael Novak, *On Cultivating Liberty: Reflections on Moral Ecology* (Lanham, MD: Rowman and Littlefield, 1999), 173.

charges against Martin Luther (1483–1546). In response, Luther criticized Mazzolini's dependence on Aquinas. Sixteenth-century historian Johannes Sleidanus, in his book *The General History of the Reformation of the Church*, reported, "[Luther] objects against him, That he alleged no Text of Scripture, and only quoted the Opinion of Thomas, who himself had handled most things, according to his own Fancy, without the Authority of Scripture." Mazzolini, according to Sleidanus, "strongly defended Thomas Aquinas, affirming, That his whole Doctrin was so well Received, and Approved of by the Church of Rome, that it was even preferred before all other Writings." Mazzolini "rebuked [Luther] for speaking with so little Reverence of so great a Man; and told him, That he looked upon it as an Honour, to be called a Thomist."[4]

And it was Mazzolini's pupil Tommaso de Vio Cajetan (1469–1534), the greatest Thomistic scholar of the sixteenth century, who was to first try Luther for heresy in Augsburg. As far as Cajetan was concerned, we were to "follow Saint Thomas, not whomsoever may come along."[5] So when Luther did come along, Cajetan rejected Luther because Luther had rejected Aquinas.

In October 1518, when Cajetan was unable to prove from Scripture that Luther was a heretic, he charged Luther with departing from the established Catholic orthodoxy of Thomas Aquinas. This charge Luther didn't deny, for he didn't pretend to agree with Aquinas. As far as Luther was concerned, Aquinas was "the source and foundation of all heresy, error and obliteration of the Gospel."[6] Luther was critical of Aquinas's dependence on Aristotle, but more importantly, he was

---

4 Johannes Sleidanus, *The General History of the Reformation of the Church, From the Errors and Corruptions of the Church of Rome: Begun in Germany by Martin Luther* (London: Edw, Jones), 3.
5 See Catetan, *Commentry on Summa Theologiae* 2a-2ae, q. 151, art. 4, no. 2. Cited in Cessario and Cuddy, *Thomas and the Thomists*, 80.
6 *Luther on Thomas Aquinas: The Angelic Doctor in the Thought of the Reformer*, trans. Denis Janz (Franz Steiner, 1989), 11.

critical of Aquinas's doctrine of justification.[7] According to Luther, Aquinas was the true heretic.

And though Luther was able to escape Augsburg without being arrested and deported to Rome, the following summer, in June 1520, Cajetan assisted Pope Leo X in crafting the papal bull, *Exsurge Domine,* that condemned Luther as a heretic. Being given sixty days to recant, Luther responded, in December 1520, by openly burning the papal bull along with the *Summa Theologica* of Aquinas.

Prior to being excommunicated by the Catholic Church, in the summer of 1519, Luther and his fellow colleague Andres Karlstadt (1486–1541) debated Thomistic scholar Johann Eck (1486–1543) at Leipzig. In attendance was Philip Melanchthon (1497–1560), Luther's friend and colleague, who wrote Johannes Oecolampadius (1482–1531) four days afterward, claiming the debate could be reduced to whether Aristotelian philosophy, introduced into the church by Aquinas, should be integrated into theology.[8] "Indeed," Melanchthon said, "this province of debate was first undertaken for no other reason than that it might be made known openly what a great difference there is between the old theology, that of Christ, and the new, Aristotelian doctrine."[9] In other words, Eck appealed to Scripture and the philosophical speculation of the Schoolmen, whereas Luther appealed to Scripture and to Scripture alone.

In the early years of the Reformation, according to Leif Grane, "Thomism was Luther's greatest enemy."[10] Luther maintained that the

7 See Alister McGrath, Reviews, *The Journal of Theological Studies,* Volume 42, Issue 1, April 1991, 390–392.

8 See Clyde Leonard Manschreck, *Melanchthon, The Quiet Reformer* (New York: Abingdon Press, 1958, 48.

9 Philipp Melanchthon, "Letter on the Leipzig Debate," in *Melanchthon: Selected Writings,* ed. Elmer Ellsworth Flack and Lower J. Satre, trans. Charles Leander Hill (Minneapolis: Augsburg Publishing House, 1962), 22.

10 Leif Grane, "Die Anfänge von Luthers Auseinandersetzung mit dem Thomismus," in *Theologische Literaturzzeitung* 95 (1970), 241–250. Quoted in Denis R. Janz, *Luther and Late Medieval Thomism,* 31.

Scholastics "mix the dreams of Aristotle with theological matters, and conduct nonsensical disputations about the majesty of God, beyond and against the privilege granted them."[11]

And Luther was not the only Reformer who rejected Aquinas. Philip Melanchthon was also critical of the Scholasticism of Thomas Aquinas.[12] "No faithful man," Melanchthon said, "has ever satisfied his mind with Scholastic theology, which has become polluted by so many human arguments, nonsense, tricks."[13] This is because, according to Melanchthon, none of the Schoolmen based their theology on Scripture alone: "In the citadels of scholasticism, one learns theology not according to the Bible but according to the pronouncements of men."[14] And after the University of Paris came out against Luther in 1521, Melanchthon spared no arrows when he fired this response back to them:

> For it is agreed that in Paris was born that profane scholasticism which they wish to be called theology. And when this has been admitted, there is no salvation left for the church. The Gospel has been obscured, faith rendered extinct, the doctrine of works received, and instead of being a Christian people, [or] a people of even the Law, [they have become a people committed to] the morals of Aristotle. And out of Christianity, contrary to every intent of the Spirit, there has been made a certain philosophical plan of living.
>
> Would that it might moisten your spiritual eyes to discern how much damage has been done to the church by that scholasticism of yours, both born and perfected among you, which the rest of Europe's schools have received from you as from your very

---

11   Martin Luther, "Disputation on Indulgence, 1517," in *Works of Martin Luther* (Grand Rapids: Baker, 1915), 1.46.

12   See Philipp Melanchthon, "Paul and the Scholastics," in *Melanchthon: Selected Writings*, 31–56.

13   Quoted in Charles Leander Hil, *Melanchthon: Selected Writing*, ed. E. E. Flack and L. M. Sa!re (Minneapolis: Augsburg Publishing House, 1962), 17–18.

14   Manschreck, *Melanchthon*, 52.

hands! It has become positively reasonable that the earth is filled with idols. And your articles assuredly testify how persistently you have philosophized all of the way from the very origin of scholasticism up to now.[15]

Just like the German Reformers, the Swiss Reformers Henry Bullinger and John Calvin criticized the Schoolmen for the same reason. The problem, according to Bullinger and Calvin, is that the Schoolmen did not limit their understanding of God to divine revelation.

Bullinger, for instance, levied this criticism while having a thorough knowledge of Aquinas's teaching. Before he embraced the doctrines of the Reformation, he studied at the oldest college in Cologne, Bursa Montis. And at this famous institution, Aristotle and Aquinas were the chief authorities. During these formative years of his life, Bullinger heard the famous Dominican apologist and Thomistic commenter Konrad Köllin lecture on the *Summa Theologica*.[16]

Köllin, moreover, was no friend of the theology flowing out of the University of Wittenberg. Along with Cajetan, he was one of the most important Catholic theologians in Germany that combated Lutherans.[17] His disdain for Luther and Melanchthon could be contrasted with his love for Aquinas. Not only did he write an important commentary on the *Summa Theologica* (1512), it was through his influence that the *Summa* became the standard textbook in universities, replacing Peter Lombard's *Sentences*.

Yet by the time Bullinger had finished his studies in Cologne in 1522, he, in God's providence, was more heavily influenced by the controversial professors of Wittenberg, Luther and Melanchthon, than

---

15   Philipp Melanchthon, "Luther and the Paris Theologians," in *Melanchthon: Selected Writings*, 22.

16   See Christian Moser, "Heinrich Bullinger's Efforts to Document the Zurich Reformation: History and Legacy," in *Architect of Reformation: An Introduction to Heimrich Bullinger*, ed. Bruce Gordon and Emidio Campi (Eugene, OR: Wipf & Stock, 2019), 217.

17   Köllin would go on to write against Luther in his *Eversio Lutherani Epithalamii* (Cologne 1527) and *Adversus caninas Martini Lutheri nuptias* (Tübingen, 1530).

he was by the renowned Thomistic professor at his own university in Cologne—Köllin. By the time he graduated, he broke away from the Catholic Church and its principal theologian, Thomas Aquinas. So, he joined the protest of Luther and Melanchthon and took his new commitment to Scripture back home to Switzerland. After following Zwingli as pastor at the Grossmünster at Zurich, he claimed, "Let this stand as it were for a continual rule, that God cannot be rightly known but by his word; and that God is to be received and believed to be such an one as he revealeth himself unto us in this holy word. For no creature verily can better tell what, and what king of one God is, than God himself."[18]

John Calvin was also no friend of Aquinas, according to the historian of the Swiss Reformation, Bruce Gordon.[19] As pointed out in chapter 1, Calvin rejected Aquinas's natural theology because of Aquinas's reliance on speculative reasoning. And according to William Bouwsma, Calvin's "sharpest attacks on philosophy were directed against Scholasticism as the most flagrant example of the attempt of philosophers to storm heaven."[20] In response to the extrabiblical philosophizing of the Schoolmen, Calvin taught, "God 'does not wish us to be too wise' but to exhibit 'sobriety': we must not seek to know more than 'it pleases him to teach us.' When he 'is our teacher and we hear him speak, he is able to give us prudence and discretion to understand his teaching, and we cannot fail in that; but when our Lord keeps his mouth closed, we must also keep our sense closed and hold them captive.'"[21]

Thus, in many ways, the Reformation was a battle between Thomism and *sola Scriptura*. If one argues that Reformed Scholasticism, as a logical method of learning, is the continuation of the medieval Scholasticism of Catholicism, they need to remember that, according to James

---

18 Henry Bullinger, *The Decades of Henry Bullinger*, 4.3 (2:125).
19 See Gordon, *Calvin*, 62.
20 Bouwsma, *John Calvin*, 156.
21 Quoted in Bouwsma, 156.

Thornwell, the Reformers rejected the most important element of medieval Scholasticism—its reliance on extrabiblical authorities:

> It may be well to guard you against confounding the Reformed Scholastics with those of the Church of Rome. They had this in common, that they were slaves to the logical method. But they differed widely in the source from which they derived their materials, and, of course, in the nature of the materials themselves. The Reformed Scholastics acknowledged Scripture as the only infallible rule of faith and practice. Their problem was to digest, under fit and concatenated heads, the doctrines and nothing but the doctrine of Scripture, with the inferences that lawfully follow from them. The Scholastic Theology of Rome, on the other hand, received as authoritative, in addition to Scripture, the opinions of the Fathers, the Decrees of Councils, the Bulls of Popes, and even the philosophy of Aristotle.[22]

Due to their relentless commitment to *sola Scriptura*, the Reformers rejected the Schoolmen of the Catholic Church. Because Thomas didn't build his theology exclusively on Scripture, the Reformers did not view Thomas as a trustworthy guide. John Owen noted that "it pleased God to bring in a reformation of the churches in several European nations, and they in turn began to radiate the light and truth of Christ by preaching the gospel in its power and simplicity. At the same time, it became an abomination and an object of hatred to many good and pious men to see the hold that the schools and academies of philosophy had over the minds of men."[23]

Consequently, where the Reformation spread, according to two contemporary Thomistic scholars, Cessario and Cuddy, the influence of Aquinas diminished: "The political fallout of the Reformation, especially the series of religious wars waged in Europe, caused much harm to the Thomist commentarial tradition. The social and material support that enabled Thomas Aquinas and his followers to work tranquilly

---

22 James Henley Thornwell, "Theological Lectures," in *The Collected Writings of James Henley Thornwell* (Edinburgh: Banner of Truth, 1986), 1:35.

23 Owen, *Biblical Theology*, 677–678.

were swept away in those places where the Reformation gained legiti-
macy. . . . In Catholic lands, however, Thomists continued to flourish."[24]

The battle between the Thomists and the Reformers would continue on past the life of Martin Luther. In 1546, as Luther lay dy-
ing in Eisleben, the nineteenth ecumenical council of the Catholic
Church had only recently been convened by Pope Paul III. There at
Trent, in northern Italy, the best Catholic theologians, mostly com-
mitted Thomists, had gathered to determine how best to counter the
Reformation.[25] The only book that was placed on the altar next to the
Bible was the *Summa Theologica*.[26] And this for good reason, for the
decrees and anathemas of the Council of Trent, which condemned all
Protestants to hell, were principally based on the *Summa*.

This was affirmed by Pope Pius IV, who presided over the final ses-
sion of the Council of Trent in 1563. On January 6, 1564, he issued a
papal bull, *Benedictus Deus*, ratifying all of Trent's decrees and anathemas. And just a few months later, on March 4, he went on to ratify the
Index of Forbidden Books, which threatened excommunication for those
reading or possessing any of the works of Luther and Calvin. And
according to the pope that followed him, Pius V, Aquinas was the authority behind the decrees and anathemas of Trent. Aquinas, claimed
Pius V, was "the most certain rule of Christian doctrine by which he
enlightened the Apostolic Church in answering conclusively number-
less errors . . . which illumination has often been evident in the past
and recently stood forth prominently in the decrees of the Council
of Trent."[27] More recently, Cessario and Cuddy claim that "at Trent,
Aquinas supplied a first-class authority."[28] These two Dominicans went

24 Cessario and Cuddy, *Thomas and the Thomists*, 87.

25 The Dominican and twentieth-century Catholic historian Angelo Walz has written on
the massive involvement of Thomists in the Council of Trent. See Angelo Walz, *I Domenicani
al Concilio di Trento* (Rome: Herder, 1961).

26 See Robert L. Reymond, "Dr. John H. Gerstner on Thomas Aquinas as a
Protestant," *Westminster Theological Journal*, 59.1 (Spring 1997): 113–121.

27 Ronald P. McArthur, "The Popes on St. Thomas," Thomas Aquinas College, accessed
October 21, 2019, https://thomasaquinas.edu/a-liberating-education /popes-st-thomas.

28 Cessario and Cuddy, *Thomas and the Thomists*, 90.

on to say, "As the presence of Thomists in influential positions at the Council of Trent suggests, anyone who wanted to exegete the main dogmatic definitions contained in the decrees of the council would have to consult Aquinas, especially his *Summa theologiae*."[29]

The decrees of the Council of Trent, moreover, would be ardently defended by another student of Aquinas—Robert Bellarmine (1542–1621). Bellarmine lectured principally on the *Summa Theologica* at Roman College and was made Cardinal Inquisitor in 1599 by Pope Clement VIII. In his massive polemical work against the Reformers, *Controversies of the Christian Faith*, Bellarmine relentlessly attacked the doctrines Luther and Calvin. His main weapon against them was the writings of his favorite theologian—Thomas Aquinas.[30]

Aquinas's Ecclesiology

Another leading theologian at the Council of Trent was the cousin of Henry VIII, Reginald Pole (1500–1558). Pole, a committed Thomist, resisted the Reformers by using the same argument employed by Aquinas against the Waldensians. When we look back to the thirteenth century, we see that Aquinas had no mercy on the Waldensians. He claimed that the Waldensians had condemned themselves to hell because of their failure to bow to the authority of the papacy.

Aquinas rooted his condemnation of the Waldensians in the unity of the Catholic Church. "It must be known," Aquinas stated, "that the Church is one. Although various heretics have founded various sects, they do not belong to the Church, since they are but so many divisions whereas the Church is one" (ST, xp, Q.40 a.6). Then Aquinas rooted the unity of the Catholic Church in the papacy. According to Aquinas, there is an unbroken chain of succession of bishops that can be traced backward to the apostle Peter, which will continue forward through

---

29 Cessario and Cuddy, 91.
30 Robert Bellarmine, *Controversies of the Christian Faith*, trans. Kenneth Baker (Keep the Faith, Inc. 2016).

the ongoing line of bishops occupying the papal office: "Though populations are different in different dioceses and cities, still, as there is one Church, there must be one Christian people. As then in the spiritual people of one Church there is required one Bishop, who is Head of all that people; so in the whole Christian people it is requisite that there be one Head of the whole Church."[31]

In other words, according to Aquinas, the Catholic Church is the only true church because only the Catholic Church is ruled by Peter's successor, the pope: "Now, although the people are distributed among various dioceses and cities, nevertheless there is but one Church, and therefore only one Christian people. Consequently, just as a bishop is appointed as the head of a certain people and a particular church, so must the whole Christian people be subject to one who is the head of the whole Church" (SCG, 4.76). "Hence, since the whole Church is one body, it behooves, if this oneness is to be preserved, that there be a governing power in respect of the whole Church, above the episcopal power whereby each particular Church is governed, and this is the power of the Pope. Consequently, those who deny this power are called schismatics as causing a division in the unity of the Church" (ST, 2.2, Q.40 a.6).

Consequently, according to Thomas, anyone who breaks away from the authority of the pope has broken away from the only true church: "Wherefore schismatics are those who refuse to submit to the Sovereign Pontiff, and to hold communion with those members of the Church who acknowledge his supremacy" (ST, 2.2, Q.39 a.1).

Just a few years after the death of Aquinas, Pope Boniface VIII declared, in a papal bull in 1302, that there is no salvation for those outside submission to the pope: "There is one holy Catholic and Apostolic Church, outside of which there is neither salvation nor remission of sins. . . . Indeed we declare, say, pronounce, and define that it is altogether necessary to salvation for every human creature to be subject to

---

31 Thomas Aquinas, *The Aquinas Catechism* (Manchester, NH: Sophia Institute Press, 2000), 77 (hereafter cited in text as TAC).

the Roman Pontiff (Unam Sanctum)." This was codified at the Council of Florence in 1442, which claimed that "outside the church, there is no salvation."[32]

Therefore, following Aquinas, Pole charged the Reformers with departing from God through splintering the unity of the one, holy, catholic church by their defiance of papal authority. "I can conceive of no greater injury you can inflict upon the church," Pole claimed, "than to abolish the head of this church from the face of the earth. You do exactly this when you deny that the Roman Pontiff is the one Head of the Church on earth, the Vicar of Christ."[33]

Consequently, Aquinas would not have been in support of the Reformation, but in the same way he deemed the Waldensians as heretics, he would have deemed the Reformers as heretics for their refusal to remain submissive to the Roman pontiff.

AQUINAS'S SOTERIOLOGY

Because Aquinas believed there is no salvation for those who deny papal authority in matters of faith and practice, Aquinas's ecclesiology is intertwined with his soteriology. For him, it is the Catholic Church, under the authority of the Roman pontiff, that has the power to give and withhold salvation. For, according to Aquinas, it is through the sacraments that God has entrusted to Peter and his successors—the papacy—that divine grace and forgiveness are bestowed on the faithful. In this way, Aquinas did not teach that salvation is through faith alone by grace alone and in Christ alone.

Denial of Penal Substitutionary Atonement

Though Aquinas believed that salvation was by grace, he didn't believe it was by grace alone. Though Aquinas believed salvation was by faith,

32 "Council of Basel-Ferrara-Florence, 1431-49 A.D.," Papal Encyclicals Online, accessed July 27, 2021, https://www.papalencyclicals.net/councils/ecum17.htm.
33 Reginald Pole, *Pole's Defense on the Unity of the Church*, trans. Joseph G. Dwyer (Westminster, MD: Newman, 1965), 9.

he didn't believe it was by faith alone. And though Aquinas believed salvation was by Christ, he didn't believe it was by Christ alone. The problem was that Aquinas failed to separate justification from sanctification, grace from works, and the merits and suffering of Christ from the merits and suffering of the saints.

This can be seen in Aquinas's rejection of penal substitutionary atonement: "If we speak of that satisfactory punishment, which one takes upon oneself voluntarily, one may bear another's punishment, in so far as they are, in some way, one.... If, however, we speak of punishment inflicted on account of sin, inasmuch as it is penal, then each one is punished for his own sin only, because the sinful act is something personal. But if we speak of a punishment that is medicinal, in this way it does happen that one is punished for another's sin" (ST, 1–2.87.8).

For this reason, the Dominican Romanus Cessario rightly concluded, "Aquinas offers no support for those who would advance a theory of penal substitution as the mechanism by which the benefits of Christ reach the human race."[34] "The function of satisfaction for Aquinas," claims Eleonore Stump, "is not to placate a wrathful God but instead to restore a sinner to a state of harmony with God."[35]

The penal substitutionary death of Christ allows for God to justify sinners on the basis of the objective merit and sufferings of Christ alone. Yet for Thomas, the suffering and death of Christ was not a legal and punitive payment for sin but a corrective punishment that was "medicinal." Punishment is a means of correction. Pain has a way of teaching obedience. Through suffering, there is healing and restoration. Accordingly, Christ's death was not a direct means of satisfying God's wrath as much as it was a means to bring healing and sanctification to

---

34   Romanus Cessario, "Aquinas on Christian Salvation," 124. See also Cessario, *The Godly Image: Christ and Salvation in Catholic Thought from Anselm to Aquinas*, Studies in Historical Theology (Petersham, MA: St. Bede's, 1989), 6: xvii, 157.

35   Eleonore Stump, "Atonement According to Aquinas," in *Philosophy and the Christian Faith*, ed. Thomas V. Morris (Notre Dame, IN: University of Notre Dame, 1988), 65.

his people. It leads to justification only indirectly as it aids in a life of obedience and good works.

Denial of Justification by Faith Alone

Consequently, though sanctification, Aquinas alleged, may lead to justification, it doesn't guarantee justification because four things are necessary for justification: "There are four things which are accounted to be necessary for the justification of the ungodly, viz. the infusion of grace, the movement of the free-will towards God by faith, the movement of the free-will towards sin, and the remission of sins. The reason for this is that, as stated above (Article 1), the justification of the ungodly is a movement whereby the soul is moved by God from a state of sin to a state of justice" (ST, 2–2.113.6).

In this we can see Aquinas did not believe justification was a legal sentence whereby God declares a sinner righteous. Subsequently, Aquinas didn't separate justification from sanctification. Like sanctification, he viewed justification as a process of "the soul [being] moved by God from a state of sin to a state of justice." This movement of the soul, moreover, takes place not by imputed grace but by infused grace: "On the part of the Divine motion, there is the infusion of grace; on the part of the free-will which is moved, there are two movements—of departure from the term 'whence,' and of approach to the term 'whereto'; but the consummation of the movement or the attainment of the end of the movement is implied in the remission of sins; for in this is the justification of the ungodly completed" (ST, 2–2.113.6).

"For St. Thomas," Allister E. McGrath states, "the nature of grace, sin and divine acceptation were such that a created habit of grace was necessary in justification by the very nature of things."[36] And David Schaff claims,

No distinction was made by the mediaeval theologians between the doctrine of justification and the doctrine of sanctification,

---

36 Allister E. McGrath, *Luther's Theology of the Cross* (Oxford: Blackwell, 1985), 82.

such as is made by Protestant theologians. Justification was treated as a process of making the sinner righteous, and not as a judicial sentence by which he was declared to be righteous. . . . Although several of Paul's statements in the Epistle to the Romans are quoted by Thomas Aquinas, neither he nor the other Schoolmen rise to the idea that it is upon the [condition] of faith that a man is justified. Faith is a virtue, not a justifying principle, and is treated at the side of hope and love.[37]

Denial of Justification by Christ Alone

But for Aquinas, not only is justification not by faith alone but it is also not by the finished work of Christ alone. Because Aquinas blended justification and sanctification, he also blended the merits of Christ with the merits of the saints. Justification requires not only what Christ did on the cross but what he does within the believer through the divine works of regeneration and sanctification.

Sacerdotalism

And for Thomas Aquinas, the "sacraments are necessary for man's salvation" (ST, 3.61.1). Regeneration and sanctification are bestowed by the Church (*ex opere operato*) through the sacraments that have been entrusted to the Catholic Church. "If we hold," Aquinas claimed, "that a sacrament is an instrumental cause of grace, we must allow that there is in the sacraments a certain instrumental power of bringing about the sacramental effects" (ST, 3.62.4). Thus, the sacraments bestow grace by the very act of them being performed: "The Sacraments both contain grace and confer it" (TAC, 4.1.A.2).

Thomas believed that baptism brings about regeneration and remits "both actual sin and Original Sin as well as all guilt and punishment which they incur" (TAC, 4.2.A.4). Confirmation, according to Thomas, imparts the Holy Spirit "to give strength" to the believer (TAC, 4.1.B.4). Because the Eucharist is "the physical body of

---

37   Quoted in Phillip Schaff, *History of the Christian Church* (Grand Rapids: Eerdmans, 1960), 5: 662, 675, 754, 756.

Christ," it effectually brings believers into "union with Christ" (TAC, 4.1.C.4.b).[38] And the sacrament of penance, which includes heartfelt contrition, confession to a priest, and works of satisfaction, effectually observes the sins that occur after baptism (TAC, 4.1.D).

Works of Satisfaction

By the right use of the sacraments, believers are empowered to perform works of satisfaction (ST, 3.62.2), which are, according to Thomas, good works and hardships and suffering incurred for the sake of Christ. These works of satisfaction verify one's contrition and assist in the believer's purification. Therefore, for Aquinas, besides the work of Christ, additional merit and works are needed for divine satisfaction and forgiveness.

Works of Supererogation and the Treasury of Merit

Some believers underperform, while others have done more than enough to satisfy divine justice. According to Thomas, the saints, because of their extraordinary holiness, have more good works than they personally need.[39] And rather than these good works (i.e., works of supererogation) going to waste, God has placed them, Thomas claimed, along with the merits of Christ, into the church's treasury: "And the saints in whom this super-abundance of satisfactions is found, did not perform their good works for this or that particular person, who needs

---

38 Aquinas stated, for instance, "The form of the Eucharist is the very words of Christ: 'This is my body' and 'This is the cup of my blood.'. . . These words spoken by the priest in the person of Christ bring into being this sacrament. In virtue of the above words, bread is changed into the Body of Christ and wine into His Blood, so that Christ is entirely contained under the appearances of bread, which remain without a subject, and He is entirely contained under the appearance of wine" (TAC, 4.2.C).

39 Thomas also supported the worship of the saints: "Now it is manifest that we should show honor to the saints of God, as being members of Christ, the children and friends of God, and our intercessors. Wherefore in memory of them we ought to honor any relics of theirs in a fitting manner: principally their bodies, which were temples, and organs of the Holy Ghost dwelling and operating in them, and are destined to be likened to the body of Christ by the glory of the Resurrection. Hence God Himself fittingly honors such relics by working miracles at their presence" (ST, 3.25.6).

the remission of his punishment, . . . but they performed them for the whole Church in general, even as the Apostle declares that he fills up 'those things that are wanting of the sufferings of Christ . . . for His body, which is the Church' to whom he wrote (Col. 1:24). These merits, then, are the common property of the whole Church" (ST, Suppl. 25.1).

According to Thomas, this treasury of merit has been entrusted by Christ to Peter and his successors, and with it the pope has been authorized by Christ to dispense the surplus merit at his own discretion to those who are in need:

> Therefore, dispensation of this treasure belongs to the one who is in charge of the whole church; hence the Lord gave to Peter the keys of the kingdom of heaven [Matthew 16:19]. Accordingly, when either the well-being or absolute necessity of the church requires it, the one who is in charge of the church can distribute from this unlimited treasure to anyone who through charity belongs to the church as much of the said treasure as shall seem to him opportune, either up to a total remission of punishment or to some certain amount. In this case, the passion of Christ and of the other saints would be imputed to the member as if he himself would have suffered whatever was required for the remission of his sins.[40]

Indulgences

Seeing that the pope has been entrusted with the keys to the kingdom and the treasury of merit, he has the power to bestow forgiveness of sins, according to Thomas. This forgiveness is not restricted to the sacraments but extends to papal indulgences, and such indulgences are sanctioned and recognized by Christ himself:

> Indulgences hold good both in the Church's court and in the judgment of God, for the remission of the punishment. . . . The reason why they so avail is the oneness of the mystical body in

---

40 Thomas Aquinas, *Quaestiones De Quolibet*, trans. Turner Nevitt and Brian Davies (New York: Oxford University Press, 2020), 2.8.2 (hereafter cited in text as QDQ).

which many have performed works of satisfaction exceeding the requirements of their debts; in which, too, many have patiently borne unjust tribulations whereby a multitude of punishments would have been paid, had they been incurred. So great is the quantity of such merits that it exceds the entire debt of punishment due to those who are living at this moment: and this is especially due to the merits of Christ: for though He acts through the sacraments, yet His efficacy is nowise restricted to them, but infinitely surpasses their efficacy. (ST, 3. Suppl. 25.1)[41]

Purgatory

If the sacraments and indulgences were not enough, Aquinas believed there was one more means of forgiveness: purgatory. Aquinas taught that if one dies without having satisfied their debt of sins, there remains hope after death. He stated, "The punishment of purgatory is intended to supplement the satisfaction which was not fully completed in the body" (ST, 3. Suppl. 71.6). He went on to say:

It is sufficiently clear that there is a Purgatory after this life. For if the debt of punishment is not paid in full after the stain of sin has been washed away by contrition, nor again are venial sins always removed when mortal sins are remitted, and if justice demands that sin be set in order by due punishment, it follows that one who after contrition for his fault and after being absolved, dies before making due satisfaction, is punished after this life. Wherefore those who deny Purgatory speak against the justice of God: for which reason such a statement is erroneous and contrary to faith . . . and whosoever resists the authority of the Church, incurs the note of heresy. (ST, appendix 2.1)

---

41 Yet according to Aquinas, for indulgence to be effective, three things must be in order: "For an indulgence to benefit anyone, however, three things are required. First, a cause that appertains to the honor of God, or for the necessity or utility of the church. Secondly, authority in him who grants it: the pope principally, others insofar as they receive either ordinary or commissioned, that is, delegated, power from him. Thirdly, it is required that the one who wishes to receive the indulgence should be in the state of charity. And these three things are designated in the papal letter" (QDQ, 1.8.2).

AQUINAS NOT AMONG THE PROTESTANTS

Aquinas condemned the Waldensians as heretics for their rejection of purgatory. But it was the Waldensians who were moving away from the heresies of the Catholic Church and uniting with the churches of the Reformation, whereas it was Thomas Aquinas who opposed the Waldensians and supplied doctrinal support for the Counter-Reformation of the Inquisition, Cajetan, Eck, Köllin, Pole, Bellarmine, and the whole Council of Trent.

"In the teachings of Thomas Aquinas," Protestant historian David Schaff claims, "we have, with one or two exceptions, the doctrinal tenets of the Latin Church in their perfect exposition as we have them in the Decrees of the Council of Trent in their final statement."[42] Schaff goes on to say, "[For] the theology of the Angelic Doctor and the theology of the Roman Catholic Church are identical in all particulars except the immaculate conception. He who understands Thomas understands the medieval theology at its best and will be in possession of the doctrinal system of the Roman Church."[43] And this is not just a Protestant notion, as Jesuit theologian Joseph de Guibert confirms: "By the very fact of anyone embracing the doctrine of St. Thomas, he embraces the doctrine most commonly accepted in the Church, safe and approved by the Church itself."[44]

Aquinas was not a pre-Reformer. As he opposed the Waldensians in his day, he would have opposed the Reformers in their day. He was a Roman Catholic through and through, and it is for good reason that popes have venerated him as their greatest theologian.[45] Until this day,

42 Quoted in Phillip Schaff, *History of the Christian Church* (Grand Rapids: Eerdmans, 1960), 5: 662, 675, 754, 756.
43 Schaff, 5: 756.
44 Joseph de Guibert, *De Ecclesia Christi* (Rome: Unversità Gregoriana, 1929), 386, as quoted in Cessario and Cuddy, *Thomas and the Thomists*, 94.
45 For instance, in the nineteenth century, Pope Leo XIII claimed, "Among the Scholastic Doctors, the chief and master of all towers Thomas Aquinas, who, as Cajetan observes, because 'he most venerated the ancient doctors of the Church, in a certain way seems to have inherited the intellect of all.'" (Quoted in Cessario and Cuddy, *Thomas and the Thomists*, xi).

Aquinas remains the theologian of the Catholic Church. "After Saint Augustine," for instance, "the Catechism of the Catholic Church refers more times to Thomas Aquinas than to any other personal authority in the Catholic tradition."[46] So, let the truth be known to all who love the truth—Aquinas is *not* among the Protestants.

CONCLUSION

Thus, to unite Thomas with the Reformers is to undo the Reformation. Aquinas, as the chief authority of the Counter-Reformation, is not friend but foe to Protestantism. Though Thomas of Aquino is called the Angelic Doctor by some, the Word of God is not so accommodating to those who pervert the gospel of Jesus Christ: "If we or an angel from heaven should preach to you a gospel contrary to the one we preached to you, let him be accursed" (Gal 1:8).

---

46 Cessario and Cuddy, *Thomas and the Thomists*, 137.

APPENDIX 2

NOT AMONG THE SCHOLASTICS

John Owen on
the Mingling of Philosophy with Theology

Excerpt Taken from *Biblical Theology*[1]

In the second chapter of his Epistle to the Colossians, the Apostle Paul most earnestly warns the faithful that they must take heed "Lest any man spoil you through philosophy and vain deceit" (Colossians 2:8). All commentators agree that it was not the use, but the abuse of philosophy which the Apostle censures in that place. But, whether the intermingling of philosophy with theology constitutes its use or its gross abuse is something on which scholars are by no means agreed. It is quite certain that there have not been lacking in all ages of the Church men who were both learned and pious, having so great a reverence for apostolic institutions and authority that they absolutely rejected all employment of philosophic concepts in divine matters. Note that neither Paul, nor anyone who has followed in his footsteps, has ever condemned any skillful, prudent, and constant contemplation of the works of God, His creation and providence, or disparaged any natural or innate feelings which discriminate between the good and the evil, the honorable and the base, and which might influence men towards obedience to God. But, as such ideas are, for the great part, corrupted, and as the fallen human intellect will inevitably misconstrue whatever

---

1 Owen, *Biblical Theology*, 668-684.

knowledge concerning God it can glean from such sources, then it is essential that all be tried by the touchstone of the sacred Scriptures.

Here we shall only consider the primary purpose and end of all knowledge—how to live acceptably before God—something over which the inborn curiosity of the human psyche will always exercise itself, but which it is incapable of understanding by force of intellect alone. I have shown, in an earlier part of this work, that these common ideas about good and evil, or the contemplation of the works of nature, were only a true theology in man's primary state, and thus all study of them, without the aid of revelation, is simply vanity now.

But such ideas are really not what we are considering at this point. Instead, we must consider philosophy as it has been developed and polished by generations of thinkers who were ignorant of God and His will. This is quite another matter and its encroachment into theology must be called sharply into question. Shall philosophy be suffered to mingle its principles, notions, hypotheses, and conclusions with the teaching of the gospel and bring into its methods, means, and con-clusions which are subservient to the naked human intellect? Shall philosophers be allowed to employ their reasonings and methodology to the interpretation, declaration, and teaching of Christian doctrine as they have refined them according to their own discretion and schools of thought?

How some learned churchmen in the past have answered these ques-tions may be shown by a few testimonies. Says Clement of Alexandria, "There are some who think that philosophy has come to be so great an evil, intended for the ruin of men, that it must have been the inven-tion of some malignant power" *(Miscellanies,* Book I). Tertullian says, "Heresies are fueled by philosophy. Valentinus had been the disciple of the Platonic philosophy, and so he makes much of his '30 eons,' which he maintains are lesser gods, to the confusion of the doctrine of the Trinity. Marcion, the heretic of Sinope, who gave himself out to be Christ, derived his teaching of a 'better god' and of 'tranquility of mind' from the Stoics. The Epicureans say that the soul is mortal, and so the resurrection of the body is vehemently denied by all under Epicurean influence. What correspondence has Jerusalem with Athens? What do the Academics have to do with the Church? What have heretics to do with Christians? And what has the teaching of Christ to do with that of the Portico?"

So also Justin Martyr, "What is common knowledge of the practices of you philosophers proves you to be full of every kind of deceit and ignorance!" So Tertullian named philosophers as "the patriarchs of heretics," and Jerome says much the same (*Continuation of Eusebius' Chronicle*, Book 2, chapter 37) (A). But it is beside our purpose to heap up further testimonies. It will suffice for our present point to have shown that there was no lack of great and holy men who voiced their opposition to the inroads of philosophy in all ages of the Church. I shall add briefly my own convictions on the subject, perhaps the more briefly as the course of this work flows swiftly now towards its conclusion.

In teaching Scriptural doctrine, two factors demand our attention—first, the divine truth itself, and second, the correct method of expounding it. I have already shown that Biblical truth itself has absolutely nothing in common with secular philosophy. But the method in which that truth was handed down and expounded from the sanctuary of the divine mind, to be encapsulated within the Scriptures, remains to be discussed. That Scripture truth is varied and various, all will agree who know anything at all of God's revealed will in His Word. Nowhere does it contain those logical rules for systematically teaching any truth which we expect from all human disciplines and studies. The doctrine here has to do with the faith and obedience of sinful men, and it emanates from a unique source, being a matter of pure and unadulterated revelation, coming straight from the bosom of the Father through Jesus Christ. So the method of expounding and interpreting it is also through and by the

Holy Spirit, making it quite unique and divine, a different species from and, therefore, in total disagreement with all merely human teaching and transmission of knowledge.

So teaches the Apostle, "My speech and my teaching was not with enticing words of man's wisdom, but in demonstration of the Spirit and power, that your faith should not stand in the wisdom of men, but in the power of God. Howbeit we speak wisdom amongst them that are perfect: yet not the wisdom of this world, nor of the princes of this world, that come to naught" (1 Corinthians 2:4, 6). Let the reader also consult Ephesians 1:8–9, 17–19 and Colossians 1:27–28, 2:2, 8–9. This, then, is a description of evangelical truth, and of the principles on which the sacred Scriptures are to be expounded. But, to this, two additional elements have crept in from secular philosophy, and they have proved themselves sufficiently troublesome to the truth.

The first was a desire to systemize theology into a pattern like those skillfully wrought out, and methodical systems which everywhere hold sway in, the schools of philosophy. By these truths which were revealed in different manners and different ways by the Spirit are regimented and reordered into mechanical formulas, and this is the result, I say, of the unnatural partnership of philosophy with theology. To this is owed almost all of the theological systems-farragoes of odd theological propositions strung together with generalized arguments, sections lifted out of divine truth and context, plausible statements and propositions derived from them, all well mixed with philosophical terms and notions, cemented with overall and rigid formulas, and dished up as Christian theology! By these means has arisen a philosophico-theology which, in the hands of some scholars, is nearer to theology and in some is nearer to philosophy, but in all of which our evangelical doctrine has been cast down from its spiritual supremacy and loses its heavenly grandeur. And yet today such philosophical theology is taught by the learned to their pupils in almost all denominations of Christians. Thus it has come about that there is almost no article of evangelical truth, although in its own nature the most plain, obvious, and clear to the eyes of the faithful, replete with all of its innate efficiency for the saints who are in communion with God in Christ, which has not been taken up by these philosophically—learned scholars under pretense of explaining it precisely and systematically, and so become entangled in terms, notions, trivialities and arguments until the Apostle Paul himself would struggle in vain to grasp or understand it—unless, that is, he was given the clue by Aristotelian learning!

Among the ancient philosophers, this hairsplitting way of arguing had the same result that no one was able any more to see the plainest truths—as was well noted and deservingly mocked by Lucian of old. Having wittily criticized their dubious reasonings he adds that "Of all these strange things, the most absurd of all is the way each one offers the most overwhelming and irrefutable arguments—to prove the most contradictory and opposite things! One proves absolutely that a substance is hot, another equally so that it is cold! As if it were not patently obvious all the time that nothing can be hot and cold at the same time!" (*Menippus* 4). For such reasons it may not be displeasing to the reader for me to trace back a little more deeply into the origin and progress of this evil.

When the gospel was first preached in the world, the teachers understood their business and knew that they had been commissioned to proclaim to others the faithfulness and love of Him who had called them from the powers of darkness and brought them into His own most marvelous light. Their religion consisted of the celebration of the riches of divine grace by which they had been justified through the shed blood of Christ, and so set free from the wrath to come, the worship and contemplation of the love of Christ the Mediator in His redeeming work, and a constant striving to imitate that sacred ex ample in glad obedience and holiness of life. These things were undertaken by the rich outpoured aid of the Holy Spirit, by whose working the redeemed come daily more to resemble Christ. Their mutual delight was fellowship among themselves, the performance of good works among their neighbors, the worship of God in spirit and truth, and the performance of the rites and duties of corporate worship in that purity and simplicity with which they were instituted by Christ. This completed their theology and practice. Those who are led of the Spirit and who rely on God's Word will do and suffer great things in accord with Christ's will in their progress in grace and through life. But they will never be deprived of the spiritual and indescribable joys necessary for their state and condition. But how little time was suffered to pass after that first proclamation of the gospel before men of wicked and corrupt minds, men whose intellects were still in bondage to spiritual darkness, began to twist and pervert these heavenly truths in many ways! As they themselves were still in the flesh, so spiritual things must seem foolish and empty to them, and so they began to alter the fashion of gospel truth until it took on the form of secular wisdom.

The initial philosophic errors, naturally, concerned the person of Christ, and soon He was being reinterpreted as a ghost, a phantom, a mere man, a spirit-controlled man, one attaining to the ranks of the gods, or one who was to be equated with the sun in the sky! Along with this came the assumption that faith itself was a sham, a supposition, or a fantastic projection. At all events it was *no science!* And so they went on, recognizing neither Father nor Son. Since they were not equipped to apprehend spiritual matters spiritually, the attempt had to be made to rationalize religious concepts by accommodating them to some prevailing philosophic teaching or other. The sacred page proves that this infection was abroad already while the Apostles—or at least some of them—still lived, and its rapid spread all of the histories of the times describe.

Finding all of his initial assaults against the truth repelled, and forced to relinquish his hold, Satan improved the opportunity of the passing of the Apostles to attempt to adulterate the truth of the gospel and, in this he found great success. What could not be gained by a head-on attack on the truth was achieved by pretending to be an expounder of the truth. With the passing away of the generation of men who had been divinely led by the infallible Spirit, the task of defending the faith fell to men who had been educated in the various schools of secular wisdom—Clement, Origen, Tertullian, and countless others. To these it seemed insufficient merely to employ the weapons formed by superhuman hands—the Word and Spirit of God—against the circling enemies of truth, but they must add arguments hammered out on secular anvils. Seeing heretics (as many philosophers falsely assumed the name of Christian) dragging the express words of Scripture into novel and unnatural meanings, they retaliated by attempting to match philosophy with philosophy, and so drive the opposers from their intellectual and words fortresses; and so new terminologies and concepts were invented for the purpose.

Then it naturally followed, with the passing of time, that the terms and vocabulary and philosophizing arguments which had been employed in defending this truth or that came to be considered as essential and necessary parts of the religion of Jesus Christ. And yet still no one had made the attempt of reducing the entire faith to a systematic form, apart from, perhaps, some parts of that formulary which goes under the name of the "Apostles Creed." The truly faithful would admit of no system and allow authority to no theological writing or catechism, however systematically arranged or philosophically adorned. Sacred Scripture alone was their criterion for settling controversies and instructing the people. They were not easily drawn away into empty conjectures because they waited patiently upon the Holy Spirit who had been promised to teach believers. But all was not so with their leaders and learned men, who daily felt more strongly the itch to mingle secular wisdom and philosophical maxims with their revealed theology. Once lacking in Spiritual gifts—or failing to sufficiently trust in them—they had no resource but human reason to support their friends or confound their enemies, and so were set on a course of calamitous destruction for the Church. There followed no generation which did not give itself to this evil until the entire foundation of the Church was undermined. Some invented new vocabulary, new terminology, while others brought in subtle and devious philosophical reasonings. Others worked out verbal dialectical knots and meshes with the design of entangling the enemies of the truth. Others were busy forcing the express words of the Holy Spirit, used by Him in expounding super-natural truths, into distorted and philosophical usages until, at last, the sacred and spiritual teachings of Jesus Christ were corrupted and over whelmed and hidden beneath the mass of worldly wisdom.

Acacius, Bishop of Berea, relates, in a letter to Cyril of Alexandria, how Apollinarius fell into schism and disgrace in the Church simply by being too hot a debater and allowing far too free a reign to philosophic subtleties in his attempts to defend the truth. See the transactions of the Council of Ephesus. "What profit," asks Acacius, "did Apollinarius gain for having been for so long a period a great champion of those contending for the faith against its enemies, when his abilities betrayed him into the mischance of relying on his own strength? Wishing to ar-gue himself out of certain seeming difficulties in our pure and spotless faith of Christ, did he not end up counted amongst the schismatics, by the catholic Church?" Which shows, at least, that some reverence for heavenly truth, some discernment, remained in the Church in the days of Apollinarius. Had that keen debater flourished in the following cen-turies, would he have been so rejected? Or had any healthy criticism then survived, would the Church have ever admitted such deformed, disconnected, muddled, and impure doctrines as it did in the place of evangelical theology? But I would dare to say that the defection from the purity of the gospel, which the orthodox were already beginning to bewail in his day, had its origin and gained its strength from the first mingling of gentile philosophy with true theology.

Once philosophy had gained a foothold in the schools of Christ, then the knowledge of God in Christ Jesus quietly withdrew as was predicted by the Spirit in the Scriptures, and confirmed in the expe-rience of many. The most special and virulent poison to bring about this effect was the Aristotelian or Peripatetic philosophy which, having lain neglected for some centuries, began again to please men devoted to "literary pursuits." In fact, it had been preserved and cultivated by the Mohammedan Arabs, and now it invaded the Christian world as quickly as it could be transmitted by word of mouth. That philosophy, especially as refined and transmitted by the Arabs, was a most apt and subtle medium for generating divisions and for instigating lawsuits, controversies, and quarrels about anything at all you please. Adopting and relying on this, the scholastics, in effect, replaced the norm and faith of evangelical theology with a barbarous and philosophical pseudo-scientific "learning." Who will deny that the subject matter of scholastic theology (most if not the whole of it) is but the boilings-down of Aristotelian metaphysics applied to the discussion of supernatural affairs? Says Cornelius Jansen of Ypres, "Those, therefore, as Veralamius so rightly says in his *New Method*, except they have reduced theology into their own order, and fashioned it into a species of art, and stretched it on the aggressive and thorny philosophy of Aristotle, they do not consider that they have arrived at a compact body of religion" *(Augustinism,* Book 2, chapter 19). Wherever they hold up their perverse and improper speculations and interpretations, it is always the name of Aristotle that they shelter behind. Would anyone have to remain silent on how Aristotle's works came into the hands of Appelicus Trius, who sold the all-but-worn-out codices to Sulla the dictator, and so they have been passed on down in a most corrupted fashion. It should also be borne in mind that the Arabs, who seem to have been so fascinated with them and to have drunk so deeply of their subtleties, were, for the most part, profoundly ignorant of both Greek and Latin. Their translations into Arabic were crude and unsophisticated, with limited vocabulary and skimped diction, in many places making no reasonable sense at all. Small wonder that Erasmus could cry, "How I do wish that all of these cold subtleties might be pruned away, and a pure and simple Christ be restored, and placed deep within the human consciousness!"

I do not deny that many of these theologians knew and used the books of Scripture, and even admitted them to be the very truth. The problem lies with their thinking which is so deeply tinged with the peripatetic [Aristotelian] philosophy that they have suffered darkness of eyes and an irresistible itch to disputation, with an overpowering need to reduce Christianity to a system of theorems satisfactory to the philosopher; all of which can in no way set forth the religion of Jesus Christ. In fact, one might characterize the whole difference between these thinkers and their earlier philosophic forebears as this—they acknowledge our sacred books among the data from which they formulate their systems, but the earlier philosophers, being ignorant of them, did not and could not do so. From this it arises that many argue that such men should be classed as philosophers rather than as theologians, as a certain saintly German points out, "I agree with Jansen that, apart from some trifles of Aristotelian philosophy the have contributed nothing at all to the science of theology," and so Erasmus bitterly complains in his writings that "Once symbols of faith were no longer inwardly felt, but instead were reduced to paper, there were soon as many varieties of the faith as there were scholars. As articles of faith increased so sincerity declined. As strife was stirred up, charity grew cold. Christian teaching, which at the first was a complete stranger to the strife of words, began to defend itself in the language of the philosophers. So the Church took a giant stride out of her ancient and original pathway." From the date when the disputes, nay, the obscurities of the scholastics began to come to the fore, sacred theology became more and more besmirched and contaminated with worldly philosophy, as Trithemius admits.

In the last century, it pleased God to bring in a reformation of the churches in several European nations, and they in turn began to radiate the light and truth of Christ by preaching the gospel in its power and simplicity. At the same time, it became an abomination and an object of hatred to many good and pious men to see the hold that the schools and academies of philosophy had over the minds of men. But now, with the passing of the years, whether the learned men and the teachers of the Reformed Churches have remained free from the contagion is something that each must decide for himself.

I shall merely cite what Johann Drusius says in his comment on those words of Peter that "the dog is turned to his own vomit again" (2 Peter 2:22). Says he, "Such are those who now turn to the things that the first Reformers vomited out, which things include the scholastic theology, which is again pursued so eagerly by many to the neglect of true theology, which is founded on the Word of God, and from which all Christian truth flows. The very degree to which theology is mingled with this human leaven, to that degree it is adulterated, and its purity is spoiled. When at long last shall these things be reformed? Until they are there will be no peace in the Church. Would that those who undertake the study of divine things would otherwise arrange their studies, learn to spurn these empty trifles, and give themselves instead to the original languages and the sacred text itself. If that should happen, we would have theologians indeed, such as we could desire to have far more than we yet have. But by this comparative neglect the Scriptures are brought into contempt in the eyes of the common people. How many do not even comprehend the texts that they hear read from the pulpit! They are wise only in commentaries and lecture notes, with the result that nothing escapes their lips which is fit to nourish a hungry soul. That term of 'washed sow' may fittingly be given him who having once been washed in reformation waters will again roll himself in sophistic, philosophical mud, to the great harm of the Church, and especially of its rising youth. From where, I ask you, do most of our disputes arise, except out of that very mud and mire? He returns to his vomit who the second time introduces and recalls the scholastic theology of the academics, mingling the bread which proceeds from the mouth of God alone with the leaven of the ancient philosophers. Such

transmute the simplicity of the faith into the subtlety and curiosity
of the disputants, each day dreaming up fresh subjects of inquiry,
the most part of which were quite unknown to the Prophets and
writers of the Epistles of old, but are the useless, vain noises which
fill the Christian world to day." So says he.

Let us also heed the author of that book entitled *The Church's
Burden*. "Pagans," he says, "still seek to overthrow the evangelical rule
of the gospel, and to this end the devil will sponsor new doctrines, and
encourage professing Christians to discover them in the pagan philosophers of old, so that the dogmas of the gentiles are married to the
pure principles of the faith, and at length the entire evangelical truth
is exploded by these sophistic devices." And, with this, agrees Erasmus,
"All of the signs seem to indicate a new and most prosperous phase for
the Church. One thing alone grips my soul, which is this, that pagan
literature, under the guise of ancient wisdom, may again raise its head
in the Church."

And thus it has been since the beginning of the Reformation. *A
philosophical method of teaching spiritual matters is alien to the gospel.* Christians were quite strangers to philosophy in the days of the
Apostles. Let the surviving writings of the earliest Christians be con-
sulted and they will be seen to have handled their theology in a quite
different manner to our recent theologians. In this the ancient way is
the far better way.

True heavenly light has an inborn quality which at once betrays its
own divinity and seizes and compels men's minds to amazement and
wonder at it. It works its way into the hearts of men with an ineffable glory and splendor which penetrates their consciences. It possesses
fullness, grandeur, and liberty, all accompanied with irresistible efficiency. Of such is the life and soul of true theology. What wonder is it
when this power and energy is obscured, weakened, and dissipated in
great degree as theology is overburdened with sophistic concepts and
philosophical terminology? All who would employ true theology have

to complain that it is compelled to progress, dragging along with it the snares and traps of philosophy, when they would fain simply practice the simple and holy faith in God which is through Jesus Christ. How marvelously is the inner voice of conscience quieted, and the spiritual sharpness which is part of evangelical truth blunted, as all should easily observe and confess, when minds are bolstered up with insuperable philosophical prejudices. In the place of spiritual wisdom is substituted I know not what varieties of barren and arid opinion, and so countless wicked, faithless, carnal, worldly men are held back from any saving knowledge of God in Christ. This we see happening all about us daily. The spiritual nature of the gospel is most wickedly eclipsed while multitudes of petty "scholars" fret themselves how they might best teach the faith within a rigidly structured, accurate, *methodical-philosophical* form! What is more, a great multitude of errors have swarmed into the Church through the reception of philosophy, like Greeks out of the belly of the Trojan horse, as we have already shown from Tertullian and others. The clear fact is that the common, Aristotelian philosophy supplied sufficient materials for an infinity of quarrels and use less disputes. The facts shout out to heaven that our little, witty, chattering sophists, in their endless wranglings over the "articles of faith," are simply raking over the embers of Aristotle's philosophy, and in so doing they "Irritate the throne of Almighty God with legal quarrels and cheap tricks. They dissect the faith with a scalpel of ambiguity, and with words having no more substance than their own breath they tie and untie the chains of their complicated syllogisms!," as Prudentius once sang of the ancient philosophers (Deification—*a hymn against the infidels*).

One wonders how well some of those who employ these concepts themselves understand them. Says Melchior Camus, "I would be ashamed to admit that I did not understand their philosophy—If I thought that those who are spouting it at all understood it themselves!" (Book 2, chapter 7). Worthy of our notice, too, is that point made by the learned Vivus, commenting on Book 18 of Augustine's *City of God*. "Theologians," says he, "all agree in teaching that God alone can create something out of nothing. But to this simple fact see what Thomas (Aquinas) adds, how and with what arguments he is refuted by Scotus, how these are straightened out and corrected by Occam, and so replaced by Occam's own opinion, which in their turn are put out of place by Peter Alicensis, and so on with the result of making a football of heavenly truth and rendering it a matter of division, faction, and heated emotions. What morals will be corrected, what depraved feelings stilled or removed, by doctrines so harnessed about with disagreements, capable of being so turned up and down by the opinions of men, and struck all out of shape by the blows and tricks of disputatious litigants?"

From this source are theological disputes generated and, once generated, perpetuated. How would all be silenced if Christian men would once but surrender themselves to the faith and direction of the divine Word, and of the Holy Spirit speaking powerfully in it! I Say "Christian men" because of their profession, although I am quite ashamed to use the word of many today. While the minds of most men who would concern themselves seriously with the subject of religion are still deeply embued with philosophy, even if that leaven stands not at the center of their thinking, disputes between believers will continue, and reconciliation between those who are really only kept apart by the most ridiculously small matters will be impossible. It is a result of this that our theological libraries are packed full of weighty tomes, and our disputes are without end, and the most about matters, assertions, and terms which the Christian world would have done far better never to have heard of—and would not have heard of if they had not happened to enter the fertile brain of Aristotle so long ago! But the full catalog, the great Iliad, of evils so produced, this is not the place to try to expound in detail.

Not so long ago, Hoornbeek wrote a treatise defending the doctrine of the Trinity against the Socinians, in which he says, "What are the terms or ideas that we can employ, when we are to approach or treat of a matter so unapproachable for the human mind, and so utterly profound? Must we employ the words and terms hammered out but recently in the schools? All these not all logical and meta-physical terms, which were shaped to describe far lesser things? When they are wont to be employed in theology is it not done with scant regard for the real and deep mysteries of the subject? Certainly these terms are completely incapable of describing such matters, being so ill-proportioned and inapt. New words are every day proposed under the pretext that they offer better and more satisfactory definitions, and convey clearer ideas. But of a certainty it is good to be continually checking one's footsteps, and I for one, do not believe that the men of old were any the less orthodox for lacking all of these modern formulas and terminology. Whenever some new verbal distinction is proposed it is at once the subject of fierce controversy, whilst the real crux of the matter is scrupulously avoided, to the great prejudice of the truth. The more foolish the idea is, the more boldly it is pressed!"

And so quarrel begets quarrel, dispute begets dispute, distinction begets distinction, and at length he who at the outset seemed to know all, is reduced to the level of knowing nothing at all. It is not for noth-ing that Jansen comments that "In truth for most Christians a knowl-edge of recent theological thought serves no purpose at all, beyond making them aware of the battles of opinion, and the great thirst men have for building reputations by promoting differences. All can see how men, laying aside Christian simplicity become the more cunning the less they possess of righteousness" (*Augustinism*, Book 2).

But I can hardly delay my course any more over these matters. Perhaps, in the long-suffering of God, opportunity will be granted to me to deal at greater length with the evils of the resurgence of philosophy in religion. I trust that I might complete this digression in as few words as possible.

Those who have impartially investigated the origin, occasions, and causes of theological disputes, willing to look at all sides and having love and goodwill rather than sectarian hatred or irritation between groups, will be at once struck with a sense of the great disgrace that this brings on the Christian name, and the offense that by it accrues to the gospel. But, alas! such unbiased men have always been so few—"Hardly in number equal to the gates of Thebes, or the mouths of the Nile!" Juvenal. *Satires*, 13, 26) (B). The long established prejudices of the ages divert the minds of men to quite another direction, while those who have attempted to settle disputes between the parties by some mutual relaxation of the hardness of their opinions, have long since come to learn that they are simply wasting time and effort. Some, indeed, attribute all this to a righteous judgment of God, abandoning such men to their own folly and vanity, and so leaving them to the combat of words since they would not surrender to the peace of the gospel. And what can be the natural outcome of this frame of mind but darkness, prejudice, lusts, and depravity? But the factor which brought in this just judgment of God on the sins of men so richly deserving it was that importation of loathsome errors, breeding within the Church, which fermented the disputes in the first place, and the great engine by which *that* was done was the intermingling of philosophy, both Platonic and Peripatetic, as we have seen, with the pure doctrines of the gospel (C). All hope of breaking free from unending disputes will be vain until our scholars learn to shake off the dust of this Babylonian confusion and return to the simplicity of the gospel. This, I say, is the great crime which professing Christians have so wickedly practiced against each other, and which is the great fount of their separations and schisms, and so it will continue until they learn to be wise only in "the spirit of revelation, in the mysteries of the gospel."

Because of these things, theology has become a thorny and confused subject of study which men think to pursue exactly as they would any other art or science; that is, without any spiritual light or the assistance of the Holy Spirit. And yet many cry out in surprise and distress that the very study of theology corrupts the minds of the students, turns them away from divine investigations and the wisdom that comes only from faith, leads them *away* from the study of God's Word and prayer, and all the holy obedience of gospel practice! Then will they not agree that the study of theology must be absolutely divorced from all intermingling with philosophy? Can we not acknowledge that it is the sovereign work of the Holy Spirit which alone can free men's minds from the bondage of inherited prejudices and the meshes of philosophy, and pluck up by the roots that "science falsely so called" which has hithertofore played so great a part in their education? Will men learn to turn their backs on the theorems of the crowds of would-be teachers, and look again to the sole aid of the Holy Spirit? Let us pray for an outpouring of the Spirit in this matter!

Bibliography

Aquinas, Thomas. "Aquinas Against the Averroists." In *On There Being Only One Intellect*. West Lafayette, IN: Purdue University Press, 1993.

———. *De quollbet* 2 8.2 ob.1–2 Edited by Raimondo Spiazzi. Turin: Marietti, 1956.

———. 'Dionysius' Divine Names and to Aquinas.' In *Librum Beati Dionysii De Nominibus Expositiio*. Edited by M. R. Cathala and R. Spiazzi. Turin: Marietti, 1964.

———. *On Being and Essence*. Translated by Armand Maurer. 2d rev. ed. Mediaeval Sources in Translation, vol. 1. Toronto: Pontifical Institute of Mediaeval Studies, 1968.

———. *Quaestiones Disputatae De Potentia Dei*. Trans. English Dominican Fathers. Westminster, MD: The Newman Press, 1952.

———. *Summa Contra Gentiles, Book I-II*. In *Latin/English Edition of the Works of Thomas Aquinas*, Vol. 11. Translated by Fr. Laurence Shapcote. Green Bay, WI: Aquinas Institute, Inc., 2018.

———. *Summa Contra Gentiles, Books III-IV*. In *Latin/English Edition of the Works of Thomas Aquinas*, Vol. 12. Translated by Fr. Laurence Shapcote. Green Bay, WI: Aquinas Institute, Inc., 2018.

———. *Summa of the Summa*. Edited and Annotated by Peter Kreeft. San Francisco: Ignatius Press, 1990.

———. *Summa Theologica*. Translated by Fathers of the English Dominican Province. Revised by Daniel J. Sullivan in "Great Books of the Western World." Gen. Ed., Robert Maynard Hutchins. New York: Encyclopedia Britannica, 1952.

———. *The Aquinas Catechism*. Manchester, NH: Sophia Institute Press, 2000.

———. *Thomas Aquinas's Quodlibetal Questions*. Trans. Turner Nevitt and Brain Davies. New York: Oxford University Press: 2020.

Aristotle. *The Metaphysics: Books X-XIV*. In *Loeb Classical Library*, Vol. 287. Translated by Hugh Tredennick. Cambridge, MA: Harvard University Press, 1997.

———. *Physics*. In *Great Books of the Western World*. Gen. Ed., Robert Maynard Hutchins. Translated by R. P. Hardie and R. K. Gaye. New York: Encyclopedia Britannica, 1952.

Augustine. *The Trinity*. Introduction and Translation by Edmund Hill. Edited by John E. Rotelle. Hyde Park, NY: New City Press, 1991.

Báñez, Dominic. *The Primacy of Existence in Thomas Aquinas: A Commentary in Thomistic Metaphysics*. Proctorville, OH: Wythe-North Publishing, 2021.

Barr, James. *Biblical Faith and Natural Theology*. Oxford, UK: Clarendon Press, 1993.

Barron, Robert. *Thomas Aquinas: Spiritual Master*. New York: Crossroad Publishing Company, 1996.

Bavinck, *Reformed Dogmatics*. 4 Vols. Translated by John Vriend. Grand Rapids: Baker, 2004.

Beeke, Joel R. and Paul M. Smalley. *Reformed Systematic Theology: Revelation and God*. Vol. 1. Wheaton, IL: Crossway, 2019.

Bellarmine, Robert. *Controversies of the Christian Faith*. Translated by Kenneth Baker. Keep the Faith, Inc., 2016.

Berkhof, Louis. *Systematic Theology*. Grand Rapids: Eerdmans, 1996.

Blankenborn, Bernhard. *The Mystery of Union with God: Dionysian Mysticism in Albert the Great and Thomas Aquinas*. Washington DC: The Catholic University Press, 2015.

Bouwsma, William J. *John Calvin: A Sixteenth Century Portrait*. (New York: Oxford University Press, 1998.

Brown, John. *Systematic Theology: A Compendious View of Natural and Revealed Religion*. Grand Rapids: Reformation Heritage Books, 2015.

Bullinger, Henry. *The Decades of Henry Bullinger*. Edited by Thomas Harding. Grand Rapids: Reformation Heritage, 2004.

Butin, Philip Walker. *Revelation, Redemption, and Response: Calvin's Trinitarian Understanding of the Divine-Human Relationship*. New York: Oxford University Press, 1995.

Cajetan, Tommansode Vio, *The Analogy of Names and the Concept of Being*. Translated by Edward A. Bushinski. Eugene, OR: Wipf & Stock, 2009.

Calvin, John. *Institutes of the Christian Religion*. 2 vols. Edited by John T. McNeill. Translated by Ford Lewis Battles. Philadelphia: The Westminster Press, 1977.

Carter, Craig A. "Contemplating God with the Great Tradition: An Interview with Craig Carter," *Credo Magazine*, Vol. 10, Issue 2. June 22, 2020. https://credomag.com/article/contemplating-god-with-the-great-tradition.

Cessario, Romanus. "Aquinas on Christian Salvation." In *Aquinas on Doctrine. A Critical Introduction*. 117–137. Edited by Thomas Weinandy, Daniel Keating, John Yocum (London: T&T Clark International, 2004).

———. *The Godly Image: Christ and Salvation in Catholic Thought from Anselm to Aquinas, Studies in Historical Theology*, Vol. 6. Petersham, MA: St. Bede's Publications, 1989.

———. "St Thomas Aquinas on Satisfaction, Indulgence, and Crusades" in *Medieval Philosophy and Theology*, Edited by Mark D. Jordan. Notre Dame, IN: University of Nota Dame, 1992.

Cessario, Romanus and Cajetan Cuddy, Thomas and the Thomists: The Achievement of Thomas Aquinas and His Interpreters. Minneapolis: Fortress Press, 2017.

Charnock, Stephen. The Existence and Attributes of God (Grand Rapids: Baker, 1996.

Chenu, M. D. *Aquinas and His Role in Theology*. Translated by Paul Philibert. Collegeville, MN: Liturgical Press, 2002.

Chesterton, G. K. *Saint Thomas Aquinas*. Nashville: Sam Torade Book Arts, 2019.

Dabney, Robert L. *Systematic Theology*. Edinburgh: Banner of Truth, 1996.

Davies, Brian. *An Introduction to the Philosophy of Religion*. Oxford: Oxford University Press, 1993.

———. *The Thought of Thomas Aquinas*. Cambridge, UK: Clarendon Press, 1993.

———. *Thomas Aquinas on God and Evil*. Oxford: Oxford University Press, 2011.

Deane, Jenifer Kolpacoff. *A History of Medieval Heresy and Inquisition*. Plymouth, UK: Rowman & Littlefield Publishing Group, 2011.

Dionysius. "The Divine Names." In *Dionysius the Areopagite on the Divine Names and The Mystical Theology*. Translated by C. E. Rolt. Berwick, MI: Ibis Press, 2004.

Emery, Gilles. *The Trinitarian Theology of St. Thomas Aquinas*, Translated by Francesca Aran Murphy. Oxford: Oxford University Press, 2007.

Feser, Edward. *Aquinas*. London: Oneworld Publications, 2020.

———. *Five Proofs of the Existence of God*. San Francisco: Ignatius Press, 2017.

———. *Neo-scholastic Essays*. South Bend, IL: St. Augustine's Press, 2015.

———. *Scholastic Metaphysics: A Contemporary Introduction*. Lancaster, UK: Editiones Scholaticae, 2014.

Fesko, J. V. *Reforming Apologetics: Retrieving the Classic Reformed Approach to Defending the Faith*. Grand Rapids: Baker Academic, 2019.

Foster, Kenelm. ed., *The Life of Saint Thomas Aquinas: Biographical Documents*. Baltimore: Helicon Press, 1959.

Fuller, B. A. G. "The Theory of God in Book V of Aristotle's Metaphysics." In *The Philosophical Review*, Vol. 16, No. 2 (March, 1907): 170-183.

Garrigou-Lagrange, Reginal. *Reality: A Synthesis of Thomistic Thought*. Translated by Patrick Cummins. St. Louis: Herder, 1950.

Gilson, Etienne. *The Philosophy of St. Thomas Aquinas.* Translated by Edward Bullough. Edited by G. A. Elrington. New York: Dorset Press, 1948.

———. *The Spirit of Mediaeval Philosophy.* Notre Dame, IN: University of Notre Dame, 1991.

Goodman, Micah. *Maimonides and the Book that Changed Judaism.* Philadelphia: The Jewish Publication Society, 2015.

Goodwin, Thomas. "A Discourse of Election," in *The Works of Thomas Goodwin.* Volume. 9. Edinburgh: James Nichol, 1864.

———. "The Knowledge of God the Father and His Son Jesus Christ," in *The Works of Thomas Goodwin.* Grand Rapids: Reformation Heritage Books, 2006.

Gordon, Bruce. *Calvin.* New Haven, CT: Yale University Press, 2009.

Grabmann, Martin. *Thomas Aquinas: His Personality and Thought.* Translated by Virgil Michel. New York: Longmans, Green and Co., 1928.

Harris, C. R. S. "Duns Scotus and His Relation to Thomas Aquinas." *Proceedings of the Aristotelian Society.* vol. 25 (1924): 219–246.

Helm, Paul. *John Calvin's Ideas.* Oxford: Oxford University Press, 2004.

———. "Nature and Grace." In *Aquinas Among the Protestants.* Oxford: Wiley Blackwell, 2018, 229–247.

Hick, John. "Ineffability." *Religious Studies.* 36, no. 1. (2000): 35–46.

Hodge, Charles. *Systematic Theology.* Vol. 1. Grand Rapids: Eerdmans, 1981.

Janz, Denis R. *Luther and Late Medieval Thomism: A Study in Theological Anthropology.* Ontario: Wilfrid Laurier University Press, 1983.

———. *Luther on Thomas Aquinas: The Angelic Doctor in the Thought of the Reformer.* Translated by Denis Janz. Franz Steiner, 1989.

Johnson, Jeffrey D. *The Absurdity of Unbelief.* Conway, AR: Free Grace Press, 2016.

Kelly, Douglas. *Systematic Theology: Grounded in Holy Scripture and Understood in Light of the Church.* 2 vols. Fearn, Ross-shire, Scotland: Christian Focus, 2008-2014.

Kilby, Karen. "Aquinas, the Trinity and the Limits of Understanding." *International Journal of Systematic Theology.* 7, no. 4, (October 2005): 414–427.

Knasas, John F. X. "Aquinas' Ascription of Creation to Aristotle." *Angelicum.* 73, no. 4, (1996): 487–505.

Leibniz, Gottfried. *The Monadology.* Translated by Nicholas Rescher. Pittsburgh, PA: University of Pittsburgh Press, 1991.

Letham, Robert. "John Owen's Doctrine of the Trinity in Its Catholic Context and Its Significance for Today." In *John Owen: The Life, Thought, and Writings of John Owen (1616–83)*. Accessed March 30, 2020. http://johnowen.org/media/letham_owen.pdf.

———. *Systematic Theology*. Wheaton, IL: Crossway, 2019.

———. *The Holy Trinity: In Scripture, History, Theology, and Worship*. Phillipsburg, NJ: P&R Publishing, 2004.

Lovejoy, Arthur O. *The Great Chain of Being*. Cambridge, MA: Harvard University Press, 1976.

Luther, Martin. 'Disputation on Indulgence." In *Works of Martin Luther*. Grand Rapids: Baker, 1915.

McCall, Thomas H. "Trinity Doctrine, Plain and Simple," in *Advancing Trinitarian Theology*. Grand Rapids: Zondervan, 2014.

Maimonides, Moses. *Guide of the Perplexed*. Translated by Shlomo Pines. Chicago: University of Chicago Press, 1966.

Manschreck, Clyde Leonard. *Melanchthon, The Quiet Reformer* (New York: Abingdon Press, 1958.

Maritain, Jacques. *St. Thomas Aquinas: Angel of the Schools*, Translated by J. F. Scanlan. London: Sheed & Ward, 1948.

Maurer, Armand. "Introduction." In *Thomas Aquinas Faith, Reason and Theology: Questions I–IV of his Commentary on the De Trinitate of Boethius*. Translated by Armand Maurer. Toronto: Institute of Mediaeval Studies, 1987.

———. *St Thomas Aquinas: Faith, Reason and Theology: Questions I–IV of His Commentary on the De Trinitate of Boethius*. Translated with by Armand Maurer. Toronto: Institute of Mediaeval Studies, 1987.

McGrath, Allister E. *Luther's Theology of the Cross*. Oxford: Blackwell, 1985.

McInerny, Ralph. *Aquinas Against the Averroists: On There Being Only One Intellect*. West Lafayette, IN: Purdue University Press, 1993.

———. *Praeambula Fidei: Thomism and the God of the Phosphors*. Washington, DC: Catholic University of America Press, 2006.

McWhorter, Matthew R. "Aquinas on God's Relation to the World." *New Blackfriars* 94, no. 1049 (2013): 3–19.

Melanchthon, Philipp. "Letter on the Leipzig Debate." In *Melanchthon: Selected Writings*. Translated by Charles Leander Hill. Edited by Elmer Ellsworth Flack and Lower J. Satre. Minneapolis: Augsburg Publishing House, 1962.

———. Luther and the Paris Theologians," In *Melanchthon: Selected Writings*. Translated by Charles Leander Hill. Edited by Elmer Ellsworth Flack and Lower J. Satre. Minneapolis: Augsburg Publishing House, 1962.

———. "Paul and the Scholastics." In *Melanchthon: Selected Writings.* Translated by Charles Leander Hill. Edited by Elmer Ellsworth Flack and Lower J. Satre. Minneapolis: Augsburg Publishing House, 1962.

Moser, Christian. "Heinrich Bullinger's Efforts to Document the Zurich Reformation: History and Legacy, In *Architect of Reformation: An Introduction to Heimrich Bullinger*, edited by Bruce Gordon and Emidio Campi. Eugene, OR: Wipf & Stock, 2019.

Muller, Richard, *Post-Reformation Reformed Dogmatics*, 2nd ed. 4 vols. Grand Rapids: Baker, 3003.

———. "Reformation, Orthodoxy, Christian Aristotelianism, and the Eclecticism or Early Modern Philosophy." *Nederlands Archief Voor Kerkgeschiedenis / Dutch Review of Church History* 81, no. 3 (2001): 306–325. Accessed July 13, 2021. http://www.jstor.org/stable/24011334.

Novak, Michael. *On Cultivating Liberty: Reflections on Moral Ecology.* Lanham, MD: Rowman and Littlefield Publishers, 1999.

O'Meara, Thomas F. *Thomas Aquinas Theologian.* Notre Dame, IN: University of Notre Dame Press, 1997.

O'Rourke, Fran. *Pseudo-Dionysius and the Metaphysics of Aquinas.* Notre Dame, IN: University of Notre Dame Press, 2010.

Owen, John. *Biblical Theology.* Morgan, PA: Soli Deo Gloria, 2002.

———. "Of the Divine Original, Authority, Self-evidencing Light, and Power of the Scripture." In *The Works of John Owen.* Edinburgh: Banner of Truth, 1968.

Pegis, Anton. "General Introduction." In *Saint Thomas Aquinas: On the Truth of the Catholic Faith, Summa Contra Gentiles, Book One: God,* Translated by Anton C. Pegis. Garden City, NY: Hanover House, 1955.

Peters, Edward. *Inquisition.* Berkeley: University of California Press, 1989.

Pieper, Josef. *The Silence of St. Thomas.* Translated by John Murray, S. J., and Daniel O'Connor. South Band, IN: St. Augustine's Press, 1963.

———. *Guide to Thomas Aquinas.* Translated by Richard and Clara Winston. New York: Pantheon Books, 1962.

Pinnock, Clark. *Most Moved Mover: A Theology of God's Openness.* Grand Rapids: Baker Academic, 2001.

Pole, Reginald. *Pole's Defense on the Unity of the Church.* Translated by Joseph G. Dwyer. Westminster, MD: Newman, 1965.

Poythress, Vern S. The Mystery of the Trinity: A Trinitarian Approach to the Attributes of God. Phillipsburg, NJ: Presbyterian & Reformed, 2020.

Purro, Pasquale. *Thomas Aquinas: A Historical and Philosophical Profile.* Translated by Joseph G. Trabbic and Roger W. Nutt. Washington, DC: The Catholic University of America Press, 2012.

Provine, William. "Scientists, Face It! Science and Religion are Incompatible." *The Scientist*, 2, no.16 (September 1988):10.

Reeves, Michael. *Delighting in the Trinity*. Downers Grove, IL: InterVarsity Press, 2012.

Reymond, Robert L. "Dr. John H. Gerstner on Thomas Aquinas as a Protestant." Westminster Theological Journal (Spring 1997): 113-121.

Russell, Bertrand. *Why I Am Not a Christian*. New York, NY: Simon & Schuster, 1957.

Schaff, Phillip. *History of the Christian Church*. Vol. 5. Grand Rapids: Eerdmans, 1960.

Schwertner, Thomas. *St. Albert the Great: The First Universal Doctor*. Post Falls, ID: Mediarix Press, 2018.

Sleidanus, Johannes. *The General History of the Reformation of the Church, From the Errors and Corruptions of the Church of Rome: Begun in Germany by Martin Luther*. London: Edw, Jones.

Stump, Eleonore. "Atonement According to Aquinas." In *Philosophy and the Christian Faith*. Edited by Thomas V. Morris. Notre Dame, IN: University of Notre Dame, 1988.

Thornwell, James Henley. "Theological Lectures." In *The Collected Writings of James Henley Thornwell*. Vol. 1. Edinburgh: Banner of Truth, 1986.

Torell, Jean-Pierre. *Christ and Spirituality in Thomas Aquinas*. Washington, DC: The Catholic University of America Press, 2011.

———. *St. Thomas Aquinas*. Vol. 1. *The Person and His Works*. Translated by Robert Royal. Washington, DC: The Catholic University of America Press, 2005.

Turretin, Frances. *Institutes of Elenctic Theology*. Translated by George Musgrave Giger. Edited by James T. Dennison, Jr. Vol. 1. Phillipsburg, NJ: Presbyterian and Reformed Publishing, 1992.

Van Til, Cornelius. *An Introduction to Systematic Theology*. 2nd ed. Edited by William Edgar. Philipsburg, NJ: P&R, 2007.

———. *The Defense of the Faith*. Phillipsburg, NJ: Presbyterian and Reformed, 1967.

Vos, Arvin. *Aquinas, Calvin, and Contemporary Protestant Thought: A Critique of Protestant Views on the Thought of Thomas Aquinas*. Grand Rapids: Christian University Press, 1985.

Vos, Geerhardus. "Theology Proper." In *Reformed Dogmatics*. Translated and edited by Richard B. Gaffin. Bellingham, WA: Lexham Press, 2012–2014.

Vost, Kevin. *St. Albert the Great: Champion of Faith and Reason*. Charlotte, NC: Tan Books, 2011.

Warfield, B. B. "Calvin and Calvinism." In the *Works of B. B. Warfield*, 10 Vols. Grand Rapids: Baker Book House, 2003.

———. *Biblical Doctrine*. Edinburgh: Banner of Truth, 1988.

INDEX OF NAMES

A

Abelard, Peter 95
Albert the Great 9, 36, 73, 75, 96, 111, 113, 135, 151
Alexander III 196
Alexander IV 112, 135
Alexander the Great 152
Ammonius Saccas 75
Anselm 17, 95, 210, 238
Aristotle 5–6, 17–18, 24, 30, 32, 35–37, 42–43, 45, 47–51, 53–74, 79, 88, 94–98, 101, 102, 108–122, 125–126, 130, 131–138, 140, 141, 146–151, 154, 158, 161,–164, 169, 172, 173, 181, 190, 192, 193, 200–203, 205, 227, 228, 232, 233
Augustine 2, 4, 9, 41, 43, 54, 71, 96, 107, 153, 158, 217, 232
Averroists 37, 72, 73

B

Barr, James 10
Barron, Robert 98
Barth, Karl 21
Bavinck, Herman 14–15, 29, 81, 91, 117, 137
Beeke, Joel R. 14, 21–22, 138, 190, 191
Bellarmine, Robert 207, 216
Benedict XV 10
Berkeley, George 55
Berkhof, Louis 138, 183, 184
Berkouwer, G. C. 21
Blankenborn, Bernhard 75
Boethius 43, 73, 95, 96, 112
Boethius of Dacia 72, 73
Bonaventure 43, 71, 72, 176

Bouwsma, William 31, 204
Brown, John 29, 186
Bullinger, Henry 31, 32, 203
Butin, Philip Walker 154

C

Cajetan, Tommansode Vio 44, 178, 200, 201, 203, 216
Calo, Peter 112
Calvin, John 6, 15–17, 29–33, 44, 47, 113, 155, 159, 164, 190, 191, 203, 204, 206, 207
Capreolus, John 113
Carter, Craig A. 156
Cessario, Romanus 205, 206, 210
Charnock, Stephen 188
Chenu, M. D. 41
Chesterton, G. K. 3, 9, 54, 73, 113, 152, 153
Chrysostom 2
Clement IV 135
Clement VIII 207
Cuddy, Cajetan 206

D

Dabney, Robert L. 146, 160, 239
Davies, Brian 40, 69, 139, 142, 148, 149, 184, 185, 214
Deane, Jennifer Kolpacoff 196
de Guibert, Joseph 216
Dionysius the Aeropagite 74–75. *See also* Pseudo-Dionysius.
Dominic of Caleruega 197

E

Eck, Johann 201, 216
Emery, Gilles 38, 141, 144, 147, 172

F

Feser, Edward 37, 97, 117, 118, 120, 170, 171, 193
Fesko, J. V. 6, 10, 20, 21
Flack, Ellsworth 201, 202, 241, 242
Foster, Kenelm 194
Frederick II 7
Fuller, B. A. G. 68

G

Garrigou–Lagrange, Reginald 97
Gilson, Etienne 17, 24, 37, 43, 72, 73, 117, 119, 126, 170
Goodman, Micah 240
Goodwin, Thomas 163, 165, 166
Gordon, Bruce 31, 203, 204, 240, 242
Grabmann, Martin 2, 17, 40, 53, 74, 112, 152, 176, 193
Grane, Leif 201
Gregory IX 198
Gregory X 176

H

Harris, C. R. S. 122, 123
Helm, Paul 47
Henry VIII 207
Heraclitus 56, 58
Hick, John 25
Hodge, Charles 119
Honorius III 197
Hume, David 55

I

Innocent III 197

J

Janz, Denis R. 200, 201
Johnson, Jeffrey D. 172, 192
John XXI 4
John XXII 53

K

Karlstadt, Andres 201
Kelly, Douglas 168
Kilby, Karen 144
Köllin, Konrad 203, 216

L

Landulf of Aquino 7, 8
le Bougre, Robert 198
Leibniz, Gottfried 168
Leo X 201
Leo XIII 53, 216
Letham, Robert 10, 11, 22, 146, 147, 155, 159
Locke, John 55
Lovejoy, Arthur O. 129, 130
Lucius III 196
Luther, Martin 199–203, 205, 207

M

Maimonides, Moses 18, 20
Manschreck, Clyde Leonard 201
Maritain, Jacques 2, 35, 36, 176, 194
Maurer, Armand 18, 39, 41, 43, 45, 51, 96, 237
Mazzolini, Sylvester 199, 200
McCall, Thomas H. 159, 160
McGrath, Allister E. 200, 211
McInerny, Ralph 36, 37, 44, 73
McWhorter, Matthew 132, 133
Melanchthon, Philipp 201, 202, 203
Mill, John Stuart 60

N

Novak, Michael 198

O

Oecolampadius, Johannes 201
O'Meara, Thomas F. 43, 44
Origen 75, 95, 225

O'Rourke, Fran 91
Owen, John 14, 16–17, 30, 32–33, 47–48, 184, 205, 219

P

Paley, William 171
Parmenides 59
Paul III 206
Pegis, Anton 42, 43
Peter of Ireland (Ibernia) 36, 95, 96
Peter Waldo 196
Peters, Edward 198
Pieper, Josef 2, 3, 9, 40, 54, 71, 107, 109, 130, 134
Pinnock, Clark 157
Pius IV 206
Pius V 53, 206
Pius XI 53
Plato 4, 24, 36, 54–56, 72–76, 78, 85, 88, 96, 106, 123, 125, 130, 136, 221, 235
Plotinus 75–78, 81, 123, 161
Pole, Reginald 207, 209, 216
Porphyry 78
Poythress, Vern S. 146, 147, 158, 161
Protagoras 56
Provine, William 169
Pseudo–Dionysius 26, 30, 43, 50, 51, 71, 74–75, 78–96, 100, 101, 103, 104, 106–110, 112, 118, 125, 126, 143, 149, 150, 154. *See also* Dionysius the Aeropagite.
Purro, Pasquale 8, 37, 95, 111

R

Rahner, Karl 155
Reeves, Michael 166
Reginald of Piperno 153
Russell, Bertrand 60, 61

S

Sabellius 141

Satre, Lower J. 201
Schaff, David 211
Schaff, Phillip 212
Scheler, Max 21
Schwertner, Thomas 9
Scotus, Michael 35
Severus 75
Siger of Brabant 72, 73
Sinibald 8
Sleidanus, Johannes 199, 200
Smalley, Paul M. 14, 21–22, 190, 191
Sproul, R. C. 10, 20, 21
Stump, Eleonore 210

T

Tempier, Stephen 4
Theodora of Aquino 7
Thornwell, James Henley 204, 205
Torell, Jean–Pierre 151, 153
Turretin, Frances 159

U

Ulrich of Strasburg 111
Urban IV 135

V

Valla, Lorenzo 75
Van Til, Cornelius 158, 164
Velecky, Ceslaus 142
Vos, Arvin 6, 44, 47
Vos, Geerhardus 164, 165
Vost, Kevin 111

W

Warfield, B. B. 13, 164, 166, 167, 190
William of Tocco 3, 7, 112

Z

Zwingli, Ulrich 203

www.ingramcontent.com/pod-product-compliance
Lightning Source LLC
Chambersburg PA
CBHW030506100426
42813CB00002B/353